Palgrave Studies in Languages at War

Languages play a crucial role in conflict. They enable or disrupt communication between the people involved. They express the identities of the participants. They convey representations and interpretations of what is happening. And sometimes language differences are a key part of what the conflict is about.

This series brings together books which deal with the role of languages in many different kinds of conflict, including international war, civil war, occupation, peace operations, humanitarian action, the preludes to conflict and its aftermath. The series embraces interdisciplinary approaches, drawing on applied linguistics, sociolinguistics, translation studies, intercultural communication, history, politics, international relations, peace studies and cultural studies. Books in the series explore conflicts across a range of times and places and analyse the language-related roles and activities involved. The Editors welcome proposals for new contributions, including monographs and edited volumes.

More information about this series at
http://www.palgrave.com/gp/series/14615

Marija Todorova • Lucía Ruiz Rosendo
Editors

Interpreting Conflict

A Comparative Framework

palgrave
macmillan

Editors
Marija Todorova
The Hong Kong Polytechnic University
Hung Hom, Hong Kong

Lucía Ruiz Rosendo
Faculty of Translation and Interpreting
University of Geneva
Geneva, Switzerland

Palgrave Studies in Languages at War
ISBN 978-3-030-66908-9   ISBN 978-3-030-66909-6 (eBook)
https://doi.org/10.1007/978-3-030-66909-6

Cover illustration: Jean-Philippe Tournut / Getty Images

This Palgrave Macmillan imprint is published by the registered company Springer Nature Switzerland AG.
The registered company address is: Gewerbestrasse 11, 6330 Cham, Switzerland

Acknowledgments

First and foremost, we would like to thank all the authors of this volume for their valuable contributions. We would also like to thank the International Association of Translation and Intercultural Studies (IATIS) as well as the European Society of Translation Studies (EST) for allowing us to organize panels at their international conferences at Hong Kong Baptist University in 2018 and the Stellenbosch University in 2019 respectively. Several of the contributions in this volume have been presented at these panels for the first time.

We are grateful to the Series Editors of the Palgrave Studies in Languages at War, Hilary Footitt and Michael Kelly for their insightful comments and suggestions, as well as for their support in making this volume yet another addition to the Series. Our special thanks to our editors at Palgravc, Alice Green and Cathy Scott, for their collegiality and their assistance in the production stage.

Praise for *Interpreting Conflict*

"A key compilation for interpreters and researchers interested in interpreting in conflict zones and related fields."

—Jesús Baigorri-Jalón, *former United Nations staff interpreter and author of* Languages in the Crossfire: Interpreters in the Spanish Civil War (1936–1939) *(forthcoming)*

"This timely volume gathers an impressive body of international research on interpreting which encompasses violent conflict and the refugee and humanitarian crises that emerge in its aftermath."

—Moira Inghilleri, *Professor of Translation and Interpreting Studies and Comparative Literature, University of Massachusetts Amherst, USA*

"A fascinating, eye-opening collection of unique studies that set the standard for research on interpreting in military and humanitarian contexts and covers an amazing array of geographical regions, including Korea, China, Japan, Afghanistan, Iraq, Lebanon, the Sahel, Italy, Spain, the US and Argentina. A must-read for scholars of translation, interpreting, intercultural communication, and a wide range of disciplines concerned with the study of conflict and its aftermaths."

—Mona Baker, *University of Oslo, Norway*

Contents

Notes on Contributors

Manuel Barea Muñoz is a professional conference interpreter, translator, and fiction writer. He completed his undergraduate training and MA in Translation and Interpreting at the University Pablo de Olavide (Sevilla), where he is working as a substitute teacher in the Translation and Interpreting Department. He is also finishing his PhD dissertation on interpreting in the Israeli-Palestinian Conflict in the FTI at the University of Geneva. His main areas of research include interpreting in conflict zones and scenarios, history of interpreting, ethics in interpreting, and interpreting in humanitarian and institutional contexts.

Lorena Guadalupe Baudo is a professor and researcher at the National University of Córdoba (UNC), Argentina. She holds a PhD in Translation and Intercultural Studies. She has presented her dissertation at the UN headquarters in NY and Geneva. She is also a Specialist in English–Spanish Interpretation. She is Adjunct Professor of Terminology, Journalistic Translation, and Consecutive Interpreting at the UNC. She is the local coordinator of a terminology collaboration between the UNC and WIPO, Switzerland. In 2020, she has been a guest professor at the Universitat de Lleida, Spain. She leads a research team working on the language of diplomacy.

María Gómez-Amich holds a PhD in Translation and Interpreting Studies from UGR, a master's degree in Intercultural Communication from UAH, and a second master's degree in Teaching Spanish as a Foreign Language by UPSA. She has taught Spanish, Translation, Literature, and Culture at Florida International University (USA), University of Cape Town (SA), and NAS Dubai (UAE) where she heads the Spanish department. Her research interests include interpreting in conflict zones, role and quality perception, life stories, conflict narratives and concept mapping. She also works as a professional translator and interpreter.

Cherine Haidar Ahmad has master's degree in Translation and Interpretation and is pursuing a doctoral thesis at University of Geneva on United Nations interpreters in field missions. She is a permanent staff interpreter at United Nations Office in Geneva, Switzerland. Before joining the United Nations, she worked as a freelance interpreter and participated in field missions especially for the European institutions. She has taught interpretation in Italy, and she teaches interpretation at ISIT, Paris. She has published several poetry and literature translations in Arabic and Italian. Her working languages are Arabic, French, Italian, English, and Spanish. Her main domain of research is field missions.

Maya Hess is the founder and CEO of Red T, a US-based non-profit organization that advocates worldwide on behalf of translators and interpreters in high-risk settings. As a forensic linguist, she provided language support and expert witness services in major US terrorism trials and experienced firsthand how vulnerable members of this profession can be. She holds an MA in Journalism from New York University, a Graduate Certificate in Terrorism Studies from John Jay College of Criminal Justice, as well as an MPhil and PhD in Criminal Justice from the City University of New York.

Hyongrae Kim is a visiting assistant professor at the Department of Foreign Languages and Literatures at Auburn University, USA. He holds a PhD in Comparative Literature from the University of Massachusetts Amherst, USA, and an MA in Translation and Consecutive Interpretation from Hankuk University of Foreign Studies, South Korea. His main research interests include interpreters in violent conflict, the sociology of translation and interpreting, and North Korean literary translation.

Gabriela Fernanda Lorenzo is a National Sworn Translator of English and Specialist in Interpretation, graduated from the School of Languages, National University of Córdoba in Argentina. Her professional experience as an interpreter includes the performance in numerous instances of consecutive, simultaneous, and liaison interpreting in conferences, meetings, business rounds, and large agricultural fairs. She is a member of P-TIAL, a research group on the language of diplomacy. She has been continuously working for ten years as a translator and linguistic advisor, along with teaching, translation, text revision, and project management for clients in Argentina and abroad.

Tian Luo is professor of Translation Studies at Chongqing Jiaotong University, MA supervisor, and vice president of Chongqing Translators Association. He received his PhD in Linguistics (English) from the University of Macau. His main research interests include military translation history, discourse analysis, corpus-assisted translation studies and multimodal translation studies. His publications include more than 30 journal articles (some in *Perspective*, *Babel* and *LANS-TTS*), two monographs, and two textbooks. He is leading a research project sponsored by the National Social Science Foundation of China after the completion of three research projects.

Estela Martín-Ruel is teaching Translation and Interpreting, and International Communication, Translation and Interpreting at the UPO in Seville, Spain, since 2005. Previously, she taught at the University of Salamanca (2003–2005), where she had graduated in Translation and Interpreting Studies. She holds a PhD in Translation and Interpreting at the University of Granada (2012). She has extensive professional experience in the public, private and institutional sectors, translating and interpreting both from and into Spanish. She is a founding member of the Interglosia research group at the UPO.

Verónica Méndez Sánchez did her graduation in French Studies and post-graduation in Translation and Intercultural Mediation from the University of Salamanca (Spain). Likewise, she has done several specialization courses among which the Management of Translation Projects and Audio-visual Translation stand out. She is an active member of the

Spanish Air Forces, which is why she focuses her interest and studies on this area. Her master's degree thesis deals with the working, development and organization of translation and interpretation processes within the Spanish Armed Forces—research based on a real practical case carried out as a soldier deployed in external operations.

Yolanda Moreno-Bello specializes on interpreting in vulnerable and conflict settings by applying transnational and intersectional approaches of sociolinguistics. She holds an international PhD from Universidad de Alcalá and Université Saint Joseph-Beyrouth. She has collaborated with a number of universities, such as the University of Nairobi and the Pan-African Consortium of Masters in Translation and Interpreting where she carried out a postdoctoral research focused on the access to women's sexual and reproductive health. Since 2017, she is a member of CETAPS, Universidade NOVA de Lisboa, and she is carrying out field research in Nigeria.

Maura Radicioni is following a PhD program in Interpreting Studies at the Interpreting Department, FTI, University of Geneva. She obtained her MA in Conference Interpreting from Bologna University, Forlì-based DIT, in 1997. Since then, she has worked as a conference interpreter and interpreter trainer, mostly at DIT (2003–2019) with additional teaching assignments at the University of Macerata and Università Politecnica delle Marche. In 2017, she was involved as a trainer in the first humanitarian interpreting pilot course carried out in Italy, jointly organized in blended-learning mode by the University of Bologna, DIT, and the University of Geneva, FTI.

Lucía Ruiz Rosendo is an assistant professor at the University of Geneva's Interpreting Department. She is also a conference interpreter working in the institutional market in Geneva. Her research has appeared in *Linguistica Antverpiensia*, *Target*, *War & Society* and *Armed Forces & Society*, among others, as well as edited collections, including the *Oxford Handbook of Translation and Social Practice* (2021). She teaches in the MA in Conference Interpreting and the MAS in Interpreter Training (University of Geneva). Her main areas of research are interpreting in conflict zones and scenarios, interpreting at international organisations and interpreter training. She is the coordinator of the project AXS (https://www.unige.ch/fti/en/faculte/departements/dint/research/axs/).

Kayoko Takeda is professor of Translation and Interpreting Studies in the College of Intercultural Communication at Rikkyo University, Japan. She is the author of *Interpreters and War Crimes*, *Interpreting the Tokyo War Crimes Trial* and *Taiheiyo-senso Nihongo Choho-sen* (Intelligence war in Japanese during the Pacific War) and a co-editor of *New Insights in the History of Interpreting*.

Marija Todorova is a visiting scholar of the RCPCE at the Hong Kong Polytechnic University and an adjunct assistant professor at the University American College Skopje. Her research has appeared in *The Translator*, *Linguistica Antverpiensia*, *Bookbird*, and numerous edited collections, including the *Oxford Handbook of Translation and Social Practice* (2021). She serves as editor of *New Voices in Translation Studies* and *Vermilion Journal for Art and Literature*. She is an executive council member of the International Association of Translation and Intercultural Studies (IATIS) (2011 –present) and Chair of the IATIS Social Media and Outreach Committee (2020 –present).

Ruiqi Zhu is MA student majoring in translation and interpreting studies at the University of Leeds, United Kingdom. Her main research interests include multimodal translation and translation history.

List of Tables

Part I

Introduction

1

Moving Boundaries in Interpreting in Conflict Zones

Lucía Ruiz Rosendo

Interpreting in conflict zones has recently received considerable attention in academic literature. The role of interpreters working in these contexts is blurred, in that the tasks they perform go beyond the oral transfer of linguistic features to encompass their role as translators, cultural mediators and even as original speakers in their own right. Usually they are alone in understanding the languages and cultures involved; often, they are civilians belonging to the community in conflict with no previous training in interpreting who are recruited by armed forces, humanitarian organizations or NGOs. In other cases, they are professional or non-professional volunteers, willing to help in humanitarian crisis situations and post-conflict development. In still other cases, they are trained interpreters who work for international organizations, such as the United Nations, but who face different circumstances when interpreting in the field; this stems from their positionality as interpreting experts and their

L. Ruiz Rosendo (✉)
Faculty of Translation and Interpreting, University of Geneva, Geneva, Switzerland
e-mail: Lucia.Ruiz@unige.ch

M. Todorova, L. Ruiz Rosendo (eds.), *Interpreting Conflict*, Palgrave Studies in Languages at War, https://doi.org/10.1007/978-3-030-66909-6_1

professional affiliation, which lead them to assume a different role as mediators.

In Translation and Interpreting Studies, scholarly interest in the complex role of interpreters in conflict settings began in the twentieth century. However, the current ubiquity of interpreting, an increasing public awareness of this activity, as highlighted by Pérez González (2012), and its prominence in scientific literature (Schäffner et al. 2013) have led to an increasing interest in the methodical study of interpreting in different conflicts. Studies tend to focus on interpreting in war settings (e.g., Baigorri Jalón 2019; Baker 2010; Inghilleri 2008, 2009; Lan 2016; Footitt and Kelly 2012, 2018; Juvinall 2013; Ozawa 2008; Stahuljak 2009) and much less on the role of interpreters who work in the humanitarian field as a subcategory of post-conflict scenario (e.g., Delgado Luchner and Kherbiche 2018; Todorova 2016, 2017). Interestingly, most of the studies on the role of interpreters in war, mainly those working for the military, have been carried out by scholars who are outsiders to the activity or, in other words, who do not have direct experience as interpreters in these scenarios, with some noteworthy exceptions (Méndez 2018; Snellman 2016). Contrastingly, many of the authors of studies conducted on humanitarian interpreting are interpreters with experience of working in these settings, although these are still scarce. Given the circumstances and conditions under which interpreters in conflict and post-conflict scenarios perform their work, we believe that it is essential to encourage a more interdisciplinary discussion that analyzes the different factors that have an impact on the interpreter's role in different contexts and settings.

Against this backdrop, this volume, which is a compilation of studies that are related to the themes of two panels coordinated by the authors, the first at the 2018 IATIS (International Association for Translation and Intercultural Studies) conference and the second at the 2019 EST (European Society for Translation Studies) conference, consists of contributions on military and humanitarian interpreting and is particularly interested in studies of an interdisciplinary nature. Contributions seek to foster interprofessional dialogue and are written not only by scholars but also by those directly or indirectly involved in the activity, such as military personnel, humanitarian interpreters and activists, with the ultimate goal of examining the topic through different lenses and from different perspectives.

The innovative nature of this book comes not only from its comparative framework of the military and the humanitarian but also from an analysis of a range of case studies based on different settings, periods and actors and through which the research questions are addressed. While recognizing that some aspects are common to both frameworks, the purpose of this book is to compare relevant notions of interpreting in conflict-related scenarios such as the specific positionality of the interpreter in these different contexts; the ethical, psychological, emotional and security implications of their work in different scenarios; the specific training needed to work for the military and for humanitarian settings and whether or to what extent this training has to be adapted to the demands; and the relations of power created between the different stakeholders. The rationale is that the term "interpreting in conflict zones," as it has been coined in the literature, is too broad, encompassing any setting in which the interpreter works and that is located in a zone that is in conflict, usually an armed conflict. It is our belief that more attention must be given to the particularities of each context. In this volume a distinction is made between the military and the humanitarian environments as two contexts representing conflict and post-conflict scenarios, along the lines of Tesseur and Footitt's (2019) examination of the role of language mediators in conflict and post-conflict contexts, and the authors' purpose of increasing our understanding of what constitutes the "profession" of interpreting by the analysis of diverse contexts and scenarios. Therefore, the chapters included in this volume draw on data stemming from different studies that investigate the role(s) of interpreters in diverse military and humanitarian scenarios in different regions (Europe, the Middle East, Asia, Africa and Latin America) through the consultation of myriad sources (archival materials, secondary sources, autobiographies, war novels and personal experiences) and the use of different qualitative methods, mainly experiential interviews with the main parties involved (military personnel, humanitarian agents, military interpreters, locally recruited interpreters and UN staff interpreters).

In the first part of the volume, a total of seven chapters focus on the role of the interpreter in military scenarios. The first chapter deals with the role of Nisei (second-generation Japanese Americans and Canadians) in the Asia-Pacific War (1931–1945) and the Allied Occupation of Japan (1945–1952). *Kayoko Takeda*'s "Dual Citizen Interpreters: Consequences of Assigned Loyalties in the Aftermath of War" analyzes the role of Nisei as linguists recruited to engage in different language-related tasks by the Japanese military, government and state news agency. Drawing on archival materials and secondary sources, the chapter examines the backgrounds and wartime activities of these Nisei linguists and their treatment by Allied powers in the post-war occupation era. The chapter brings to the fore aspects that are relevant today and allows us to understand the scope of language issues in armed conflicts, such as the complex issues faced by dual citizens of warring states, the liability of being a heritage speaker in war, and the ethical and legal implications of interpreting in criminal acts.

The next chapter belongs to this same period but addresses the role of linguists from a different perspective. *Tian Luo and Ruiqi Zhu*'s "To Be or Not to Be Loyal: Loyalty of Military Interpreters Serving the Japanese Army in the Second Sino-Japanese War" explores the states of interpreters' loyalty in this conflict by focusing on interpreters who served the Japanese army during the Second Sino-Japanese War (1931–1945). The authors analyze 80 narratives from historical archives and autobiographies of interpreters and come to the conclusion that interpreters demonstrated four distinct states of loyalty: fervent, feinted, shifted and divided loyalty. These were shaped by different interrelated factors such as ethnic identity and nationality, the chance of survival in the war, linguistic competence, economic reward, position in the power structure, temporary social status, ideology and prospects of war. The chapter offers a complex examination of loyalty and its ethical implications in military contexts.

After these two chapters, the focus of this volume remains in the first half of the twentieth century, but shifts to a different conflict, focusing on the three stages of the Korean War, that is, the preparatory phase, the US/USSR military occupation of Korea (1945–1948); the engagement phase, the confrontation between the militaries of North and South Korea and their respective allies (1950–1953); and the conclusionary phase, the Korean Armistice Negotiations (1951–1953). *Hyongrae Kim*'s "Interpreting the Korean Conflict (1945–1953)" examines the shifts in the interpreter's positionality during the aforementioned phases, drawing on Bourdieu's field theory and Inghilleri's (2005) analysis of the existence of a zone of uncertainty in which the interpreter's work takes place. The chapter concludes that these different positionalities, the different tasks the interpreter carries out, the existence of diverse needs, and power structures and the norms dictating the interpreter's work in different periods and locations show that there is a need to reconsider traditional notions of the interpreter's identity and functionality.

Moving to the second half of the twentieth century and the twenty-first century, a total of four chapters deal with conflicts in the Middle East and Africa. *María Gómez Amich*'s "Local Interpreters Versus Military Personnel: Perceptions and Expectations Regarding the Local Interpreter's Role and Agency Within the Afghan Conflict" examines the role of the interpreter in the context of military operations conducted by internationally deployed armies that required interaction with Afghan security forces and civilians. Drawing on narrative interviews with Spanish troops deployed in Afghanistan and Afghan interpreters, the chapter examines relevant issues of trust, allegiance, identity, ideology and interdependency that challenge the traditional view of the interpreter as a neutral linguistic mediator.

Subsequently, *Yolanda Moreno Bello*'s "Negotiating Ideologies in Conflict Zones: The Case of the Interpreter in Lebanon" draws on interviews with interpreters who worked in the conflicts in Lebanon between 1975 and 2006 and applies Baker's (2006) frame analysis to examine how interpreters negotiate ideologies found in discourse. The author comes to the conclusion that the interpreter plays an essential role in negotiating conflict ideologies, although they show different levels of autonomy in doing so.

In "The Spanish 'Military Interpreter': A Practical Application in International Operations Arising from Armed Conflicts," *Verónica Méndez Sánchez* draws on her insightful knowledge and experience as both a soldier and a language mediator in international missions to explore the main factors shaping the military interpreter's status when working in sensitive zones such as the Africa's Sahel region. She analyzes different factors inherent in the work of military interpreters, including workload, thematic fields, responsibility, military discipline and multifunctionality of the position and highlights the specific characteristics of this category of interpreter as a connoisseur of the military profession and of the different topics and jargon dealt with in the armed forces. The author posits that interpreting is an indispensable activity as it is an instrument of conflict prevention and mitigation.

Moving to the Iraq war, "Narrative Representations of the Interpreter in Wartime," by *Lucía Ruiz Rosendo*, applies narrative analyses to two war novels about the Battle of Najaf. Both narratives focus on the experiences of the Spanish soldiers serving in Iraq, but the author analyzes the two novels in terms of how they depict the role of the military interpreter. One of the issues that both novels tend to agree on is that interpreters in war zones and scenarios are usually locally recruited interpreters who are paradoxically considered to be an ambivalent resource. This arises because they are indispensable for communication but, at the same time, belong to the community in conflict and, therefore, arouse the mistrust of the military. The chapter also highlights the interpreter's identity as a central theme and the problematic issue of the lack of protection for interpreters who have served for Western armed forces in the Middle East.

The last chapter in this section, "After the Towers Fell: The Fate of Two Arabic Linguists" by *Maya Hess*, the founder and CEO of RedT, focuses on the paramount notion of trust through the socio-psychological lens on the US prosecutions of Ahmad Al Halabi and Mohamed Yousry, two translators/interpreters who were tried in a military and federal court, respectively. It analyzes court documents, trial records and observations in the trials of two Arabic language translators/interpreters in US military and federal courts to conclude that as a result of the 9/11 attacks, the treatment of Arab American interpreters in high-risk settings is shrouded in a distrust and stereotyping largely rooted in Islamophobia and the profession-specific Translator-Traitor Mentality (TTM).

The second part of the volume includes six chapters which look at interpreting in a humanitarian setting arising as a direct consequence of war and conflicts, most often resulting in displacement of civilians. These chapters constitute an overview of the reality of the role of interpreters in different contexts around the world, from Spain and Italy to the Middle East and South America.

In "Psychological Aspects of Interpreting Violence: A Narrative from the Israeli-Palestinian Conflict," *Manuel Barea Muñoz* draws on semi-structured interviews with 11 interpreters working at international organizations within the Israeli-Palestinian conflict to create a paradigmatic narrative which reveals the interpreter's complex positionality as an actor embedded in the conflict. The author points out that the interpreter's role goes beyond the traditional notion of being an impartial and neutral conduit to adopt a more active stance. The author highlights the emotional reactions of the interpreters and their response to psychological conditions that may subsequently linger due to repeated exposure.

Remaining in the same region, the next chapter focuses on the positionality of interpreters employed by the United Nations Office at Geneva to work in the field during events associated with the "Arab Spring." *Cherine Haidar*'s "United Nations Interpreters in the Arab Spring" compares the interviews with two professional UN interpreters, and similar to the findings presented in the previous chapter, she comes to the conclusion that interpreters who work in their own country are under significantly emotional stress, which may be understood not only as the natural outcome of interpreting accounts of harsh events but also as the result of a deliberate effort the interpreter makes to abide by an internalized code of conduct. Interestingly, the positionality of UN interpreters is different to that of other categories of interpreters in that, due to their status as international staff, they enjoy certain immunities when on duty. This provides them with some degree of protection and makes it less likely that they will fall victim to abusive power relations in the triangle of United Nations users, third party users and interpreters.

Moving on to a different region, *Maura Radicioni*, in "Interpreter-Mediated Encounters in Complex Humanitarian Settings: Language and Cultural Mediation at Emergency ONG Onlus," focuses on the role of interpreters who work for NGOs in complex humanitarian settings, such as the refugee crisis in Italy. Radicioni takes an ethnographic approach to look at the role of cultural mediators at an Italian NGO that provides medical assistance to civilian victims of war, migrants and asylum seekers. The very name of the cultural mediators defines their role as cultural brokers above their language mediation tasks. The author states that in healthcare interpreter-mediated encounters, cultural differences are better overcome when mediation is carried out by a language professional who shares a cultural background with the beneficiary. She concludes with the powerful remark that language mediation is a form of humanitarian aid, promoting peace, solidarity and respect for human rights.

From the south of Italy to the south of Spain, in "Andalusia, the Principal Gateway to Europe for Migrants and Refugees Arriving by Sea: Access to the Right to Interpreting Services in Agencies Receiving Asylum Seekers," *Estela Martín Ruel* presents the results of an investigation on the right to access to interpreting services provided at five Spanish organizations in charge of receiving asylum seekers in Andalusia. The author comes to the conclusion that the role required of interpreters by the different entities varies greatly in terms of the higher or lower levels of visibility and intervention, and that most of the existing challenges stem from a lack of training and professionalism and are associated with a lack of understanding of the interpreter's role and professional ethics.

The next chapter, "Interpreting for Refugees in Hong Kong" by *Marija Todorova*, moves the discussion to a different continent, presenting a comparative study of the humanitarian crises following the violent conflict in Vietnam and the current situation with interpreters for refugees in Hong Kong. Drawing on oral histories of interpreting during the Indochina refugee crisis and interviews with contemporary interpreters who have worked as interpreters for refugees and asylum seekers in Hong Kong, the study identifies common issues arising in interpreting for refugees across temporal and spatial boundaries that stem from the complexity of the communicative situations and the usual recruitment of non-professional ad-hoc interpreters, such as emotional stress, trust-related issues and training needs. The author concludes with the insightful remark that, in these environments, the issues of neutrality, objectivity and trust all gain new meanings which must be renegotiated.

The last chapter continues the discussion related to the refugee crisis but, focusing on South America, diverts from the previous chapters to provide a different perspective on humanitarian interpreting. Entitled "Latin American Interpreters Working in a Safe Country: Specific Training and Emotional Implications," this chapter by *Lorena Guadalupe Baudo* and *Gabriela Fernanda Lorenzo*, although not directly connected to a crisis situation, lays out the experiences and decisions of interpreters working at an international conference organized by the United Nations Development Programme (UNDP) and the Government of the Argentine Republic in which refugees, migrants and other actors participated. The authors analyze the role of the interpreter as a modeling agent, their human dimension and their activism in mediating in these conflicts and becoming involved in the values, feelings and meanings that should be transferred from one language/culture to another. The authors explore the linguistic and emotional challenges faced by the professional interpreter in preparing for such an event, as well as strategies that can be used to successfully deal with such difficulties.

Interpreting Conflict: A Comparative Framework aims to go beyond the traditional notion of interpreting in conflict to a more nuanced and precise notion that takes account of the specific context in which interpreters work and that allows us to adopt a more granular approach to the study of linguistic mediation in these contexts, using detailed empirical evidence and bringing together the thoughts of scholars, activists and practitioners. The contributions in this volume, taken as a whole, strengthen the idea that interpreting is a situated practice and that, as such, it depends on the context and setting in which it is practiced. Although all interpreting is interpreting, the particularities of the context, setting and organization/institution have a clear impact on the interpreters' positionality and on the decisions taken by them.

Despite an evident increasing interest in these issues and a body of existing research, more research has yet to be carried out to elucidate certain key concepts—ethics, neutrality, positionality, professionalism and identity—that are of paramount importance in this field. Consequently, more discussion is needed regarding the categories of interpreters working at each stage of different conflicts and the position they adopt; the actors with whom the interpreters interact in each situation; how the former perceive and define the role of the latter, and the power relations that develop between them; the specific tasks carried out by interpreters in each stage and communicative situation; the underlying factors that influence their decisions, how these decisions are related to considerations of ethics and, in particular, neutrality; and the existence of common patterns in the role of interpreters across geopolitically and geographically different regions.

With this volume we aim to make three key contributions. Firstly, the volume will offer further evidence of the situated nature of interpreting and the role of interpreters through a meaningful comparison of different conflict and post-conflict contexts in different regions. Secondly, it aims to deepen our understanding of the different factors shaping the interpreter's positionality and status. Finally, the volume will contribute to current debates about the complexity of training interpreters in these contexts.

References

Baigorri Jalón, Jesús. 2019. *Lenguas entre dos fuegos. Intérpretes en la Guerra Civil española (1936–1939)*. Granada: Comares.

Baker, Mona. 2006. Contextualization in Translator- and Interpreter-Mediated Events. *Journal of Pragmatics* 38 (3): 321–337

———. 2010. Interpreters and Translators in the War Zone. *The Translator* 16 (2): 197–222.

Delgado Luchner, Carmen, and Leila Kherbiche. 2018. Without Fear or Favour? The Positionality of ICRC and UNHCR Interpreters in the Humanitarian Field. *Target* 30 (3): 408–429.

Footitt, Hillary, and Michael Kelly. 2012. Eds. *Palgrave Studies in Languages at War*. London: Palgrave Macmillan.

———. 2018. Translation and War. In *The Routledge Handbook of Translation and Politics*, ed. Fruela Fernández and Jonathan Evans, 162–176. Abingdon/New York: Routledge.

Inghilleri, Moira. 2005. Mediating Zones of Uncertainty: Interpreter Agency, the Interpreting Habitus and Political Asylum Adjudication. *The Translator* 11 (1): 69-85.

———. 2008. The Ethical Task of the Translator in the Geo-political Arena: From Iraq to Guantanamo Bay. *Translation Studies* 1 (2): 212–223.

———. 2009. Translators in War Zones: Ethics Under Fire in Iraq. In *Globalisation, Political Violence and Translation*, ed. Esperanza Bielsa and Christopher W. Hughes, 207–221. London: Palgrave Macmillan.

Juvinall, Ben. 2013. Heaven or Hell? The Plight of Former Wartime Interpreters of the Iraq and Afghanistan Conflicts Living in the U.S. *Michigan State Journal of international Law* 21: 205–227.

Lan, Shichi. 2016. 'Crime' of Interpreting: Taiwanese Interpreters as War Criminals of World War II. In *New Insights in the History of Interpreting*, ed. Kayoko Takeda and Jesús Baigorri Jalón, 193–223. Amsterdam/Philadelphia: John Benjamins.

Méndez, Verónica. 2018. *La traducción en las Fuerzas Armadas: el traductor militar en Senegal*. MA diss., Salamanca: University of Salamanca.

Ozawa, Tomoko. 2008. Nisei Interpreters/Translators of the US Military. *JICA: Journal of the Japanese Overseas Migration Museum* 3: 37–50.

Pérez González, Luis. 2012. Translation, Interpreting and the Genealogy of Conflict. *Journal of Language and Politics* 11 (2): 169–184.

Schäffner, Christina, Krzysztof Kredens, and Yvonne Fowler. 2013. *Interpreting in a Changing Landscape*. Amsterdam/Philadelphia: John Benjamins.

Snellman, Pekka. 2016. Constraints on and Dimensions of Military Interpreter Neutrality. *Linguistica Antverpiensia* 15: 260–281.

Stahuljak, Zrinka. 2009. War, Translation, Transnationalism: Interpreters in and of the War (Croatia, 1991–1992). *Translation Studies* III: 345–374.

Tesseur, Wine, and Hilary Footitt. 2019. Professionalisms at War? Interpreting in Conflict and Post-Conflict Situations. *Journal of War & Cultural Studies* 12 (3): 268–284.

Todorova, Marija. 2016. Interpreting Conflict Mediation in Kosovo and Macedonia. *Linguistica Antverpiensia* 15: 227–240.

———. 2017. Interpreting at the Border: "Shuttle Interpreting" for the UNHCR. *Clina* 3 (2): 115–129.

[illegible]

Part II

Interpreting for the Military

2

Dual Citizen Interpreters: Consequences of Assigned Loyalties in the Aftermath of War

Kayoko Takeda

1 Introduction

During the Asia-Pacific War (1931–1945)[1] and the Allied occupation of Japan (1945–1952), there were *Nisei* (literally 'second-generation' but in this context individuals born in the United States or Canada to Japanese immigrant parents) who used their language skills to serve various military and government organizations, performing tasks such as translating captured documents, interrogating prisoners of war (POWs), monitoring enemy communications and teaching Japanese to intelligence officers. Collectively, they are called *Nisei* linguists here, following the precedent

[1] The Asia-Pacific War refers to the wars Japan engaged in, covering the period from the Mukden Incident (1931) through the Second Sino-Japanese War (1937–1945) and the Pacific War (1941–1945).

K. Takeda (✉)
Rikkyo University, Tokyo, Japan
e-mail: kayokotakeda@rikkyo.ac.jp

M. Todorova, L. Ruiz Rosendo (eds.), *Interpreting Conflict*, Palgrave Studies in Languages at War, https://doi.org/10.1007/978-3-030-66909-6_2

set in relevant primary sources.[2] The most well-known and researched of *Nisei* linguists are Americans trained in the US Army's Military Intelligence Service Language School, who played a vital role in language-related Allied missions on the battlefield, at intelligence posts and in postwar operations in occupied Japan (McNaughton 2006). In addition to American *Nisei*, Takeda (2018) discusses Canadian *Nisei* translators, interpreters and Japanese instructors in the British and Canadian war efforts.

On the opposing side of *Nisei* linguists within Allied organizations, however, there were *Nisei* who used their English proficiency for Japanese intelligence and military operations in the fight against their birth countries. Although some references to such *Nisei* have been made in historical studies of Japanese Americans, the Asia-Pacific War and subsequent war crimes trials (e.g., Azuma 2005; Shibusawa 2006; Takeda 2016), the experiences of *Nisei* linguists within wartime Japanese organizations have not been a focus of research, nor have the consequences these individuals faced in the aftermath of the war. This chapter attempts to fill the gap by shedding light on the backgrounds and wartime activities of these *Nisei* linguists and on their treatment by Allied powers in the postwar occupation era. The records of postwar trials against *Nisei* interpreters for treason and war crimes are drawn on to examine in particular the nature of tasks assigned to heritage language speakers.[3] Although this is a case study based on close readings of archival materials and relevant secondary sources, special attention is paid to its relevance to issues faced by present-day interpreters by exploring the role of interpreters in violent conflict and social and legal concerns of heritage language speakers as military linguists.

[2] Primary sources for *Nisei* linguists are mostly found in the Records of the Allied Operational and Occupation Headquarters, World War II (Record Group 331), US National Archives and Records Administration.

[3] A heritage language is a minority language that a person is exposed to at home as a child.

2 *Nisei* Linguists in the Japanese Military, Government and State News Agency

2.1 Nisei *in Japan in the 1930s*

Although no official records are available, up to 50,000 *Nisei* were estimated to be living in Japan in the mid-1930s (Azuma 2005; Ichioka 1997; Yamashita 1938). Azuma (ibid., 136–138) categorizes them into three groups. The vast majority were among the first group of those who had moved to Japan due to their parents' decision to return to their homeland or who had been sent by their parents to live with relatives and be educated in Japan. The timing and duration of their schooling varied as did the motivation for it. Some immigrant parents wished for their children to learn the language and culture of their ancestral land while others sought to ease the burden of economic hardship.

The second group represented a few hundred *Nisei* professionals working in mass media, the Japanese government, academia and private corporations. Due to the severe economic downturn and to discrimination against people of Japanese ancestry during the Great Depression (1929–1939), *Nisei* struggled to secure decent jobs in their home countries, even with university degrees. Taking advantage of their English proficiency and expertise, educated *Nisei* found a land of opportunities in Japan.

The third group consisted of about 4000 *Nisei* students who crossed the Pacific specifically to attend high school or university in Japan. During the 1930s there was a spike in the number of *Nisei* studying in Japan (Yamashita 1935, 1938), fed by anti-Japanese sentiment in North America and the yen's depreciation as a result of Japan's abandonment of the gold standard (Morimoto 1995). Additionally, Azuma (ibid., 138–139) argues that this transnational education of *Nisei* was supported by the idealistic internationalism envisioned by some *Issei* (first-generation Japanese immigrants) who hoped that *Nisei* would serve as a bridge across the Pacific. This narrative was also embraced by Japanese officials with imperial ambitions for global expansion.

2.2 Nisei *in the State News Agency*

The earliest cases of *Nisei* involvement in language-related roles in the Japanese war effort can be found among those employed at national news agencies. As Japan emerged as an imperial power, leaders in industry, the press and the government established national news agencies in the mid-1920s to secure the ability to transmit Japan's views and standing to the world to counterbalance the news provided by dominant Western media. In response to the international condemnation of Japan's actions following the 1931 Mukden Incident[4] in northeastern China, these agencies were consolidated into Domei News Agency in 1936 to fully function as a state news agency backed by the Japanese government.

During the early years of Domei, several *Nisei* worked on the English edition, including Clark H. Kawakami, who was educated at Harvard and Geneva; Ken Murayama, a graduate of George Washington University; Tosuke Yamasaki, who graduated from the University of Missouri; and Tamotsu Murayama, a former reporter for Japanese newspapers in San Francisco. Seeking professional positions in Japan, these highly educated *Nisei* demonstrated their ability to translate Japanese news into English and produce English-language news.

In fact, the Japanese government established a boarding school called Heishikan in Tokyo in order to train *Nisei* aged between 20 and 30 in Japanese language and culture as well as translation for two years so that they could work in the press and government agencies as English-speaking defenders of Japan. With generous scholarships as incentives and contributing to US/UK-Japanese friendship as the stated purpose,[5] the recruitment of students started in the United States and Canada in 1939 in coordination with Domei. As the hostility with the United States intensified, from 1940 onward the recruitment of *Nisei* was carried out within Japan and Southeast Asia. In total, 68 *Nisei* were enrolled in Heishikan

---

[4] Also called the Manchurian Incident, it marked the start of Japanese aggression into northeastern China and led to the establishment of Manchukuo, a Japanese puppet state in 1933.

[5] This purpose of establishing Heishikan is stated in the inaugural issue of The Heishikan News (1940).

and 47 graduated. Most of them went to work for Domei, translating and producing Japanese propagandistic news in English.

2.3 Nisei *Stranded in Japan*

While the *Nisei* discussed above voluntarily took up roles on the Japanese side, there were *Nisei* who were stranded in Japan and conscripted or made to serve as linguists in Japanese military and government organizations. In the midst of the heightened nationalism and militarism of late-1930s Japan, police surveillance and harassment of *Nisei* as suspected American spies intensified. Fearing being conscripted by the Japanese military and losing their North American citizenship, several hundreds of *Nisei* rushed back to their birth country by the end of 1940 (Azuma 2005, 158). There were, however, *Nisei* students, workers and visitors still in Japan when the Pacific War broke out in 1941. While some had chosen to live there permanently or stay for study, work or family reasons, others had been unable to return home in the chaos following Japan's attack on Pearl Harbor and were stranded in Japan.[6] Eventually, they were either conscripted or compelled to join the Japanese war effort as soldiers,[7] *gunzoku* (civilian members of the Japanese military, such as interpreters and translators), radio monitors and propagandists.

2.4 Issue of Citizenship

Prior to 1924, *Nisei* born in the United States could automatically acquire dual citizenship because the United States granted citizenship to individuals who were born in the United States regardless of their ancestral origin (right of the soil) while Japan granted citizenship to individuals

---

[6] Iva Toguri D'Aquino, also known as Tokyo Rose, was among the *Nisei* who were stranded due to paperwork problems. She participated in English-language radio programs that aimed to demoralize Allied soldiers during the war and was convicted by the United States for treason after the war. See Duus (1977) for details. According to Duus (ibid.), there were an estimated 7000–10,000 *Nisei* strandees in Japan.

[7] See Kadoike (2010), Kadota (2011), McDonald and McDonald Mazawa (2011), NHK (2013) and Tachibana (1994) for more on *Nisei* students conscripted by the Japanese military, including those who became *kamikaze* suicide attackers.

whose father was a Japanese national regardless of their birthplace (right of the blood). Likewise, Canadian-born *Nisei* were also automatically citizens of Japan and Canada (and therefore Britain).[8] However, following the 1924 US immigration law which effectively stopped further immigration from Japan, the Japanese government revised its nationality law to require *Issei* parents to register their children (*Nisei*) with a Japanese consulate to obtain Japanese nationality. Dual citizenship was no longer automatic. At the same time, the revised Japanese law relaxed restrictions on *Nisei* renouncing their Japanese nationality. Previously, *Nisei* males within the ages of compulsory military service were not allowed to renounce their Japanese citizenship and were conscripted if residing in Japan. Under the revised law, *Nisei* of any age could renounce their Japanese citizenship and avoid being conscripted by the Japanese military.

While many *Nisei* in North America renounced their Japanese citizenship,[9] those who chose to stay in Japan presumably kept dual nationality until they lost US or Canadian citizenship by serving the Japanese military and voting in Japan. With its relationship with Allied nations rapidly deteriorating, the Japanese government started requiring foreign residents, including *Nisei* with American or Canadian citizenship, to report to the local police, so the authorities presumably had a sense of *Nisei*'s whereabouts within Japan.

2.5 Nisei *Linguists in the Japanese Military*

Considering that *Nisei* were under surveillance, it would not have been difficult for the Japanese military to locate potential linguists for its war operations. While the exact numbers of *Nisei* who served in the Japanese military are unknown, there are firsthand accounts that offer some estimates. For instance, in an NHK TV documentary (2013) on American *Nisei* in the Japanese army, Teri Morinaka talks about 20 young *Nisei* women, including her own sister Yoshiko, who worked in the Japanese Second General Army's special intelligence unit in Hiroshima to monitor

[8] Canadian-born *Nisei* were denied the right to vote, along with other Asian Canadians, until 1949.

[9] Just before the outbreak of the Pacific War, about 70% of *Nisei* in the United States held only US citizenship (Lyon 2012, 18).

shortwave broadcasts. All of them were killed by the atomic bomb. According to Shigetsugu Tsuneishi (1978, 261), a former intelligence officer in the Japanese Army, about 200 *Nisei* were hired as temporary workers by a special intelligence unit of the Army General Staff Office.

The archival documents that are most revealing of the tasks carried out by *Nisei* military interpreters are those from postwar trials for Japanese war crimes. The records of trials in which wartime interpreters testified as defendants[10] and witnesses bring to light that there were *Nisei* civilian interpreters attached to the *Kempeitai* (military police),[11] POW camps and private corporations that utilized Allied POWs as forced laborers under the Japanese military's supervision. These interpreters delivered their superiors' orders to POWs and local residents and worked in interrogations and torture of POWs and locals suspected of being anti-Japanese elements in Japanese-occupied areas.

In addition, there are memoirs by and publications on *Nisei* soldiers in the Japanese military that indicate that their duties included language-related tasks such as monitoring enemy communications and interpreting communication to local civilians (e.g., Kadoike 2010; Tachibana 1994). For instance, Teiji Takemiya, as a *Nisei* university student in Tokyo, was conscripted into the Japanese Navy in 1943 and was assigned to a suicide mission unit. Because of his English proficiency, however, he was transferred to the Navy's General Staff Office to monitor overseas shortwave radio programs (Takeda 2018).

2.6 Nisei *Interpreters Recruited from the Exchange Ship*

Records of the trial of Masayoshi Nigo,[12] an American *Nisei* interpreter, indicate one avenue the Japanese military resorted to for recruiting *Nisei*

[10] Over 100 wartime interpreters associated with the Japanese military were prosecuted at postwar Allied military trials for Japanese war crimes (Takeda 2018)

[11] *Kempeitai* was a Gestapo-like military police that notoriously terrorized POWs and local civilians with harsh interrogations and torture.

[12] WO 235/891 Trial of Haruzo Sumida and 20 others (including Masayoshi Nigo). Transcript (Nigo Trial, hereafter), 397–398. UK National Archives.

linguists. Almost immediately after the Pacific War broke out, the United States and Japan started negotiating exchanges of government officials and other civilians who were stranded on the 'wrong' side, completing two of the three planned exchanges. In the second exchange in September 1943, the *Gripsholm* (a Swedish cruise ship) and the *Teia Maru* (a Japanese troop ship) met at Mormugao, India, to swap their passengers and cargos, then returned to the United States and Japan respectively. Of the 1516 passengers who moved from the *Gripsholm* to the *Teia Maru* at Mormugao, 314 had come from internment camps,[13] including over 100 *Nisei* (Murakawa and Kumei 1992, 21). When the *Teia Maru* arrived at Singapore and Manila, *Nisei* men were urged to get off the ship and work as interpreters. Military officers would visit the ship repeatedly, threatening young *Nisei* with conscription into the army upon arrival in Japan if they declined to work as interpreters.[14] Thus, some *Nisei* took the job under duress (ibid., 105). According to Nigo's testimony during his trial, he worked for the *Kempeitai* in Singapore where three or four out of nine or ten English-speaking interpreters were American *Nisei* (Nigo Trial, 398).

2.7 Nisei *Linguists in Intelligence Gathering*

Outside the military, over 100 *Nisei* utilized their English skills for monitoring and transcribing overseas shortwave radio programs and wired messages at intelligence gathering sections of the Ministry of Foreign Affairs and the Ministry of Communication. Domei sorted and translated the transcribed information to be distributed to relevant military and government organizations. According to a postwar report submitted from the Japanese government to the Superior Commander for the Allied Powers (SCAP) on 10 April 1946,[15] there were 90 *Nisei*, including 21

[13] Nearly 120,000 Japanese and Japanese Americans on the west coast of the United States were forcibly relocated to internment camps in 1942.

[14] A total of 96 passengers from North America disembarked in Singapore (Ministry of Foreign Affairs of Japan 1943).

[15] American-born Japanese now in Japan, a report from the Imperial Japanese Government Central Liaison Office to General Headquarters of the Supreme Commander for the Allied Powers, dated 10 April 1946. *General Headquarters G-2, Far East Command, Jan-Dec 1946.*

women, working as shortwave broadcasting monitors, translators and typists at the Foreign Ministry during the war. About 20 of them were those trained at Heishikan (Ikeda 1981/2015). Additionally, the report lists 29 *Nisei*, including five women, who were employed by other government organizations, such as a quasi-official communications section of the Ministry of Navy, the War Prisoner Intelligence Bureau and the Ministry of Communication.

3 Postwar Experiences of *Nisei* Linguists on the Losing Side

3.1 Dual Citizenship and Treason Charges

Perhaps the most well-known American *Nisei* interpreter associated with Japan's war effort is Tomoya Kawakita, who was convicted for treason in the aftermath of the war. The following story is based on Kawakita's trial records[16] and biographical information included in Shibusawa (2006) and Shimojima (1993).

Kawakita was born in California in 1921. Although he was automatically eligible for dual citizenship, Kawakita's father never registered him with a Japanese consulate. With his US passport, Kawakita crossed the Pacific for schooling in Japan in 1939. As an American citizen, he was under Japanese police surveillance. Remaining in Japan following his graduation from Meiji University in 1943, Kawakita formally filed an entry into a Japanese family census register, allowing him to secure employment and circumvent police surveillance as a Japanese citizen. From 1944 through the end of the war, Kawakita worked as an interpreter at a mine and metal processing plant that utilized Allied POWs, including 400 Americans, as forced laborers. After the war, Kawakita briefly assisted the Allied occupation forces as an interpreter, renewed his American passport by claiming that he was registered in the family census under duress and moved back to California. In 1946, a former POW spotted him and informed the FBI. Kawakita was arrested and charged

[16] See *Kawakita v. United States*, 343 U.S. 717 (1952) (Kawakita Trial, hereafter).

with treason on account of his ill-treatment of American POWs. The prosecution argued that Kawakita never lost his US citizenship and owed his allegiance to the United States. He was found guilty and sentenced to death. His US citizenship was revoked in 1948. In 1953, Kawakita's sentence was commuted to life imprisonment, and in 1963, President John F. Kennedy ordered his release from prison on the condition that he would leave the United States and never come back. He lived in Japan following his deportation.

3.2 War Crimes and Treason: Two Trials of Kanao Inouye

Like Kawakita, the treason case of Kanao Inouye, a Canadian *Nisei* interpreter, involved the issue of dual citizenship. Extraordinarily, Inouye was also prosecuted for war crimes in a British military trial in Hong Kong prior to the treason trial. Inouye is known as the first Canadian charged with war crimes and one of only two Canadians ever convicted and hanged for high treason. Here is a summary of Inouye's story based on his testimonies and statements at the two trials.[17]

Kanao Inouye was born in British Columbia in 1916. In 1935, his grandfather, a prominent businessman in Japan, urged Inouye to move to Japan as his father had died. Inouye enrolled in Waseda International Institute[18] in 1936 to learn Japanese. In the following year, he was enlisted in a Manchurian unit of the Japanese Army but subsequently took a leave for health reasons. In 1942, he was conscripted as a civilian interpreter and dispatched to Hong Kong where he worked at POW prisons from May 1942 to December 1943. After assignments at other military posts, discharge and employment at a trading company, Inouye returned to Hong Kong in June 1944 and worked for the *Kempeitai* as an interpreter through February 1945.

---

[17] See WO 235/927 Trial of Kanao Inouye (Inouye War Crimes Trial, hereafter), UK National Archives, and *Supreme Court of Hong Kong, Rex v. Inouye Kanao*. (Inouye Treason Trial, hereafter).

[18] A Japanese school for *Nisei* and other international students operated by Waseda University from 1935 to 1945, mainly as a preparatory school to enter the university.

In the British war crimes trial of Inouye in May 1946 in Hong Kong, he was accused of ill-treating and torturing POWs and local civilians while working as an interpreter. Inouye defended himself by stating that he was just interpreting and following the orders of his superiors. In the end, he was convicted and sentenced to death.[19] Then, Inouye's lawyer argued that Inouye had Canadian citizenship and could not be tried in a war crimes trial against Canada's enemy. His conviction was overturned, but Inouye was then sent to the Supreme Court in Hong Kong and charged as a British subject for high treason. This time, he claimed that he was a Japanese citizen devoted to the Emperor. He also referred to the discrimination and prejudice he experienced in Canada. Rejecting his claim, the court found him guilty and sentenced him to death.[20] In August 1947, he was hanged in Hong Kong.

3.3 'American-speaking' Interpreter as War Criminal

Masayoshi Nigo was another *Nisei* interpreter who was convicted for war crimes in a British military trial. As previously mentioned, Nigo was recruited by the Japanese army from the exchange ship to work as an interpreter in Singapore in 1943. The following is based on Nigo's testimony and statements at his trial and his interview included in Murakawa and Kumei (1992).

Born in California in 1919, Nigo was in an internment camp when his father, who had returned to Japan, arranged for him to be on the exchange ship. He decided to leave the ship in Singapore because 'just using his mouth' as an interpreter would be better than facing Americans in combat (Nigo Trial, 398; Murakawa and Kumei 1992, 22). He was assigned to the *Kempeitai* and was involved as an interpreter in harsh interrogations and torture of local civilians. At his trial in March and April 1946 in Singapore, Nigo was charged with the ill-treatment of local civilians. In witness testimonies during the trial, he was identified as an 'American-speaking' interpreter who was kind to British POWs (Nigo Trial 33, 44,

[19] For details, see Inouye War Crimes Trial.

[20] For details, see Inouye Treason Trial.

49, 307, 312). Nigo stated that he was just interpreting and denied the charges but was ultimately found guilty and sentenced to life imprisonment. He was transferred to Sugamo Prison in Tokyo and later released for clemency in 1961.

3.4 Working for the Occupation Forces

Although the three *Nisei* interpreters discussed above faced severe consequences for their wartime actions in the aftermath of the war, most of the *Nisei* linguists associated with the Japanese war effort were able to escape condemnation from their birth countries (now the occupiers of defeated Japan) as traitors for assisting the enemy. In fact, many of them ended up working as interpreters and translators for the occupation forces. Concerning *Nisei* who worked for the Japanese during the war, the SCAP G-2 (intelligence section) reported to Washington on 22 May 1946[21] as follows:

> most of the jobs described were of a temporary emergency nature and ... Japanese nationality was not a prerequisite. ... The majority of the Nisei contacted allege that they were forced to take the employment indicated under threat of considerable personal harm. They further state that whether they wanted to or not they had to remain in Japan and keep themselves alive, and that since they were not permitted to repatriate to the United States and were not interned by the Japanese, they of necessity secured such employment as was available to them.

Faced with severe shortages of interpreters and translators to assist with the implementation of its occupation policies (Takeda 2016), the SCAP seems to have accepted the *Nisei*'s claims described in the report and made it possible to tap them as competent linguists who also had the advantage of being familiar with the inner workings of Japanese organizations. The case of Teiji Takemiya shows how the US occupiers chose to

[21] American-born Japanese now in Japan, a correspondence from the Military Intelligence Section, General Staff G-2, General Headquarters, United States Army Forces, Pacific to Assistant Chief of Staff, General Headquarters G-2, War Department General Staff, Washington, dated 22 May 1946. *General Headquarters G-2, Far East Command, Jan-Dec 1946.*

overlook *Nisei*'s past involvement in the Japanese war effort. As previously mentioned, American-born Takemiya was trained to become a suicide attacker in the Japanese Navy. Right after the end of the war, he was assigned to the role of an interpreter on the Japanese side during the negotiations with the United States concerning the signing ceremony of the Japanese surrender. Impressed by his linguistic ability, the US Navy then recruited Takemiya as an interpreter and later as a civilian administrator at its base in Yokosuka (TKU 2011). Some *Nisei* linguists regained their US citizenship and returned to their birth country following the US Immigration and Nationality Act of 1952 (NHK 2013).

Some of the Heishikan-trained *Nisei* who used to work at the radio monitoring section within the Foreign Ministry established Radiopress, a news agency, in January 1946, encouraged by US officials and supported by the Japanese Foreign Ministry. Radiopress continued the work of monitoring overseas radio programs, translating relevant information and delivering it mostly to government organizations, which contributed to Japan's Cold War intelligence (Torii 2014). Radiopress now is a North Korea expert.

4 Discussion

The experiences of *Nisei* linguists discussed above shed light on the nature of tasks assigned to heritage language speakers, the muddled and risky aspects of dual citizenship, and the visibility of interpreters in war. With a range of bilingual and bicultural backgrounds, *Nisei* in wartime Japan were in a unique position to meet the linguistic needs of Japan's intelligence gathering, propagandistic activities and military operations. Even before the outbreak of the Pacific War, working as an interpreter and translator was a viable career option for *Nisei* living in Japan.[22] In the escalating conflict with Anglophone nations, English was deemed 'the enemy language', and English classes were being drastically reduced in

[22] For instance, newsletters of the Waseda International Institute ran an ongoing advertisement offering student translation and interpreting services (Waseda Hoshien 1935-1945). A 1939 survey conducted with 437 *Nisei* in the Tokyo area indicated that 'Translator, interpreter, and guide' ranked third on the list for possible occupations open to *Nisei* women (Keisen Girls' School 1940).

schools (Erikawa 2008) even as the value of knowing it was increasing. As tasks involving translation became more urgent and voluminous, the Japanese government took advantage of *Nisei*'s citizenship status to mobilize them for its war effort. Those young men who were formally registered in a family census were conscripted into the Japanese military, which was supposed to mean automatic renunciation of their US or Canadian citizenship. Even those who kept the citizenship of their birth country were compelled to serve the Japanese government as they were treated as loyalists by virtue of their father's nationality. *Nisei*, including those stranded in Japan, were now driven to take the Japanese side.

It was not only their English proficiency but also their familiarity with the social and cultural norms of the enemies and their presumed loyalty to the ancestral homeland that made *Nisei* linguists valuable assets to Japan's war effort, whether it be by monitoring American radio programs or producing propagandistic news in English. In contrast to *Issei*'s idealistic expectation of *Nisei* becoming a bridge across the Pacific and Heishikan's front of training 'goodwill ambassadors',[23] these *Nisei* were assigned to Japan's cause and carried out missions to defeat their birth countries.

Kawakita's story showcases the personal toll assigned loyalties take on dual citizens of nations at war with each other. Kawakita was an interpreter employed as a Japanese citizen by an organization under control of the Japanese army in Japan. The court, however, determined that, as a US citizen, Kawakita should have maintained his allegiance to the United States, even in Japan. As in the treason case of Inouye, considering the fact that a number of *Nisei* left North America to escape discrimination and forcible relocation to internment camps, one could point to the hypocrisy of a government charging with treason a member of a group it designated as enemy aliens. Inouye was even called 'the guest of the Dominion of Canada' by the judge of his war crime trial (Inouye War Crimes Trial, 149) despite the fact that he was born in Canada. While some may find the ways Kawakita and Inouye claimed their own

[23] This term was used by Yoshio Shimogaki, a former Heishikan student, during his interview in McDonald and McDonald Mazawa (2011).

citizenships opportunistic, others may view their behavior as a desperate act to survive through difficult and extraordinary circumstances.

There were many other *Nisei* with dual nationality who took part in Japan's war effort, but why were Kawakita and Inouye among the very few who were convicted for treason?[24] Why were Nigo and Inouye charged for war crimes, along with other wartime interpreters? Granted, the trial records of Kawakita, Inouye and Nigo contain a number of testimonies describing their abusive behavior toward POWs and local civilians, including their participation in torture as interpreter in the cases of Inouye and Nigo. However, attention should also be paid to the visibility of interpreters and the immediate performativity of their work as plausible factors contributing to their fate. Interpreters who had been in close contact with Allied POWs and local civilians victimized by the Japanese military were in a vulnerable position in war crimes investigations since they were easily remembered and identified. In particular, American-born and Canadian-born interpreters seem to have left even greater impressions on the victims' mind, as reflected in references to them in the trial records. The fluency and accent of their English was a constant reminder of where they came from. Nigo was identified as the 'American-speaking' interpreter by witnesses (Nigo Trial, 33, 44, 307, 312). Canadian POWs in the Hong Kong prisons nicknamed Inouye 'Kamloops Kid' after his hometown in Canada (Inouye War Crimes Trial, 321). It was alleged that *Nisei* interpreters expressed bitterness over the abuse they had suffered in their birth countries, that they were lashing out in vengeance at their 'fellow countrymen' and took pleasure in seeing white men being degraded by the Japanese.[25] In the postwar war crimes investigations, they were an easy target of hostility and viewed as traitors by American and Canadian POWs. Also, the immediate performativity of interpreting led to the view of the interpreter as accountable for the action they enabled instead of perceiving them as mere messengers, reflected in the following statement from the judge in the Kawakita case: '[Kawakita's]

[24] Iva Toguri D'Aquino and Kawakita were the only Americans and Inouye the only Canadian convicted for treason in the context of the Pacific War. Toguri D'Aquino was pardoned in 1977.

[25] For details, see the transcripts of the Kawakita and Inouye War Crimes trials.

exhortation helped force prisoners to mine more ore for the Japanese war effort' (Kawakita Trial, 5003, 5028).

As discussed before, however, being a bilingual dual citizen did not prove to be a liability for all *Nisei* who found themselves on the losing side. Many *Nisei* who had worked for the Japanese war effort, including as trained suicide attackers, became interpreters and translators for the Allied forces in occupied Japan after the war. In short, their services were in demand on both sides. How the trustworthiness of *Nisei* linguists was viewed by Japanese organizations during the war and by Allied occupation forces in the postwar period will be examined in future studies by drawing parallels and comparisons with the case of *Nisei* linguists within the Allied organizations (cf. McNaughton 2006; Takeda 2018).

Examination of *Nisei* linguists who served wartime Japanese organizations brings to the fore issues relevant even to today's contexts, such as the complex and risky issues faced by a dual citizen of warring states, the asset and liability of being a heritage language speaker in war, the ethical and legal implications of language mediation in criminal acts, and the consequences of transnational human movements in the midst of international conflict. Against the backdrop of post-9/11 world affairs and ongoing conflicts, scholars have paid sustained attention to issues around the recruitment and training of military linguists as well as the risks they encounter,[26] and activists have been promoting their support and protection.[27] Historical references to *Nisei* linguists during the Asia-Pacific War may prove to be helpful in achieving a fuller understanding of the language issues bred in environments of international armed conflict.

---

[26] For instance, see Footitt and Kelly (2012a, 2012b) and other titles in the Palgrave Studies in Languages at War.

[27] For instance, RedT is a non-profit organization that advocates for the protection of interpreters and translators in high-risk settings. https://red-t.org/

References

Primary Sources

American-born Japanese now in Japan, a report from the Imperial Japanese Government Central Liaison Office to General Headquarters of the Supreme Commander for the Allied Powers, dated 10 April 1946. 211: *General Headquarters G-2, Far East Command, Jan-Dec* 1946a. Japanese Diet Library digital library. http://dl/ndl/go.jp/titleThum/info:ndljp/pid/3540498

———, a correspondence from the Military Intelligence Section, General Staff G-2, General Headquarters, United States Army Forces, Pacific to Assistant Chief of Staff, General Headquarters G-2, War Department General Staff, Washington, dated 22 May, 1946. 211: *General Headquarters G-2, Far East Command, Jan-Dec* 1946b. Japanese Diet Library digital library. http://dl/ndl/go.jp/titleThum/info:ndljp/pid/3540498

Heishikan. *Heishikan News*. No. 1. 10 August 1940.

Ministry of Foreign Affairs of Japan. 1943. *Nichibei dainiji-kokan: Shonan gesen-sha*. Diplomatic Archives of the Ministry of Foreign Affairs of Japan. Tokyo.

Record Group 331, Records of the Allied Operational and Occupation Headquarters, World War II. US National Archives and Records Administration, College Park, Maryland.

Supreme Court of Hong Kong, Rex v. Inouye Kanao. Government Record Service, The Government of Hong Kong Special Administrative Region, Public Records Office, Kowloon.

United States v. Tomoya Kawakita, 343 U.S. 717 (1952).

Waseda Hoshien. 1935–1945. *Waseda kokusai gakuin ho* (Waseda International Institute). Tokyo.

WO 235/891 Trial of Haruzo Sumida and others. UK National Archives, Kew.

WO 235/927 Trial of Kanao Inouye. UK National Archives, Kew.

Secondary Sources

Azuma, Eiichiro. 2005. *Between Two Empires: Race, History, and Transnationalism in Japanese America*. Oxford: Oxford University Press.

Duus, Masayo. 1977. *Tokyo Rose*. Tokyo: Simul Shuppankai.

Erikawa, Haruo. 2008. *Nihon-jin wa eigo-o do manandekitaka*. Tokyo: Kenkyusha.

Footitt, Hilary, and Michael Kelly. 2012a. *Languages and the Military*. London: Palgrave Macmillan.

———. 2012b. *Languages at War*. London: Palgrave Macmillan.

Ichioka, Yuji. 1997. Special Issue: Beyond National Boundaries: The Complexity of Japanese-American History. *Amerasia Journal* 23 (3): 1.

Ikeda, Norizane. 1981/2015. *Puropaganda senshi*. Tokyo: Chuo Bunko.

Kadoike, Hiroshi. 2010. *Nihongun heishi ni natta America-jin-tachi*. Tokyo: Genshu Shuppansha.

Kadota, Ryusho. 2011. *Sokai ni kiyu*. Tokyo: Shueisha.

Keisen Girls' School. 1940. *The Nisei: A Study of Their Life in Japan*. Tokyo: Keisen Girls' School.

Lyon, Cherstin M. 2012. *Prisons and Patriots*. Philadelphia: Temple University Press.

McDonald, Mary, and Thomas McDonald Mazawa. 2011. Nisei Stories of Wartime Japan (DVD). Mary McDonald.

McNaughton, James C. 2006. *Nisei Linguists: Japanese Americans in the Military Intelligence Service during World War II*. Washington, DC: Department of the Army.

Morimoto, Toyotomi. 1995. The American Nisei in Japan prior to WWII. *Surugadai University Studies* 11: 43–65.

Murakawa, Yoko, and Teruko Kumei. 1992. A Study on the 'Japanese' Repatriates and Expatriates from the United States during and after World War II. Toyota Foundation Research Report.

NHK. 2013. Nagai tabiji: Nihon-hei ni natta Amerika-jin (TV documentary).

Shimojima, Tetsuro. 1993. *America kokka hangyaku-zai*. Tokyo: Kodansha.

Shibusawa, Naoko. 2006. *America's Geisha Ally: Reimagining the Japanese Enemy*. Cambridge, MA: Harvard University Press.

Tachibana, Yuzuru. 1994. *Teikoku-kaigun shikan ni natta nikkei Nisei*. Tokyo: Tsukiji Shokan.

Takeda, Kayoko. 2016. Guilt, Survival, Opportunities, and Stigma: Japanese Interpreters in the Postwar Occupation Period (1945–1952). In *New Insights in the History of Interpreting*, ed. Kayoko Takeda and Jesús Baigorri-Jalón, 225–246. Amsterdam/Philadelphia: John Benjamins.

———. 2018. *Taiheiyo-senso, Nihongo choho-sen*. Tokyo: Chikuma Shobo.

TKU. 2011. Hyakunen no omoi, sedai o koete (TV documentary).

Torii, Hideharu. 2014. *Kokusaku-tsushinsha 'Domei' no kobo*. Tokyo: Kadensha.
Tsuneishi, Shigetsugu. 1978. *Shinri-sakusen no kaiso*. Tokyo: Tosen Shuppan.
Yamashita, Soen. 1935. *Nikkei-shimin no Nihon ryugaku jijo*. Tokyo: Bunseisha.
———. 1938. *Nichibei o tsunagu mono*. Tokyo: Bunseisha.

3

To Be or Not to Be Loyal: Loyalty of Military Interpreters Serving the Japanese Army in the Second Sino-Japanese War (1931–1945)

Tian Luo and Ruiqi Zhu

1 Introduction

Translators and interpreters play roles much more significant than we imagine in wars between/among countries. Baker (2006) remarks that the very process of mobilizing military power and management of conflict depends on continuous acts of translation to a large extent. Being aware of the importance of military translation and interpretation, academic interest in military translation is on the rise recently (cf. Footitt and Kelly 2012; Footitt and Tobia 2013; Inghilleri 2008; Salama-Carr 2007; Stahuljak 2000).

The Second Sino-Japanese War (1931–1945) (hereinafter referred to as SSJW), also referred to as China's War of Resistance against Japanese Aggression, began with the Japan's invasion of northeast China in

T. Luo (✉)
Chongqing Jiaotong University, Chongqing, China

R. Zhu
University of Leeds, Leeds, UK

M. Todorova, L. Ruiz Rosendo (eds.), *Interpreting Conflict*, Palgrave Studies in Languages at War, https://doi.org/10.1007/978-3-030-66909-6_3

September 1931 and ended with Japan's surrender in September 1945. Unexceptionally, this conflict involved the participation of a large number of linguists, mainly interpreters, working for both sides of the war. It provides an interesting site where military interpreters can be researched.

However, among the large body of research literature on military translation and interpretation, only a few papers focus on the interpreters in China's War of Resistance against Japanese Aggression. For instance, Luo (2016) looks into the role of over 4000 interpreters in SSJW who helped increase combat power and eventually contributed greatly to the victory of the Alliance. Guo (2015, 2016), drawing upon Bourdieu's theory of sociology, discusses how interpreters, with their capitals, managed to survive the war by serving different interest groups. None of these researches discussed concept of loyalty with earnest attention although it was mentioned occasionally in passing.

Among a wide range of themes and topics still need to be examined concerning military interpreters, loyalty is a long-neglected but worthwhile theme for investigation since loyalty greatly determines for which side military interpreters may serve with what function and to what effect. This chapter, therefore, tries to look into the loyalty of military interpreters working for the Japanese forces during SSJW.

2 Loyalty in Military Context

Loyalty is a rather complicated theme that (re)surfaces rather frequently in popular discourses, from newspapers to television drama, from code of conducts to political speeches. Loyalty becomes critical when interests are in conflict and one is required to choose a side. It travels across social time and space, occurring within micro and macro sociological interactions (Connor 2007, 1). Before we look into this complicated issue of interpreter's loyalty in military settings, it is essential to gain a comprehensive view of the loyalty in the general sense. In the following section, some basic concepts of loyalty will be examined, including the definition, layers and the functions it may play.

2.1 Loyalty: Definition, Functions and Layers

Although the concept of loyalty denotes diverse connections and relationships and thus "appears to be almost too broad a term to have a definitive meaning" (Connor 2007, 2), some scholars managed to come up with certain definitions. Connor (2010, 279), for instance, defines loyalty as "an emotion that is central to group and individual identity formation" and crucial to social action. Philosopher Keller (2007, 21) believes that loyalty is "the attitude and associated pattern of conduct that is constituted by an individual's taking something's side, and doing so with a certain sort of motive."

Our research agrees to Keller's comprehensive and plausible definition that sees loyalty as not only an attitude or emotion but also some motived behaviors and actions for the following reasons. On the one hand, since emotion is rather abstract, elusive, even ambiguous in most cases, it needs to be testified or to find its expression in concrete actions. On the other hand, action needs emotion as its guidance and support. Without the support of emotion, loyal action seldom persists. An individual can only be said to be loyal when he displays such a trait in both emotion and conduct.

Loyalty has multiple functions like "regulating social intercourse, defining roles, informing identity and giving reason for action" (Connor 2007, 8). For instance, loyalty is vital in informing and furnishing individual and collective identity primarily because it denotes membership and belonging (Connor 2007, 49). Loyalty also motivates action; put it another way, it provides a justification for action, behavior and cognition. These claims help build an overall picture of what loyalty is and how it functions (Connor 2007, 5).

Loyalty exists in multiple layers since individuals involve a great variety of social interactions in a multitude of relationships. A person can easily have many loyalties toward different objects, such as loyalties to family, friends, colleagues, sports, politics, religion, class, organizations and nations (Coleman 2009; Connor 2007, 2). He can be loyal to his wife in his marriage and at the same time to his institution where he is employed. In most cases, a person is expected to be loyal at more than one level;

however, not all loyalties share the same importance or status. "Some loyalties are generally seen to be more important than others; some loyalties even have legal protection" (Coleman 2009, 110). Some individuals may choose to engage certain layers, which means that particular loyalties become the salient ones under some circumstances (Connor 2007, 47). For instance, war and international sports are likely to provoke a nationalistic layer of loyalty. A threat to the survival of a company may elicit employer loyalty, and an ethnic food festival could reinforce the actor's ethnic loyalty.

Different layers of loyalties can sometimes clash, which forces people into two different solutions. On the one hand, an individual may negotiate these layers and adheres to one layer after a number of processes in which the most dominant level is determined. If these layers of loyalty do not constitute clashes or oppositions of interests between two sides, such choice of one loyalty over another does not lead to "a consequence being disloyal" (Coleman 2009, 110). On the other hand, if there is a harsh confrontation of interests between two opposite sides, and a person leaves the side he used to serve, abandons the bonds of loyalty, and turns to another side for reasons that are self-serving (Kleinig 2017, 10), he becomes disloyal to the side he previously serves. To betray is usually considered a profound moral vice (Connor 2010, 278) by the ingroup members.

Loyalty can be a virtue in some cases and a vice in other ones. According to Coleman (2009, 110), factors such as the character of the person, object of loyalty and consequence of loyalty are extremely important in determining whether loyalty is in fact a virtue or a vice. Loyalty may be used as an incentive for a noble cause. A person "loyal to the ideals of a benevolent organization, such as the International Red Cross, is demonstrating a virtue as a result of that loyalty" (Coleman 2009, 110).

Loyalty can be abused for a bad, evil purpose. As Wahlke (1952) finds out, the US government employed loyalty oaths to remove communist and left-leaning academics and public servants in the McCarthy era. A person loyal to a malevolent ideal or to an evil person is not demonstrating a virtue. For instance, people ardently loyal to the malpractice of the Klu Klux Klan cannot be considered to be virtuous (Connor 2010, 110). The Nazi Party has incited and affirmed fever loyalty among its adherents by means of massive rallies, spectacles and rituals. However, such loyalty ultimately led to the genocide of Jews and ill-treatment of other minorities and became destructive for the social order of Germany and the world. With its consequence of violence, death and destruction, "this loyalty with its expression in war is obviously, from a moral perspective, wrong and bad" (Connor 2007, 44–45).

2.2 Loyalty in the Military Context

In most cases, loyalty is usually considered as the highest of military virtues, especially by military personnel. Winslow (1998, 345) argues that loyalty is "encouraged at all levels as military values and structures grant primacy to collective goals" since strong interpersonal ties and small unit cohesion are considered necessary for the army. Jones (2010, 292) states that loyalty is "a paramount military virtue, especially on the part of enlisted combat soldiers on active service."

It has to be noted that group loyalty becomes the primary option for military in many situations. Group loyalty and cohesion are not only part of military culture but also important for combat effectiveness and closely related to soldier's life, adaptability and well-being (Elizur and Yishay-Krien 2009, 282–283). The military seeks to limit layer-based clashes of loyalties and assert the primacy of group loyal service and giving one's autonomy over to the needs of the group (Connor 2010, 287). Insofar as military operation and success are collective, regimental loyalties knit with loyalties that go up the chain of command and are incorporated into the more abstract loyalties to state leaders or national constitution (Jones 2010, 293).

Since loyalty is usually believed to be a primary military virtue, constant efforts are taken to ensure that officers and soldiers remain loyal to the regiment, state and constitution. These measures may include good salary, prospect of professional development, strong monitoring and punishment (Albrecht and Ohl 2016, 42). Military establishment will go to considerable lengths to protect those whose loyalties remain firm through adversity and to punish soldiers whose loyalty may be in doubt (Jones 2010, 302). To be specific, the penalties imposed for disloyal actions may range from admonishment, extra duties, monetary fines, demotion and termination of service, to (life) imprisonment (Jones 2010, 295).

Disloyalty in military context may occur however hard the military establishments try to maintain loyalty among officers and soldiers. Disloyalty is manifested in a range of breaches that are peculiar to the military: treason, defection, mutiny, desertion, exist, resistance, insubordination, failure to comply with lawful orders, aiding and assisting the enemy, imperiling the success of operations, endangering morale, assaulting a superior and malingering (Jones 2010, 295). For instance, military defection occurs when government soldiers, instead of fighting for the regime, desert or fight for the opposition (McLauchlin 2010, 333).

One important issue concerning military loyalty is that it is often used as an excuse for actions that are morally wrong. In some cases, moral values have become subsumed under the overwhelming group loyalty and norm (Connor 2010, 285), and such practice may bring about a bolstering effect that encourages blind obedience (Kelman and Hamilton 1989). Therefore, it is warned that although "loyalty is demanded and is expected to be manifested in obedience to (lawful) orders, it is not to be equated with blind allegiance" (Jones 2010, 293). It is not acceptable to use loyalty to justify moral harm. In other words, "loyalty as a moral norm neither requires nor permits the violation of the rights of others" (Driver 2007, 597). Loyalty is not an excuse for harm, yet too often loyalty is the explanation (Connor 2010, 287). To prevent oneself from being indulged in blind loyalty, one need to take into consideration the object and outcome of his loyalty, and to make his own choice that is morally righteous.

Another important issue concerning military loyalty is that some professionals in the military are often faced with the challenge of dual loyalty or divided loyalty (e.g., Dai 1944; Bergen 2012). In some cases, when the interests of two sides do not accommodate, divided loyalty surfaces and professionals in military have to make their own choices on which side he shall be loyal to, professional ethics or military-ones. For instance, physicians in military have to look at the interests of the individual soldier-patient as well as the state and the military in general. If a physician chooses to do in favor of the soldier-patient, such action could lead to conflict with a military superior. Professionals' decisions are varied depending on their identity, education status, personal ideology, group affiliation and different situations which they are involved in.

3 Narratives of Interpreters Serving Japanese Forces

This section gives a brief introduction to the interpreters serving Japanese military during the war, the data source of our analysis and the analytical procedures.

3.1 Interpreters Serving Japanese Military

Although no accurate record of total number of interpreters serving Japanese military during the SSJW has been found, an estimation can be made that the amount was undoubtedly huge, possibly exceeding 5000. During the war, Japan maintained a strength of 800,000 to 1,000,000 soldiers in China (Barrett 1970, 8). Their operations had to depend heavily on interpreters' assistance in many aspects: from military supply to intelligence collection, to battle commands and to liaison between Japanese military and Chinese puppet forces. A Japanese squadron usually consisted of 200 soldiers, and therefore, there were roughly 4000 squadrons operating in China. If we suppose two interpreters worked for each squadron, there would be 4000 interpreters.

From 1931 onward, Japan began to capture piece by piece the majority of northern, eastern and central parts of China. By the end of the war, above one-third of Chinese territory, or 3.5 million km^2, fell into Japanese hands, including more than 600 cities and counties. After the occupation of each piece of Chinese territory, Japan had to endeavor in suppressing resistance, fighting back guerrilla attacks and tightening its control of occupied areas. Puppet governments at various levels were set up under Japanese control to maintain social order, educate people with colonizing ideology and rake in resources that might feed into the war machine. If two interpreters worked in each county, that number would be 1200 at least.

The estimated number of interpreters serving Japanese army can be evidenced to some extent by a few historical archives. For instance, according to the statistics gathered up from the archives concerning Japanese forces and puppet government in Qinghuangdao, a stronghold city in northern China, there used to be at least 40 interpreters serving 14 units of Japanese military and puppet troops from 1933 to 1945 (Liu 1988, 69–95; Kang and Zhang 1998, 103–114). Similarly, there were more than seven interpreters working for the Japanese special agents and other military units stationed in Handan, a county in Hebei Province (Hao 1989, 110–115), and six interpreters working in Zhangdian, a town in Shandong Province (Wu and Zhu 1991, 61–66).

Interpreters serving the Japanese military came from two major sources. The first source were Japanese individuals who were able to speak Chinese fairly enough to perform the interpreting tasks, including students of Chinese studies. Early before the war, colleges and institutions had been set up in Japan as well as in China to train Japanese citizens into linguists of Chinese language. Among them, a typical example was Japan's East Asia Common Culture Academy (東亜同文書院, or Toa dobun Shoin) in Shanghai, established in 1907 and then relocated to Nagasaki shortly after the Marco Polo Bridge Incident on July 1937. It trained a large number of experts in Chinse language and culture. To answer to the demand of military interpreters, the administration of the institute, including the head of the institution Chozo Ouchi (大内暢三), encouraged students to join the army (Rokkaku 1992, 257). From September to November 1937, about 100 students went to the battle front providing linguistic support to Japanese forces fighting in China. Most of them worked several months (Zhao 2002, 53; Zhou 2006, 56–7).

The second source was individuals of other nationalities than Japan. They were civilians who were capable of speaking both Chinese and Japanese, recruited locally from Korea, Taiwan or other parts of China, as these places were occupied by Japan before the war or at its earlier stages. For instance, Taiwan was colonized by Japan in 1895, Korea was annexed to Japan in 1910, and Manchuria was occupied by Japanese Kwantung Army in 1931. In these areas, puppet governments at different levels were established under Japan's dominance. Puppet troops were rallied to put down resistance and to maintain the colonizing order. A large number of interpreters of this type worked for them for several reasons: firstly, there was a short supply of interpreters of Japanese ethnicity; secondly, these interpreters had a good command of local dialects which Japanese soldiers were ignorant of; thirdly, they had a close connection with the local community which might help Japanese to strengthen their control of occupied areas.

A majority of these interpreters of Chinese or Korean nationality were trained at schools set up locally by Japan or puppet governments. For instance, after Japan's occupation of Peking, a puppet government was set up which rallied the North China Peace Preservation Corps headed by Qi Xieyuan. Qi set up an interpreter training school in neighboring counties of Peking, which recruited Chinese high school graduates with basic knowledge of Japanese and offered courses in Japanese grammar, military and internship for 6–12 months. From June 1939 onward, about 200 students graduated and were sent to work as interpreters for puppet officers above lieutenant rank (Ma 1996, 14–24).

3.2 Relevant Narratives

Our research is based on a body of literature which narrate the interpreters serving Japanese military in SSJW. Specifically, we gathered up 82 texts of public and private narratives, published or authored in a large span of time from 1941 to 2018. These texts record what interpreters have done during the war and give clues to interpreters' loyalty, some written and collected by Chinese individuals and governmental organizations and others by Japanese individuals. They come from a variety of sources and are varied in genres, such as autobiographies, oral history, journal papers, monographs, news reports and archive files.

Among the 82 texts, there are 27 historical accounts of past events collected by governments at various levels of China (a majority of them published in 1990s), 10 texts from the edited collection of archival files, 10 books (most of them are documentary writings) by Chinese authors, 9 autobiographic texts written by Japanese who worked as interpreters during the war, 9 news items issued between 1939 and 1947 reporting execution or assassination of interpreters in Japanese army, 9 academic texts investigating the issue of military interpreters during the war and 8 oral historical accounts reported by Chinese soldiers. More than a half of these texts include "interpreter" (翻译、翻译官 or 通译 in Chinese) into their titles, and they focus on what these interpreters have done during the war. Over 150 interpreters serving Japanese forces were referred to by these texts.

3.3 Analytical Procedures

Our investigation of interpreters' loyalty in the war is done by means of content analysis of the texts at the following five steps. Firstly, we identify the subject of loyalty, namely, who are the interpreters serving the Japanese forces in the war and what their identities are (such as linguistic, ethnic, religious and national identities). This step can be easily performed since there are always linguistic items indicating interprets' names, ancestry, place of birth, nationality or the language they spoke.

The second issue involves finding out the object of loyalty, that is, to whom or what the interpreters were loyal. This can be judged by the fact that on which side they worked for and whose interest they actually defended. It has to be noted that interpreters could be loyal to Japanese army or to Chinese counterpart, or even to both on rare occasions.

Thirdly, we detect the outcome of loyalty, which means to find out what impact and effects were brought out by the loyal or disloyal interpreters. These impacts may include the failure of success of a military operation, the death of soldiers and civilians or lifesaving of people, the interrogation or prosecution of prisoners of war.

At the fourth step, we examine the status of loyalty. Here, we find out whether interpreters were constantly loyal, occasionally disloyal or mired in divided loyalty by looking at the behaviors of these interpreters during the whole process of war and discovering if any significant changes occurred which might divert interpreters to work for the other side. The diachronic change of loyalty status is the focus of this step.

Finally, we try to figure out the motivation of interpreters' loyalty or discuss the factors that may influence interpreters' choice on loyalty. This requires a closer reading of the texts so as to find out what encouraged, impelled or forced the interpreters to make their choices on loyalty. These factors may be economic, social, ideological or cultural and exist in combinations.

After the analysis of the loyalty of these interpreters, we sum up and classify them according to their states of loyalty.

4 Loyalty of Interpreters Serving the Japanese Forces

Our investigation finds out that a large number of interpreters with different identities served the Japanese forces during SSJW, displaying different states of loyalty: fervent, feigned, shifted and divided loyalty.

4.1 Fervent Loyalty

Among all interpreters serving Japanese military during the war, a majority of them displayed fervent loyalty to Japanese forces although they were varied in nationalities, identities, consequences of and motivations for their service.

A large number of linguists of Japanese ancestry served as interpreters on important positions during the war. A typical example was Nakagawa Hiroshi (中川博) from Yamaguchi of Japan, then on active service in the Special Information Team of Headquarters of Japanese forces in North China from August 1935 to September 1945. Responsible for extracting information from varied sources, he worked earnestly to translate and interpret telegraphs gathered from Chinese forces. He detected radio intelligence from the 1st, 2nd, 3rd, 8th and 10th battle zones in China, from Xinhua News Agency as well as from communist armies in different parts of Hebei Province in northern China (Shanxi People's Procuratorate 1995, 451). He submitted his collection of information concerning Chinese battle plans and military deployment to Japanese army headquarters to be used as important references. For that purpose, he traveled frequently across China to gather information under orders. He once accompanied Lieutenant Naofumi Mori (森尚文) to survey the coal resources in the southeast of Shanxi Province of China. In November 1935, he followed Lieutenant Iwasaki (岩崎) to investigate damages to railways. In December, he accompanied Lieutenant Nakajima (中島) to inspect the flooding of Yellow River in Ji'nan of Shandong Province. Nakagawa's constant loyalty was testified by what he had done for the Japanese army, together with his linguistic capacity and diligence.

Another example was Aizawa Yangsan (相沢养三) from Sendai City, Japan. He interpreted for the military police of Eighth Battalion, the 3rd Independent Mixed Brigade of the Japanese Expeditionary Army in North China. In addition to his interpreting job, he killed 37 Chinese civilians and participated in arson, setting fire on 2483 civilian houses (Shanxi People's Procuratorate 1995, 430–431).

Among these devout interpreters of Japanese nationality, some were students working as temporary interpreters in the forces. For instance, Anazawa Kotobuki (穴沢一寿), a student at East Asia Common Culture Academy, considered military service in Japanese aggressive army a great honor. Like many other students, Anazawa (2007) joined the Japanese Army and worked for 20th Infantry Squad of 16th Division. He aided lieutenants in interrogation of Chinse civilians, witnessed the abuse of Chinese citizens by Japanese soldiers, and later the great human tragedy brought about by Japanese forces in the Nanjing Massacre. However, as he was taught to maintain absolute allegiance to the emperor, to his militarist state and to his invading army, Anazawa did nothing to stop, to avoid or to resist such hideous acts.

These interpreters of Japanese blood, with a close tie to Japanese culture, viewed their interpreting job as a form of voluntary allegiance to the emperor of Japan. Most of them, on the one hand, worshiped Bushido, the traditional codes of loyalty and friendship by which the samurai lived and, on the other hand, practiced Japanese militarism. As these interpreters engaged mainly in military information collection, surveillance, interrogation of prisoners of war, their actions of group loyalty usually contributed to the victories of the Japanese forces who committed unprecedented atrocities and brought about heavy losses on the Chinese side.

In addition to interpreters from Japan, those of Chinese and Korean nationality who were recruited locally also displayed fervent loyalty. One typical example was Yao Yuxiu (姚玉秀), who was born in Xingtang County, Hebei Province in 1918 (Wang 1998, 721–722). After Xingtang fell into the Japanese hands, Yao became an interpreting officer for Japanese after some training. In 1939, he was enlisted into the interpreter training school set up by puppet peace preservation corps in Tongxian, Peking, and afterward, he resumed his interpreting job and pledged allegiance to Japanese army. He led Japanese and puppet troops into local villages in mopping up operation, searching and arresting resistance strength, blackmailing civilians, raping women, burning houses and killing innocent civilians. According to confirmed sources, he ordered to kill over 40 resisting Chinese and enticed several resistance leaders to capitulate. After Japan surrendered in 1945, Yao disappeared and his whereabouts became unknown.

Qiu Shengxing (邱盛兴) was another typical example of interpreter who worked faithful for Japanese forces (Qianxi Historical Archives Office 1985, 129–133). He was born in Gaoxiong, Taiwan, in 1913, where he received primary education in Japanese language and culture. When he was seeking a living in Changchun in 1938, he was recruited into the Manchurian puppet army and dispatched to Tianjing. After a short training session, he was sent to Tangshan and worked as an interpreter in a regimental information office of Japanese Force 2902. In Feb. 1939, Qiu was dispatched to Qian'an County and interpreted for a Japanese brigade. Soon, he served Lieutenant Honma (本间), the head of the first squadron stationed in Yangdianzi. In winter 1939, he paid his service to Lieutenant Hiraiso (平鸠保), who was officer of the third squadron stationed in Shaheyi. As an interpreter, Qiu remained loyal to the Japanese military throughout the war, assisted in arresting, interrogating, torturing and killing Chinese resistance and innocent civilians, causing the death of 36. After Japan's surrender in August 1945, Qiu fled to Tianjin and attempted to hide his whereabout. He was arrested in 1955, found guilty after a trial by the People's Court of Qianxi County and executed in September 1958. The so-called Great East Asia Co-prosperity

Circle taught in schools run by Japanese in regions occupied. These schools aimed to cultivate local civilians that might remain submissive to the Japanese dominance, faithful to Japanese ideology and useful in their further military expansion and colonizing rule. Young individuals with linguistic talent were attracted into Japanese classes with material rewards, such as a meager supply of food which was valuable during difficult times of war. Unlike Japanese interpreters who believed themselves patriots, Chinese and Korean interpreters were mainly motivated by the material gains, privilege and power far superior to the local civilians that could only be obtained by means of cooperation with Japanese. Without strong outside interferences, their loyalty to Japanese army was self-sustaining and could remain intense and steady.

4.2 Feigned Loyalty

Some interpreters serving Japanese military demonstrated feigned loyalty from the very beginning. A typical instance was Chen Mingxue (陈敏学), who was an interpreter with pretended loyalty toward Japanese forces (Chen 2001, 40–41). Chen was born in 1930 in Shenzhen, Guangdong Province where a Japanese language school was set up when he was ten years old. Children were asked to receive education there and those who refused to go would be killed, while those who agreed would get a handful of rice each day as reward. To survive the war and famine, Chen went to learn Japanese for two years. In 1943, he secretly joined in a communist resistance troop in Dongjiang and began working in disguise of an interpreter. Much military information was delivered in time about Japanese deployment, battle plans, weapons and facilities, which enabled resisting Guerrilla forces to fight against Japanese with foreknowledge and initiatives. Chen occasionally handed out guns, ammunitions and other supplies to meet the demand of resistance. He was also active in stirring up rebellions among the Japanese forces and successfully disrupted a special agent team of Chinese who serve Japanese forces.

According to the memoir of Zhou Yuefa (Zhou and Guo 1996, 90–93), Fu Zhigan (傅之干) was an interpreter who worked with feigned loyalty for the puppet police of Datong City, Shanxi Province. In

September 1942, Fu delivered a detailed report of the deployment of Japanese forces in Datong, and after half a month, he handed out another piece of intelligence about the relocation of a puppet force from Inner Mongolia to Datong. Fu's great contribution to the intelligence collection of resistance forces was accomplished under the disguise of his fake loyalty to Japanese.

These two examples of Chen and Fu showed that thanks to the unique role in communication, interpreters were able to participate in important military decisions, to be informed of military deployment and to get access to battle plans. Under the disguise of interpreting job, they worked actually as special agents for resistance forces, being disloyal to the Japanese from the very beginning. They accessed and sent out confidential military intelligence, contributing to the weakening and defeat of Japanese army. Such feigned loyalty came from interpreter's clear knowledge of both sides in the war and their voluntary choice, thus such fake loyalty would be difficult to change and could last as long as interpreters could continue their work with their identities remaining secret. However, once the pretended loyalty was detected by the Japanese, interpreters would face extreme dangers like life threat.

4.3 Shifted Loyalty

The third type of interpreters had loyalty shifted from one side to another during the war. For instance, Lang Xuan (郎宣), a Manchurian born in Qiqihaer, Heilongjiang Province, was an interpreter with altered loyalty (Lang et al. 1996, 57–68). After his graduation at a senior high school with a good command of Japanese, he started to work as an interpreter for Arai Squadron (新井中队) stationed in Taigu County, Shanxi Province, under the recommendation of another interpreter. In the beginning of 1944, he worked for Captain Nakamura of a dispatched team stationed in a village. In May, he was arrested by the Eight Route Army, a communist resistance force, and was sent to Yan'an. There, he joined Eight Route Army, converted his belief and became loyal to Chinese resistance ever since. In another fighting the same year, he was captured by Japanese army and appointed again as an interpreter for Japanese troops in Yuci, Shanxi. Taking advantage of his position, he aided in secrecy the resistance, rescued many officers of the resistance strength, set free a large number of Chinese militiamen and passed on important military intelligence. He became a member of communist party during this period and went back to Chinese communist army after the war was over. He experienced a dramatic change in the object of his loyalty.

Another example is Gong Baoshou (龚宝寿), an interpreter serving Japanese Yokota Detachment in Taixing, Jiangsu Province. In Autumn 1943, he was captured by a communist resistance force led by information liaison Lv Jiliang (Lv et al. 1999, 7–8). After being persuaded, Gong decided to work for the resistance and promised to provide military intelligence. Later, he delivered important information about the changes in the military strength, designation of military units, relocation of forces and the "wiping-out" operations plans. In addition, Gong handed out leaflets encouraging fighting against Japanese militarism and recommending giving up invasion. Such leaflets were even handed out to the office of Yokota, commander in chief of the Detachment.

These two examples of Lang and Gong showed that at the beginning some interpreters pledged their loyal service to Japanese army, although they might be suspicious of the ethic ground of Japanese Aggression. After close contact with resistance forces, they were aware of what Japanese forces have done to China and forecasted the doomed failure of Japan in China. They realized that it was morally wrong for them to assist Japan invading China since they were of Chinese nationality. Either out of their own will or under persuasion of resistance forces, they chose to exit, resist or defect Japanese military. Their loyalty was diverted to the Chinese side even though they had to work for Japanese for the time being. The shift of loyalty from Japan to China was evident among a large number of Chinese interpreters, which suggested that loyalty could be altered when people decided to do so.

4.4 Divided Loyal

Divided loyalty existed among a few interpreters in war who worked for both sides at the same time as double agents. Xia Wenyun (夏文运) was a typical example of dual loyalty. His voluntary choice to interpret for Japanese at the very beginning of the war was most likely influenced by his early education and life experience in Japan. Xia was born and grew up in Dalian, a northern city in China under Japanese control since 1905. He finished his higher education in Imperial University of Kyoto, Japan, under the sponsorship of South Manchurian Company. His command of Japanese language and exposure to Japanese culture enabled him to become an interpreter working for the Manchurian puppet government in 1931. On the post, Xia became acquainted with many senior Japanese military officers, among whom was Wachi Takaji (和知鷹二), who once headed the Japanese wartime intelligence agency in Shanghai (Xia 1999, 1–3).

Wachi and other senior Japanese officers were looking for unofficial secret political cooperation with the Chinese southwest clique headed by local and military officials who were pro-Japanese and in discord with the central government (Xia 1999, 2: 77). Xia was chosen to be the interpreter to help contact with these Chinese officials. Xia arranged more than 100 meetings between Japanese and Chinese officials. His loyal service then won praises from Wachi: "Xia is my secretary, interpreter, and bodyguard, and sometimes he is also my teacher" (Xia 1999, 1: 78).

However, Xia turned out to serve another master later. While working for Wachi, Xia get acquainted with General Li Tsung-jen (李宗仁), head of the Chinese Nationalist forces in Guangdong (Li and Te-kong 1979, 316–317). General Li invited Xia for a private talk and asked him why he chose to serve the Japanese army. Xia "burst into tears" and answered "if there is a chance to serve the motherland, I am ready to die for it without hesitation" (ibid., 317). At the invitation of Li, Xia agreed to work for Chinese Kuomingtang (KMT) government in intelligence collection.

From then on, Xia became an interpreter and a double agent with divided loyalties. With his personal radio station, he kept communicating with both Japanese intelligence agencies and Chinese KMT government in Chongqing. From 1934 to 1941, he delivered Chinese government much timely and accurate information about the Japanese forces, contributing greatly to China's victory in some operations. Xia's work in intelligence was highly valued by the Chinese government (Xia

1999, 4: 76; 5: 78; 2000, 2: 96; Li and Te-kong Tong 1979, 178). At the same time, Xia did not stop his earnest work for the Japanese.

Xia's divided loyalty, concealed carefully, won him rewards and benefits from both sides. On the Japanese side, he was able to participate socio-political activities at a higher level. He could enjoy benefits such as free opium, luxury accommodation, a personal bodyguard, free transportation and evening entertainment; on the Chinese side, he received praises and a huge monetary reward (USD 300,000) from Chiang Kaishek, the KMT's military and political head (Xia 1999 6: 77). Xia was motivated by the benefits from such divided loyalty, but at the same time, he was aware that if anything happened to expose his dual loyalty, he would face severe penalties from either side.

5 Concluding Remarks

In the Second Sino-Japanese War, Japanese military recruited interpreters of a wide range of linguistic and ethnic identities in order to fulfill various functions for its military operations and colonizing rule in China. The war has demonstrated an extreme situation in which the demand for neutrality of interpreters was almost replaced by that of loyalty. It is most likely that in conflict scenarios, loyalty becomes ever more significant for interpreters to survive hardships and for military to ensure that interpreters will finish their interpreting and other assigned tasks.

Japanese military might have taken a series of measure to prevent officers, soldiers as well as interpreters from becoming disloyal. In most cases, interpreters were closely monitored and guarded by ideological education, economic bait, coercion or other means. However, interpreters' choices of loyalty were different and sometimes changeable. As our study reveals that there were four states of loyalty: some interpreters sustained their fervent allegiance to the Japanese aggressive army throughout the war; some owned feigned loyalty at the onset, working as secret agents for Chinese side to gather military intelligence; some have shifted their loyalty to Chinese, breaking away from the Japanese forces they used to serve even they were clearly aware that such conversion might cost their lives; and others were plunged into divided loyalties, working for and torn by two sides.

The study demonstrates that interpreters' choices of loyalty in war are shaped by a web of interrelated factors and no factor alone can decide the state of loyalty. Ethnic identity or nationality alone cannot ensure that interpreters may maintain the same level of loyalty from the beginning to the end of the war. Factors that motivate interpreter's choice of loyalty may include chance of survival in the war, interpreter's linguistic competence, economic reward, position in the power structure, temporary social status, ideology such as nationalism and militarism, and prospects of war. Some of these factors may become more prominent than others at a particular moment and that variance in degree of importance can generate a changed state of loyalty.

It is definitely not an easy job to make a decision over loyalty since in most cases there is an ethical dilemma behind that choice. However, it is also the obligation of an interpreter to "work out what is the right thing to do in that particular situation" (Coleman 2009: 106). When an interpreter is mired and get confused in ethic confrontations, he has to prioritize the humanitarian principles of justice and peace.

Acknowledgments This work was supported by the National Social Science Foundation of China under Grant Number 17BYY200.

References

Albrecht, Holger, and Dorothy Ohl. 2016. Exit, Resistance, Loyalty: Military Behavior during Unrest in Authoritarian Regimes. *Perspectives on Politics* 14 (1): 38–52.

Anazawa, Kotobuki [穴泽一寿]. 2007. Professor Nozaki: A Dissenter against Students Joining in the Army as Interpreters [翻译从军论的反对者——野崎教授] (trans. Feifei Zhou and Lin Ye [周菲菲、叶琳译]). In *Truths of Nanjing Massacre, Historical Archives from Japan Volume 3 [南京大屠杀真相日方史料(中)]*, ed. Xianwen Zhang and Jing Lv [张宪文、吕晶编], 220–232. Nanjing: Jiangsu People's Press [南京: 江苏人民出版社].

Baker, Mona. 2006. *Translation and Conflict*. London: Routledge.

Barrett, David. 1970. *Dixie Mission: The United States Army Observer Group in Yenan, 1944*. Berkeley: The Centre for Chinese Studies, University of California.

Bergen, Leo van. 2012. "For Soldier and State: Dual Loyalty and World War One". *Medicine, Conflict and Survival* 28(4): 317–334.

Chen, Mingzhe [陈明哲]. 2001. Interpreter for Japanese Army During Colonizing Period [沦陷时期 "日军翻译" 人民天下 "编外公安"]. *Source [源流]* 10: 40–41.

Coleman, Stephen. 2009. The Problems of Duty and Loyalty. *Journal of Military Ethics* 8 (2): 105–115.

Connor, James. 2007. *The Sociology of Loyalty*. Canberra: Springer.

———. 2010. Military Loyalty: A Functional Vice? *Criminal Justice Ethics* 29 (3): 278–290.

Dai, Bingham. 1944. Divided Loyalty in War. *Psychiatry* 7 (4): 327–340.

Driver, Julia. 2007. Cosmopolitan Virtue. *Social Theory and Practice* 33 (4): 595–608.

Elizur, Yoel, and Nuphar Yishay-Krien. 2009. Participation in Atrocities Among Israeli Soldiers During the First Intifada: A Qualitative Analysis. *Journal of Peace Research* 46: 263.

Footitt, Hilary, and Michael Kelly. 2012. *Languages at War: Policies and Practices of Language Contacts in Conflict*. Hampshire: Palgrave Macmillan.

Footitt, Hilary, and Simona Tobia. 2013. *War Talk: Foreign Languages and the British War Effort in Europe, 1940–47*. Hampshire: Palgrave Macmillan.

Guo, Ting. 2015. Interpreting for the Enemy: Chinese Interpreters in the Second Sino-Japanese War (1931–1945). *Translation Studies* 8 (1): 1–15.

———. 2016. *Surviving in Violent Conflicts: Chinese Interpreters in the Second Sino-Japanese War 1931–1945*. London: Palgrave Macmillan UK.

Hao, Xinhua [郝新华]. 1989. Secret Service in Hangdan for Japanese Military [日军在邯郸的特务组织]. In *Handan Historical Accounts Volume 6 [邯郸文史资料 第6辑]*, ed. Handan Historical Accounts Research Committee [中国人民政治协商会议河北省邯郸市委员会文史资料研究委员会编], 110–115.

Inghilleri, Moira. 2008. The Ethical Task of the Translator in the Geo-Political Arena: from Iraq to Guantánamo Bay. *Translation Studies* 2: 212–223.

Jones, Mitchell. 2010. Loyalty in the Military: Some Preliminary Reflections. *Criminal Justice Ethics* 29 (3): 291–305.

Kang, Zicheng, and Aiman Zhang [康子成、张艾蔓]. 1998. The Chinese Youth Cooperation Society and Iron Spear Team [我所知道的中国青年协

进社与铁矛队]. In *Qinghuangdao Historical Archives Collection Volume II Special Issue for China's War of Resistance against Japanese Aggression [秦皇岛文史资料选辑 第2辑 抗日战争专辑]*, ed. Qinghuangdao Historical Accounts Research Committee [中国人民政治协商会议河北省秦皇岛市委员会文史资料研究委员会编], 103–114.

Keller, Simon. 2007. *The Limits of Loyalty*. Cambridge: New York.

Kelman, C. Herbert, and V. Lee Hamilton. 1989. *Crimes of Obedience: Toward a Social Psychology of Authority and Responsibility*. New Haven: Yale University Press.

Kleinig, John. 2017. Loyalty. *The Stanford Encyclopedia of Philosophy* (ed. Edward N. Zalta). https://plato.stanford.edu/archives/win2017/entries/loyalty. Accessed 1 October 2019.

Lang, Xuan, Shaoying Wen, and Yizhi Pu [郎宣、温绍英口述, 浦一之整理]. 1996. From an Interpreter for the Japanese Army to a Communist [从日军翻译到共产党员]. In *Yuci Historical Accounts Volume. 17 [榆次文史资料第17辑]*, ed. Yuci Historical Accounts Volume Committee [中国人民政治协商会议榆次市委员会文史资料委员会], 57–68.

Li, Tsung-jen, and Te-kong Tong. 1979. *The Memoirs of Li Tsung-jen*. Boulder: Westview Press.

Liu, Juanqi [刘锩琦]. 1988. Japanese Military and Puppet Organizations in Qinghuangdao During China's War of Resistance Against Japanese Aggression [抗日战争时期驻秦皇岛地区的日伪军警宪特组织]. In *Qinghuangdao Historical Accounts Selection Volume 2 Special Issue: China's War of Resistance Against Japanese Aggression [秦皇岛文史资料选辑 第2辑 抗日战争专辑*], ed. Qinghuangdao Historical Accounts Research Committee [中国人民政治协商会议河北省秦皇岛市委员会文史资料研究委员会编], 69–95.

Luo, Tian. 2016. "Augmenting Combat Power: Military Translation in China-Burma-India Theater". *Linguistica Antverpiensia, New Series – Themes in Translation Studies* 15: 143–161.

Lv, Jiliang, Zhenghua Yan, and Shiqing Chen [吕继良、闾振华、陈诗庆]. 1999. Jiliang Lv Outwit Interpreters Serving Japanese Army [吕继良巧计利用日寇翻译]. *Heroes of Jiangsu in People's Revolutionary Struggle Taixing [江苏人民革命斗争群英谱 泰兴分卷]*, ed. Zhanjiang Wang, Taixing Editorial Board [王湛江主编; 泰兴分卷编辑委员会编]. Nanjing: Jiangsu People's Press [南京: 江苏人民出版社], 7–8.

Ma, Chongtao [马重韬]. 1996. Qixieyuan and Puppet Forces in North China [齐燮元与华北伪军]. *Chinese Historical Accounts Series Political and Military*

Volume 5 [中华文史资料文库 政治军事编 第五卷], 14–24. Beijing: Chinese History and Literature Press [北京: 中国文史出版社].
McLauchlin, Theodore. 2010. Loyalty Strategies and Military Defection in Rebellion. *Comparative Politics* 42 (3): 333–350.
Qianxi Historical Archives Office [中共迁西县委党史资料征集办公室]. 1985. Crimes Committed by Qiu Shengxin, an Interpreter for Japanese Military [罪大恶极、死有余辜——侵华日军翻译邱盛兴罪行简介]. *Selected Historical Archives of Qianxi Revolutionary Struggle (Special Issue: Atrocities Made by Japanese Invading Troops) [迁西县革命斗争史料选(侵华日军暴行专辑)]*, 129–133.
Rokkaku, Tsunehiro [六角恒広]. 1992. *A Historical Study of Chinese Language Education in Japan [日本中国语教育史研究]* (trans. Hongshun Wang [王洪顺译]). Beijing: Beijing Languages College Press [北京:北京语言学院出版社].
Salama-Carr, Myriam, ed. 2007. *Translating and Interpreting in Conflict*. Amsterdam: Rodopi.
Shanxi People's Procuratorate [山西省人民检察院编著]. 1995. *Records of Investigation and Interrogation of Japanese War Criminals in Taiyuan [侦讯日本战犯纪实 太原]*. Beijing: Xinhua Press [北京:新华出版社].
Stahuljak, Zrinka. 2000. Violent Distortions: Bearing Witness to the Task of Wartime Translators. *TTR* 1: 37–51.
Wahlke, John C. 1952. *Loyalty in a Democratic State*. Boston: Heath and Compnany.
Wang, Yongde, ed. [王永德主编]. 1998. *Chronicles of Xingtang County [行唐县志]* (ed. Local Chronicles Committee [行唐县地方志编纂委员会编]: 721–722). Beijing: China Translation and Publishing Co. [北京:中国对外翻译出版公司].
Winslow, Donna. 1998. Misplaced Loyalties: The Role of Military Culture in the Breakdown of Discipline in Peace Operations. *The Canadian Review of Sociology and Anthropology* 35 (3): 345–367.
Wu, Shouzuo, and Yukui Zhu [武守祚、朱昱奎]. 1991. Some Secret Service in Zibo and Their Major Criminal Activities [日本侵略军占领张店后设立的部分特务组织及其主要罪恶活动]. *Zhangdian Historical Accounts Volume 1[张店文史资料 第1辑]*, ed. Zibo Historical Accounts Research Committee and Zibo Zhangdian Archives Bureau [淄博市张店区政协文史资料研究委员会,淄博市张店区档案馆], 61–66.
Xia, Wenyun [夏文运]. 1999. *A Different World: Untold Stories in Japan's Invasion of China* [黄尘万丈: 日本侵华秘录 (1–6)] (trans. Zhao Xiaosong

[赵晓松] and Zhao Liantai [赵连泰]). *Heihe Journal [黑河学刊]* 1: 77–81; 2: 77–81; 3: 77–81; 4: 68, 76–80; 5: 76–80; 6: 76–80.

——— [夏文运]. 2000. *A Different World: Untold Stories in Japan's Invasion of China* [黄尘万丈: 日本侵华秘录 (7–10)]. Translated by Zhao Xiaosong [赵晓松] and Zhao Liantai [赵连泰]. *Heihe Journal [黑河学刊]* 1: 68–73; 2: 96–100; 3: 90–94; 4: 94–100.

Zhao, Wenyuan [赵文远]. 2002. Shanghai East Asia Common Culture Academy and the Japanese Invasion in Modern History 上海东亚同文书院与近代日本侵华活动. *History Studies Monthly [史学月刊]* 9: 52–57.

Zhou, Dexi [周德喜]. 2006. *A Study on the East Asia Common Culture Academy [东亚同文书院研究]*. PhD Dissertation, Tianjing: Nankai University.

Zhou, Yuefa, and Sijun Guo [周悦法口述 郭思俊整理]. 1996. My Memoir of Underground Intelligence Collection [我做地下情报工作的回忆]. In *Yuci Historical Accounts Volume 17 [榆次文史资料 第17辑]*, ed. Yuci Historical Accounts Volume Committee [中国人民政治协商会议榆次市委员会文史资料委员会], 90–93.

4

Interpreting the Korean Conflict (1945–1953)

Hyongrae Kim

1 Introduction

Over the past two decades, research conducted within Translation and Interpreting Studies (TIS) has examined violent conflicts, such as the First and Second World Wars, the proxy wars fought during the Cold War era, and, more recently, the wars in Iraq and Afghanistan (Stahuljak 2000; Baker 2006; Rafael 2007, 2012; Salama-Carr 2007; Inghilleri 2008, 2009, 2010; Takeda 2010; Footitt and Kelly 2012, 2017; Kelly and Baker 2013; Baigorri Jalón 2014; Guo 2016; Ruiz Rosendo and Persaud 2016; Todorova 2016; Kelly et al. 2019). This work has revealed the many roles and responsibilities interpreters and translators assume during military campaigns, the ethical dilemmas they face, and the complexities of their social positioning.

Despite the upsurge in research, the role of interpreters during the Korean War has remained a relatively under-studied subject within the field. The few publications that examine this war have focused almost

H. Kim (✉)
Auburn University, Auburn, AL, USA

M. Todorova, L. Ruiz Rosendo (eds.), *Interpreting Conflict*, Palgrave Studies in Languages at War, https://doi.org/10.1007/978-3-030-66909-6_4

exclusively on the Korean Armistice Negotiations (Fernández Sánchez 2010, 2012; Wang and Xu 2016). Though these studies have provided much needed insight into the role interpreters played in the resolution of the Korean conflict, little is known about how interpreters contributed to the outbreak and progression of the war.

This chapter seeks to address this lacuna in research by engaging in a comparative study of all three stages of the Korean War, namely,

1. the *preparatory phase*—the US/USSR military occupation of Korea (1945–1948),
2. the *engagement phase*—the violent confrontation between the militaries of North and South Korea and their respective allies (1950–1953), and
3. the *conclusionary phase*—the Korean Armistice Negotiations (1951–1953).

By expanding the scope of research to include the events that led to the war, the period of direct military engagement, and the circumstances that prompted its discontinuation, this chapter will reveal how the identity of the interpreter and what it meant to interpret was oriented, disoriented, and reoriented by the shifting structures of hierarchy and power within the military field in Korea.

2 Interpreting in the Military Field: A Zone of Uncertainty

The circumstances of warfare lend themselves to sociological study and analysis as the tensions between institutions and social agents, which might remain hidden or implicit in a civil setting, are explicated under the pressures of war. Much of the research conducted on violent conflict within TIS has borrowed from the central concepts of French social theorist Pierre Bourdieu (Inghilleri 2003, 2005a, 2005b; Gouvanvic 2005; Wolf 2007a, b; Guo 2016). In particular, Bourdieu's notions of field, *habitus*, and capital have proven to be a powerful theoretical framework for conceptualizing interpreter practices, especially their "reproductive or transformative roles in particular historical and socio-cultural contents" (Inghilleri 2005a, 126).

Bourdieu posits a social world comprised of multiple fields, with larger fields capable of being further divided into subfields. Each subfield, though it follows the overall logic of the larger field in which it is situated, also has its own internal logic, rules, and regularities. All fields, both large and small, are profoundly hierarchized, with dominant agents and institutions holding considerable power to determine what happens within them. Social agents operate in these confrontational spaces where both individuals and institutions struggle for the production, attainment, and dissemination of capital. Here, capital refers to that which the social agents within a field view as valuable and can be associated with both material and symbolic wealth. An agent's *habitus* is formed based on their position in the field, which is dictated by the type and amount of capital they possess, and can be understood as an acquired schemata, set of dispositions, or "a sense of the game, ordinarily described as a 'spirit' or 'sense' (philosophical, literary, artistic, etc.)" (Bourdieu 2000, 11).

It is important to note that the current study does not consider interpreting events as taking place within a separate "field of interpreting," but rather adopts the view, proposed by Inghilleri (2005a), that interpreting occurs in "zones of uncertainty" where different fields converge and where interlocutors interact with other agents and assert with varying levels of certainty the validity of their social beliefs and practices, or *habitus*. In interpreted events, contradictions emerge due to a convergence of different fields in which their associated *habitus* can be momentarily upset, but, more importantly, these spaces and the specialized knowledge and networks of power contained therein, are brought into a new relationship and can come together as new forms of knowledge or sets of understandings.

Typically, social agents and institutions in possession of larger amounts of capital, and therefore power, will dictate the terms under which the norms of interpreting are established. Nonetheless, it is always possible for more dominant networks of power to be rendered unable to forcefully assert its authority during interpreted events if its position of power is challenged by the presence of an interpreter or other interlocutors who may diminish the value of the symbolic capital they possess. When the authority of dominant institutions is challenged, an interpreting *habitus* that rejects the dominant institution's views regarding normative behavior may emerge. In this case, the role of the interpreter and what constitutes legitimate interpretive practice can be brought into question or redefined.

3 The Korean War: A Brief Summary

Before delving into the topic of the (re)construction of the interpreting *habitus* during the Korean War, this section first provides a brief historical summary of that conflict. Such an approach has been adopted because the structures of relations between the positions occupied by agents and institutions, and the *habitus* of these agents, can only be revealed after the field in which they are located has been fully analyzed (Bourdieu and Wacquant 1992, 104–105). The conditions of the military field in Korea, as well as the relationships between interlocutors engaged in interpreted events, however, varied greatly depending on the phase of the war, which is why the historical contexts of all three stages of the war are delineated below.

The preparatory stage of the Korean War began in 1945, following the Japanese surrender to the allies, after which the Korean peninsula was immediately placed under the occupational control of the Soviet Union and the United States. The territories formed north and south of the 38th parallel were governed by the Soviet Civil Administration (SCA) and the United States Army Military Government in Korea (USAMGIK), respectively. This arrangement was meant to be temporary, but the Cold War rivalry that had begun brewing between the two emerging superpowers intensified in the following years. As part of their efforts to extend and solidify their spheres of influence, in 1948, the Soviet Union created the Democratic People's Republic of Korea (DPRK) in the north, and the United States installed the Republic of Korea (ROK) in the south. The militaries of the two superpowers withdrew from the peninsula in 1949, but left behind diametrically opposed governments, each claiming sovereignty over the whole of Korea, thus setting the stage for the ensuing war.

A period of direct military engagement was initiated on June 25, 1950, when the Korean People's Army (KPA) crossed the 38th parallel and attacked the Republic of Korea Army (ROKA). The UN Security Council labeled the attack "a breach of the peace" and requested "that the Members of the United Nations furnish such assistance to the Republic of Korea as may be necessary to repel the armed attack and to restore international peace and security in the area" (United Nations 1950, 224). The Council further recommended that all UN members providing military forces should "make such forces and other assistance available to a unified command under the United States" (United Nations 1950, 230.) While these decisions were being made by the Security Council, the DPRK military rapidly advanced southward, pushing the ROK's line of defense to the southeastern corner of the peninsula. In September, the tides of the war turned when, following the success of the Inchon Landing, the United Nations Command (UNC) and the ROKA were able to force the KPA northward, across the 38th parallel, and in retreat toward the Chinese border. In October, answering the DPRK's calls for support, the Chinese People's Volunteer Army (PVA) joined the war, and by December, the UNC/ROK alliance was driven out of North Korea. The intervention of the People's Republic of China created a pseudo "balance of power" on the Korean peninsula, and by the spring of 1951, the war took the form of trench warfare, with the front line close to the original border.

By the summer of 1951, all signs indicated that neither side would be able to readily achieve victory on the battlefield, and so, both sought to bring an end to the fighting via truce talks at the negotiation table. The conclusionary phase of this internecine conflict began on July 8, 1951, when a US-led UNC negotiation team met with the communist delegation at the city of Kaesong (Bailey 1992, 70). The venue was later moved to Panmunjom as the communist forces gained control over the region. Originally, both sides believed that a ceasefire would be arranged within a few weeks, but contrary to such forecasts, the Korean Armistice Negotiations dragged on for over two years, before a final agreement was reached on July 27, 1953. Although a peace treaty was never signed, the signing of the armistice brought the Korean War to a *de facto* end.

The Korean War and the circumstances that preceded and followed it constitute a particularly fertile ground for research on interlingual communication under conditions of warfare because it was the first "hot war" of the Cold War era and the first "United Nations War" (Edwards 2013, 1). The military presence of the two superpowers and the linguistic diversity within the UNC and communist coalition created conditions under which the services of interpreters were central to the success of the dual occupations, multinational military actions, and trilingual negotiations. As a tentative step toward better understanding the role of language and linguistic mediators during this war, the following three sections will examine interpreters working with or for the US military during the Korean conflict. While the dominant institution in all three contexts was the US military, the objective of interlingual communication as well as the social, economic, and political conditions of the military field was reoriented as the war progressed. Thus, the availability of linguistic mediators, the positionality and power of the interlocutors engaged in interpreted events, the professional obligations of the interpreter, and the norms of interpreting distinguished themselves across the three phases of the war.

4 The United States Army Military Government in Korea (1945–1948): A Government *of*, *for*, and *by* the Interpreter

Throughout its military occupation of South Korea, the United States Army Military Government in Korea (USAMGIK) was thoroughly reliant on the services of Korean civilian interpreters for its administrative duties. This was a result of a lack of preparation on the part of the US military, which entered South Korea in September 1945 "without trained Korean language personnel in their ranks" (Fishel and Hausrath 1958, 8). In October, the military belatedly sought to train Korean linguists at the US Military Intelligence Service Language School, and the Korean-language class was created with "eight students under a Korean American officer" (McNaughton 2006, 417), but this was a classic instance of too-little-too-late. In the face of an absolute shortage of trained linguists, the

USAMGIK had little choice but to employ Korean civilians to provide the interlingual services required for the daily operations of a foreign occupational government. Unfortunately, the number of Koreans capable of conversing in English was likewise in short supply. This was caused by the fact that in 1939 the Japanese imperial government declared English an enemy language and "under the highly discouraging atmosphere the colonial government created against the English language, both the quality and the quantity of English language education suffered a great deal" (Kim-Rivera 2002, 272). Thus, the US military was plagued with a perpetual dearth of interpreters throughout the occupation.

In a classified military report on the language problems encountered by the US military during the hostilities in Korea, it was determined that the shortage of trained US linguists had a number of serious consequences: (a) it put civil affairs personnel at the mercy of their Korean interpreters; (b) it made the Korean interpreter, unprepared by training and experience, the key man in civil affairs field operations; (c) it posed serious problems because of the difficulty of adequately screening interpreters under Korea conditions; and (d) it exalted the influence of Koreans who spoke English and therefore were able to obtain direct access to civil affairs personnel (Fishel and Hausrath 1958, 8–9). This led to the Military Government earning the moniker the "interpreter's government" and generated criticism that the USAMGIK was a "government of, for, and by interpreters" (Taylor 1948, 372).

The Korean public viewed the empowerment of Military Government interpreters with great pessimism. At the time, it was widely believed that the US military had simply replaced Imperial Japan as the most recent foreign power to forcefully occupy the peninsula. So too was the view that Military Government interpreters were the next generation of foreign collaborators. This claim gained weight because the majority of USAMGIK interpreters were educated overseas during the Japanese occupation, while "only one-fifth or so interpreters had learned English in Korea" (Dong 2005, 112), implying that they were from families that had grown wealthy by colluding with the colonial authorities. To the Korean people, it appeared that these interpreters were now using their advantageous position within the USAMGIK to further perpetuate the structures of power formed under Japanese colonialism. The public perception of the triadic relationship between the US Military Government, Japanese collaborators, and Korean interpreters is aptly represented in the following description of a poster seen by US Colonel Glenn Newman of the US Military Government (Historical Office of the US Command in Korea 1948, n.p.):

> An American soldier, blindfolded, is shaking hands with a Korean who holds a Japanese flag and a bundle of 100 Yen notes. Between the two is an interpreter labeled as "Bribed by Traitors and Pro-Japs."

In the poster, the American soldier was drawn wearing blindfolds to suggest that the US military was oblivious to the circumstances in Korea, while the Korean holding a Japanese flag and a bundle of Japanese money was a representation of former Japanese collaborators, now intent on forging ties with the United States. Finally, the interpreter, positioned at the center, was shown bridging the two, thus ensuring that the existing social hierarchy would prevail under the new regime.

The notion that interpreters were actually the ones in charge of the administrative duties of the occupational government became so widespread that one Korean political organization even claimed that the idea for the occupation itself originated "[f]rom the interpreters of the US Army and Military Government who are of the opinion that in Korea we have no leader who is capable of leading us and therefore our independence should be delayed" (Historical Office of the US Command in Korea 1948, n.p.). Although this claim was most certainly untrue, the comment is demonstrative of public perceptions concerning the clout and corruption of USAMGIK interpreters.

US Military Government officials likewise harbored suspicions regarding the loyalty of its civilian interpreters. Throughout the occupation, from a command point of view, "no separation had been made between the Japanese and Korean occupations [and] there was a tendency to place both Japan and Korea in the same category" (Meade 1951, 76). In fact, the commander of the occupational forces, Lieutenant General Hodge was widely quoted as calling Koreans "the same breed of cat" (Cumings 1981, 138) as the Japanese. Thus, for a member of the USAMGIK, hearing "one's interpreter and a Korean conversing at a greater length than demanded by the translation at hand" (Historical Office of the US Command in Korea 1948, n.p.) was cause for anxiety, as it appeared that the Koreans were conniving against the United States. US military officials asserted that "the basis of this suspicion was a feeling that the interpreters were not politically honest and were trying to influence policy" (ibid.). Despite such misgivings, however, Military Government staff could not enforce a conduit model of interpreting, which they viewed as normative practice, and instead were forced to grudgingly accept claims that "the rendition of an American thought into Korean terms was more than a mere exchange of words" (ibid.) because the institution lacked the personnel to select, train, or monitor its interpreters.

The interpreting *habitus* that emerged during the occupation was one that allowed local Korean interpreters to actively participate in interpreted events as active mediators, activists, and negotiators, thus assuming responsibilities that lay outside what is often thought of as their normative duties:

> Many Military Government officials came to rely heavily on interpreters for the conduct of business far beyond that of mere translation. It can readily be understood how an interpreter could in time come to know his principal's job almost as well as the principal and, if granted enterprise, act on his own in answering questions and reaching decisions while interpreting, or even independently while his principal was absent (Historical Office of the US Command in Korea 1948, n.p.)

Korean political leaders and US military personnel collectively sought out measures to regain control over the situation by reasserting their respective *habitus*. The most representative case being the Joint Korean-American Conference, a meeting held between US military officials and Korean political leaders to identify major social issues that were the "cause of disturbances" within Korea. The "effects of interpreters in government" was listed as a personnel problem alongside complications related to law enforcement, Japanese collaborators, corruption, and agitation. At the conference, the head of the Korean delegation, Kim Kiu-sic, made the following suggestions regarding the selection and management of

Military Government interpreters (National Archives and Records Administration November 4, 1946, 2):

1. Language qualifications to be tested by both Koreans and Americans before employment.
2. Duties and activities should be outlined, and he should be told how far his responsibilities go. The trouble is that these interpreters are used sometimes as informers, advisors, liaison officers, and so on.
3. Classification:

    (a) Interpreters or translators attached to the higher officials of M.B.
    (b) Those attached to bureau chiefs and governors of provinces
    (c) Those attached to sub-officials such as section chiefs.

Kim's recommendations, calling for the testing of the language skills of interpreters, clarifications of the interpreter's duties and responsibilities, and the hierarchical categorization of interpreters by skill level, might appear to be the most basic of requirements for an organization employing their services. The fact that such recommendations had to be made at such a high-level meeting, however, indicates that this was not the case during the occupation. In the absence of clear structures of operation, the dominant military institutions were unable to enforce their views regarding the norms of interpreting. Thus, although the Military Government maintained a monopoly over administrative and military power, interpreting took place amid much uncertainty regarding what constitutes normative behavior. Under such conditions, civilian interpreters, whose dominance over the channels of interlingual communication remained unchallenged, were granted the latitude to facilitate communication by whatever means they deemed necessary.

5 The Korean War: A Parrot Perched on a Rifle

When the United States deployed troops to the Korean Peninsula following the DPRK's attack of the ROK, the military decided to rely on the linguistic services of Korean military interpreters rather than train its own linguists. The country's military brass and policymakers were confident that US intervention would bring about a swift end to the conflict and did not see the need to invest in the training and maintenance of its own group of Korean-language specialists. The interpreters assigned to work with US officers were called UN Liaison Group officers, but despite the group's name, they were actually first lieutenants in the South Korean military. The primary task of these officers was mediating between ROKA unit commanders and United States Korea Military Advisory Group (KMAG) advisors.

The KMAG was a military unit deployed to South Korea to help train and provide logistical support to the ROKA. KMAG advisors did not hold the authority to issue direct orders to the ROK military unit to which they were assigned. Rather, KMAGers "were expected to control training or operations by influence, suggestion, and guidance [...] What they accomplished depended largely upon their powers of persuasion and on the esteem in which they were held by their Korean counterparts" (Sawyer 1962, 60). These US officers were often required to advise a ROKA commander "one to three levels above their own rank—captains and majors advised regiments, majors and lieutenant colonels advised divisions" (Ramsey 2006, 13). Nonetheless, while the ROKA unit commander may have held a higher rank than their US counterpart, the playing field was leveled out by the inverted hierarchical relationship which existed between the US and ROK militaries. It was due to the lopsided power relation between the US and South Korean militaries that "at the time it was widely believed that colonel-level officers had to be close to their KMAG advisor if they were to be promoted to general" (Eom 2018, 168, *my translation*). As a result, a higher-ranking ROKA advisee could not blatantly disregard the advice of a lower-ranking KMAG adviser, regardless of military rank.

The construction of the joint US-ROK military force saw the creation of another "zone of uncertainty," a result of a convergence of two ideal bureaucracies, each with their own systems of operation and regulations. Confusion arose within this multilingual organization because neither the KMAG advisors nor the ROKA advisees were certain about how they should occupy and operate in this newly formed social space in which the hierarchy of power was made ambiguous. While trying to bring order to the confusion, US and ROK military personnel competed for the authority to reproduce and distribute what each felt were legitimate values and regulative principles. Because this could only be done via the intermediary services of UN Liaison Group officers, interpreting events became a locus for struggle as both parties sought to assert control over the interpreting *habitus*.

The fact that UN Liaison Group officers were members of the ROKA provided South Korean military officers with a decisive advantage when dealing with KMAGers. As an example, former interpreter Rhee Younghee wrote that although many Korean officers engaged in corrupt activity, regardless of how they felt about such misconduct, UN Liaison Group officers "had to do [their] best to prevent the KMAGer from seeing or hearing about the various delicate situations happening in the unit, which was always a source of agony for [them]" (Rhee 2005, 218–219). The falsification of information did not go unnoticed, as KMAGers complained that interpreters "distorted" or "modified" what was said during exchanges because "the interpreters figure that when we [the Americans] go, they've 'had it' if they alienate their ROK commander" (Hausrath 1957, 70). Such practices were thought to be a threat to military operations as they implied that advice issued by KMAG personnel was not being conveyed in their entirety, which could stymie the US military's ability to work in step with their Korean counterparts.

On the other hand, the possibility that the UN Liaison Group officer might shift their loyalties to the KMAGer was a constant source of anxiety for ROKA personnel. The following excerpt (Rhee 2005, 215–216; *my translation*) shows that in order to maintain control over the interpreting *habitus*, South Korean military officers sought to fortify their position of dominance by implementing tactics to disempower the interpreter with the goal of reaffirming their subordinate position within the hierarchy of the ROKA:

> Although they assigned me the rank of "ROKA first lieutenant," in reality, I was only half a first lieutenant. I wore the insignia of first lieutenant on one of my collars, but unlike the other branches of service, I did not have a badge to indicate my area of service. Interpreter officers were half-civilian, half-military personnel. It was more than a year later that we were assigned badges, which were parrots sitting atop rifles. The "parrot perched on a rifle" was truly symbolic. It seems that an ignorant group of combat officers in the Army HQ had out of spite come up with the idea. It was perhaps an attempt to cunningly insult the group of frail intellectuals in the military.

Contrary to expectations, this approach was met with resistance from UN Liaison Group officers, who in turn refused to acknowledge the prestige of the military rank that their superiors held. The ROK military had only been officially launched in 1948, after the USAMGIK handed over power to the Korean government, and many of the senior staff had limited military experience when the war broke out but were rapidly promoted due to the lack of available leadership in the face of a rapidly expanding military. Many interpreters used this as the basis to dispute the authority of their superiors, as is indicated in the memoir of former UN Liaison Group officer Kim Il-pyeong (2012, n.p.; *my translation*):

> There were even ROKA officers and generals who hadn't graduated from middle school before joining the Japanese military as soldiers during the "Greater East Asia War" (1941–45). Some of them had been drafted as soldiers and transferred to the National Defense Guard after the country's liberation. These simple men were made officers and generals. Some were promoted rapidly during the Korean War. Generals were awarded a new star every 3 to 6 months [...] officers claimed that being a commissioned officer meant you were on the same level as a college graduate. Some of these officers were insolent and incredibly ignorant.

The dissonance between the views of the ROKA commissioned officer and UN Liaison Group officer regarding the other's authority was the cause of continued friction, and throughout the war, "interpreter officers treated ROKA officers with disdain, and ROKA officers treated interpreters with contempt" (Rhee 2005, 217; *my translation*).

KMAG advisors were mindful of the fact that as members of the ROKA, the UN Liaison Group officer's "primary loyalty [...] is to the Republic of Korea rather than to the US Government" (Fishel and Hausrath 1958, 62), putting them at a disadvantage in dictating the terms under which information would be exchanged during interpreted events. Thus, the most frequent suggestion made by KMAGers when asked how interlingual communication could be improved was that UN Liaison Group officers should be assigned to the staff of the US KMAG advisor rather than to their ROKA counterparts. Advisors who favored this shift in the interpreter's affiliation argued that the change would have the effect of "protecting interpreters from possible reprisals or disciplinary action by their ROKA superiors, and would also structure the situation so that the interpreter's primary duty clearly would be to further the advisory mission by seeing that the advisor received complete and accurate information and by interpreting for him in the same spirit" (Hausrath 1957, 71).

Such an attempt was made in June 1953 in the 8th ROK Division when the commander, General Song, "ordered control of the ROKA interpreters in the division shifted from his own G1 to the KMAG G1 advisor in the division" (Hausrath 1957, 130). Reportedly, one military interpreter informed the senior KMAG advisor that he was happy the change had been made, and he declared that although "The majority of the interpreters in ROKA are better educated than most Koreans," they are "used like dogs" by ROKA officers (ibid., 131). KMAG advisors also reported that UN Liaison Group officers reacted enthusiastically to being reassigned to the US military and claimed that it resulted in a "100 percent improvement in morals and effectiveness of the interpreters" (ibid., 130–131).

This change was made only a month before the signing of the armistice; it is thus unclear how the change of affiliation would have affected the interpreting *habitus* in the long term. What is clear is that throughout the Korean War, UN Liaison Group officers operated within a zone of uncertainty in which the dominant institution of power, the US military, was unable to assert its authority in the context of the power struggle between KMAG advisers and ROKA advisees. In an effort to tip the balance of power in their favor, US and ROK military officers sought to secure the loyalty of the interpreter by reaffirming or acquiring operational control over UN Liaison Group officers.

6 The Korean Armistice Negotiations: A Faithful Echo

The Korean Armistice Negotiations was the longest and one of the most complex negotiated armistices in history, involving "159 plenary sessions and some 500 hundred meetings at a subsidiary level" (Bailey 1992, 70), all of which required the mediatory presence of interpreters who worked between the three official working languages: Korean, English, and Chinese (Ekvall 1960, 20). In preparation for the negotiations at Kaesong, the US military issued a call for Grade A linguists to serve as interpreters at the armistice talks. Grade A linguists were defined as "personnel operating at this highest level must be completely fluent in an Asiatic language and in English as well [...] capable of simultaneous translations (interpretation) to and from English. In addition to linguistic fluency they must have a deep understanding of the appropriate Asiatic culture, area, and psychology. This is a 'super' category, the personnel in which would be competent to handle interpretation, advising, and even negotiating at high-level meetings such as those which US military representatives have been engaged at Kaesong and Panmunjom since 1951" (Fishel and Hausrath 1958, 13). Unfortunately, it was soon revealed that "the U.S. Army had no competent career-service language personnel available to handle the 2-yr truce negotiations at Kaesong and Panmunjom" (ibid., 8).

As a result, the military had to turn to "Reserve officers who [were] recalled to active duty for the express purpose of handling interpretation chores at the negotiations" (Fishel and Hausrath 1958, 16). Richard F. Underwood, a first lieutenant in the US Army Reserve, and his brother Horace G. Underwood, a lieutenant in the US Navy Reserve, served as the primary English-Korean interpreters while Lieutenant Kenneth Wu, and his replacement Lieutenant Colonel Richard Ekvall, served as the principal English-Chinese interpreters. Aside from Ekvall, all were essentially "untrained interpreters" (Fernández Sánchez 2012, 118–122) who had little to no training or experience working as interpreters but, according to Wu, were abruptly tasked with juggling exchanges that "cover[ed] every province of semantics—military science, political hocus-pocus, geographical jaw-breakers, political jargon, philosophical abracadabra, and torrential tirades of penetrating oral defamation couched in diplomatic sugarcoats" (Fishel and Hausrath 1958, 15). For interpreters who were—as is often the case in a military setting—required to learn while on the job, the task of navigating this linguistic maze proved to be tremendously strenuous, and most felt themselves linguistically ill-equipped to meet the challenges of serving as interlingual mediators at the negotiation table. For instance, Richard Underwood recalled that he "did have very great problems at the formal meetings because all of a sudden, we came up with all sorts of technical language that I had no competence to interpreter, and it was a really, really, miserable time" (Underwood 2010, n.p.). Horace Underwood likewise experienced "initial difficulty in meeting the requirements of his job satisfactorily" (Fishel and Hausrath 1958, 16), and even Ekvall, who was already a seasoned military interpreter at the time, "found his Chinese, fluent though it normally was, inadequate for the needs of the demanding task at Panmunjom for several weeks after he arrived" (ibid.).

These principal interpreters headed a team of linguists that was severely understaffed and overworked. The following chart (Fishel and Hausrath 1958, 57) indicates that there was a total of only 76 UNC military linguists working for the language division at Panmunjom in July 1953 (Table 4.1).

Table 4.1 Interpreting the Korean conflict (1945–1953)

Interpreters, Korean	26
Interpreters, Chinese	11
Translators, Korean	7
Translation, Chinese	6
Interpreter-translators, Korean	14
Interpreter-translators, Chinese	12
Total	76

The following comments made by Ekvall (1960, 46) about the state of affairs in Panmunjom in early 1953, however, suggests that the situation was much more dire than even these scant numbers suggest:

> I found myself chief of a would-be language division whose table of organization called for 140 linguists. Instead, we numbered twelve, including translators and Chinese and Korean typists.

Given the importance of interlingual communication at the negotiation table, it is hardly surprising that UNC linguist supervisors and intelligence division chiefs found their number to be "assertedly insufficient" (Fishel and Hausrath 1958, 57). As a result of the lack of personnel, the more capable interpreters "often interpreted for eight or more hours a day" (Ekvall 1960, 46). These long working hours proved to be taxing for the interpreters, who often began to "blackout" after about two hours without rest (ibid., 48). Thus, it became necessary to stagger the schedule of those meetings so that "the interpreters, could go from one meeting to the next" (ibid., 46). It is conceivable that the lack of linguistic specialist might even have had the adverse effect of extending the talks.

In addition to the linguistic challenges of interpreting at the armistice talks, interpreters operated under the constraints of being firmly positioned within the military hierarchy as US military personnel. This was unlike the circumstances seen during the occupation or the war in which case the civilian or military interpreters were foreign nationals, which provided them with a measure of insulation from the pressure that the US military might place on them to adhere to what they viewed as normative interpretive behavior. At Kaesong and later Panmunjom, however, the interpreters were US military staff, and their position of power during interpreted events was determined not by the value of their linguistic services but by their military rank. This proved to be a hurdle for interpreters, especially those who were not officers, as their junior status deprived them of the authority to provide council to their superiors on linguistic and cultural matters. This led one linguist to make the point,

"Perhaps we ought to be given field-officer rank for these negotiations so that we could deal with our own negotiators on relatively equal terms. As it is, generals and admirals often won't ask or take advice from a sergeant or a lieutenant regardless of his ability or his degree of experience" (Fishel and Hausrath 1958, 17). Nonetheless, officers-level interpreters were not free from the pressures and constraints placed on them due to their embeddedness in the US military. For instance, Ekvall also recalls a denunciation that he was nothing but a "parrot": "He [the speaker] says 'Squeak, squeak, squeak,' and you say 'squawk, squawk, squawk.' A hell of a job!" (Ekvall 1960, 70).

This comment also shows that throughout the negotiations, interpreters were expected to "parrot" the source-language message, without adding, omitting, simplifying, or embellishing what was said. At times, this practice was pushed to the extreme, and the strict reproduction of the original was pursued, even at the expense of the comprehensibility of the interpretation. In his memoir *Faithful Echo*, Ekvall (1960, 103) describes a staff meeting in which he was forced to interpret "the most amazing jumble of contradictions ever muttered." Although he was tempted "to add, if not a sentence, just a phrase or even a word," he forced himself to "[hold] true to the words of [his] principal." It was later revealed that the negotiator had been "purposefully fuzzing it up" and commended Ekvall for his precise interpreting skills, adding that "If they had understood I would have known that you were misinterpreting. They weren't supposed to understand." This event confirms the fact that the interpreter, under pressure to act as a neutral conduit, could be more concerned with form than function, even when such an approach did little to facilitate interlingual communication.

The "interpreter as conduit" norm was so fiercely upheld at the negotiation table because divergence from the original could be interpreted as an indication of disobedience toward the senior officer who had made the statement, which, within the context of a military at war, was a serious offense. This is best represented in the example of Sul Jeong-sik, the Korean-English interpreter of the communist negotiation team. In an interview, Underwood recalled:

> He continually tried to "gild the lily" of [Chinese] Liaison Officer (Col. Chang)'s remarks. For example: Col. Chang said quite calmly on one inspection trip "Here are three of the Chinese People's Volunteers [i.e. Chinese soldiers] killed by your soldiers," but Sul [the interpreter] said words to the effect, "Here you see, in pools of their own blood these brave volunteers who left home and family to come to this foreign land in sacrifice for the noble cause of our side in this war."
>
> After he did this several times I turned to Col. Chang (against all protocol, for interpreters exist only to speak for their masters) and asked him if he indeed meant what Sul said, or what he himself said. Chang glared at a third officer (who had shown no evidence of speaking English) who gave him a quick nod, meaning I was telling the truth. At that Col. Chang blew up at Sul and ordered him to go—get out of my sight. (Harris 2010, n.p.)

The historian Millet wrote that Sul, who he described as a "turncoat Seoul high school teacher" (2002, 260), was later executed because of his poor performance. Although alternate historical records indicate that Sul did not meet his demise simply because of his tendency to embellish when interpreting but as part of a political purge, more relevant to the current study is the fact that the UNC interpreters believed that misinterpreting had life-or-death implications. Given these circumstances, it is hardly surprising that interpreters abided by demands that they function as a "faithful echo" to their principals.

7 Conclusion

This chapter has examined the role of the interpreter and the shape the interpreting *habitus* assumed during the entirety of the Korean War, including the preparatory, engagement, and conclusionary phases of the conflict. The findings reveal that the US military suffered from an acute shortage of linguistic mediators for the whole of the war. The institution's inability to furnish sufficient numbers of interpreters in an environment where interlingual communication with its allies, enemies, and the local populace was integral to the success of the war effort severely limited the

US military's ability to assert the full authority typically enjoyed by a dominant military force.

During the occupation, the USAMGIK's dominance during interpreted events was challenged by Korean civilian interpreters, who could manipulate an exchange for their personal or political gain. While the interpreter's position of power was a source of anxiety for US military and Korean political leaders, they relied on these linguistic mediators to assume roles typically thought to lie outside the linguistic duties of an interpreter because the Military Government was ill-equipped to perform these tasks. The interpreter was made a scapegoat by both the US military and the Korean public and was blamed for the circumstances unfolding on the Korean peninsula, when, in fact, these were the result of ill-planning by the occupational forces and the pre-existing power structures formed during Japanese colonialization.

During the engagement phase of the Korean War, KMAGers were placed at a disadvantage during interpreted events because UN Liaison Group officers were members of the ROKA, and thus owed their loyalty to the ROKA unit commander. Korean military interpreters were pressured by their superiors to distort the exchange of information to favor them. KMAGers requested that the UN Liaison Group officer be assigned to their command, while ROKA officers tried to double down on their control over the interpreter by devaluing their service and reaffirming their subordinate position within the Korean military, a move that was met by push back on the part of interpreters, who questioned the authority of their superiors.

Finally, during the Armistice Talks, the interpreters at the negotiation tables were US military personnel and were thus susceptible to the pressure applied on them by the American military body to abide by a conduit model of interpreting. The total lack of Grade A linguists meant that the few capable interpreters present at Kaesong and Panmunjom were severely overworked, which might have negatively affected the talks. Because the interpreters themselves were US military personnel, the US military was able to dictate the norms of interpreting. The interpreters were stripped of the ability to negotiate approaches to interlingual communication because their position as military personnel obligated them to abide by the orders of their superiors. Thus, rather than employ various measures to better facilitate the exchange of meaning, their focus was placed on self-preservation, which was achieved by strictly following the designated norms of interpreting. Ironically, the interpreter's adherence to this rigid practice was enforced not by their military superiors but by enemy interpreters who were able to monitor whether what the interpreter said matched the original statement.

The variation in who acted as an interpreter, the different tasks interpreters were assigned and expected to perform, and the diverse norms that dictated how interpreters as social agents should act and react during interpreted events that took place in different periods and locations during the conflict demonstrate the plasticity of the definition of what constitutes normative interpretive activity, indicating a need to reconsider traditional notions of the identity and functionality of the interpreter, as both are dictated by the needs and power structures that exist between all the social agents that converge within a zone of uncertainty.

References

Baigorri Jalón, J. 2014. *From Paris to Nuremberg: The Birth of Conference Interpreting*. Amsterdam: John Benjamins.

Bailey, Sydney D. 1992. *The Korean Armistice*. New York: St. Martin's Press.

Baker, Mona. 2006. *Translation and Conflict: A Narrative Account*. London and New York: Routledge.

Bourdieu, Pierre. 2000. *Pascalian Meditations*. Cambridge: Polity.

Bourdieu, Pierre, and Loïc J.D. Wacquant. 1992. *An Invitation to Reflexive Sociology*. Cambridge: Polity.

Cumings, Bruce. 1981. *The Origins of the Korean War: Liberation and the Emergence of Separate Regime, 1945–1947*. Princeton: Princeton University Press.

Dong, Yongha 동용하. 2005. *Migukgwa chinhan sarameun doneul mani beoreosseoyo*미국과 친한 사람은 돈을 많이 벌었어요 [Those Close to the US Made a Lot of Money]. In *8·15ui gieok: haebanggongganui punggyeong, 40inui yeoksacheheom* 8·15의 기억:해방공간의 풍경, 40인의 역사체험 [Memories of August 15: Landscape of the liberated space, the historical experience of 40 people], ed. Jaean Moon, et al., 112–115. Seoul: Hangilsa

Edwards, Paul M. 2013. *United Nations Participants in the Korean War*. Jefferson, NC: McFarland.

Ekvall, Robert B. 1960. *Faithful Echo*. New Haven, CT: College & University Press.

Eom, Injong 엄인종. 2018. *Naneun jogugeul saranghaenneunga (I)* 나는 조국을 사랑했는가 (I) [Did I Love my Nation (I)]. Seoul: Joeun Communication

Fernández Sánchez, María Manuela. 2010. Understanding the Role of Interpreting in the Peacemaking Process at the Korean Armistice Negotiations (Panmunjom 1953). *Journal of Interpreting and Translation Studies* 13 (2): 231–249.

———. 2012. A Bilingual Officer Remembers Korea: A Closer Look at Untrained Interpreters in the Korean War. In *Languages and the Military: Alliance, Occupation, and Peace Building*, ed. Hilary Footitt and Michael Kelly, 115–130. Basingstoke: Palgrave Macmillan.

Fishel, Wesley R., and Alfred H. Hausrath. 1958. *Language Problems of the US Army during Hostilities in Korea*. Chevy Chase, MD: The John Hopkins University, Operations Research Office.

Footitt, Hilary, and Michael Kelly, eds. 2012. *Languages and the Military: Alliances, Occupation and Peace Building*. Basingstoke: Palgrave Macmillan.

———, eds. 2017. *Languages at War: Policies and Practices of Language Contacts in Conflict*. Basingstoke: Palgrave Macmillan.

Gouvanvic, Jean-Marc. 2005. A Bourdieusian Theory of Translation, or the Coincidence of Practical Instance: Field, 'Habitus,' Capital and 'Illusio'. *The Translator* 11 (2): 147–166.

Guo, Ting. 2016. *Surviving in Violent Conflicts: Chinese Interpreters in the Second Sio-Japanese War 1931–1945*. Basingstoke: Palgrave Macmillan.

Harris, Brian. 2010. Panmunjom at First Hand. http://unprofessionaltranslation.blogspot.com/search?q=underwood. Accessed 6 June 2015.

Hausrath, Alfred H. 1957. *The KMAG Advisor: Roles and Problems of the Military Advisor in Developing an Indigenous Army for Combat Operations in Korea*. Chevy Chase, MD: The Johns Hopkins University Operations Research Office.

Historical Office of the US Command in Korea. 1948. History of the United States Armed Forces in Korea, 1945–48. http://db.history.go.kr/item/level.do?sort=levelId&dir=ASC&start=1&limit=20&page=1&pre_page=1&setId=-1&prevPage=0&prevLimit=&itemId=husa&types=o&synonym=off&chinessChar=on&brokerPagingInfo=&levelId=husa_001_0040_0090&position=-1. Accessed 1 July 2016.

Inghilleri, Moira. 2003. Habitus, Field and Discourse: Interpreting as a Socially Situated Activity. *Targets* 15 (2): 234–268.

———. 2005a. Mediating Zones of Uncertainty: Interpreter Agency, the Interpreting Habitus and Political Asylum Adjudication. *The Translator* 11 (1): 69–85.

———. 2005b. The Sociology of Bourdieu and the Construction of the 'Object' in Translation and Interpreting Studies. *The Translator* 11 (2): 125–145.

———. 2008. The Ethical Task of the Translator in the Geo-political Arena: From Iraq to Guantánamo Bay. *Translation Studies* 1 (2): 212–223.

———. 2009. Translators in War Zones: Ethics Under Fire in Iraq. In *Globalization, Political Violence and Translation*, ed. Esperanca Bielsa and Christopher Hughes, 207–121. Houndmills: Palgrave Macmillan.

———. 2010. "You Don't Make a War Without Knowing Why": The Decision to Interpret in Iraq. *The Translator* 16 (2): 174–195.

Kelly, Michael, and Catherine Baker. 2013. *Interpreting the Peace: Peace Operation, Conflict and Language in Bosnia-Herzegovina*. Basingstoke: Palgrave Macmillan.

Kelly, Michael, Hilary Footitt, and Myriam Salama-Carr, eds. 2019. *The Palgrave Handbook of Languages and Conflict*. Basingstoke: Palgrave Macmillan.

Kim, Il-pyeong 김일평. 2012. *Migun beongkeo soge jamdeulda jeogui bakgyeok-potan serye batgido* 미군 벙커 속에 잠들다 적의 박격포탄 세례 받기도 [Baptism by Enemy Mortar While Sleeping in an US Military Bunker]. http://www.kyosu.net/news/articleView.html?idxno=25644. Accessed 19 November 2014.

Kim-Rivera, E.G. 2002. English Language Education in Korea under Japanese Colonial Rule. *Language Policy* 1 (3): 261–281.

McNaughton, James C. 2006. *Nisei Linguists: Japanese Americans in the Military Intelligence Service during World War II*. Washington, DC: Department of the Army.

Meade, E. Grant. 1951. *American Military Government in Korea*. New York: King's Crown Press, Columbia University.

Millet, Allan R. 2002. *Their War for Korea: American, Asian, and European Combatants and Civilians, 1945–1953*. Washington, DC: Brasseys.

National Archives and Records Administration. 1946. Minutes of the Ninth Meeting of the Joint Korean-American Conference Held at Duk Soo Palace at 1330, 4 November 1946. RG 554. Container 86. Declassified NND 745070.

Rafael, Vincente L. 2007. Translation in Wartime. *Public Culture* 19 (2): 239–246.

———. 2012. Translation and the US Empire. *The Translator* 18 (1): 1–22.

Ramsey, Robert D. 2006. *Advising Indigenous Forces: American Advisors in Korea, Vietnam, and El Salvador*. Fort Leavenworth, Kansas: Combat Studies Institute Press.

Rhee, Young-hee 리영희. 2005. *Daehwa: han jisiginui samgwa sasang* 대화: 한 지식인의 삶과 사상 [Dialogue: The Life and Philosophy of an Intellectual]. Paju: Hangilsa

Ruiz Rosendo, Lucía, and Clementina Persaud. 2016. Interpreters and Interpreting in Conflict Zones and Scenarios: A Historical Perspective. *Linguistica Antverpiensia* 15: 1–35.

Salama-Carr, Myriam, ed. 2007. *Translating and Interpreting Conflict*. Amsterdam and New York: Rodopi.

Sawyer, Robert K. 1962. *Military Advisors in Korea: KMAG in Peace and War*. Washington, DC: US Army Center of Military History.

Stahuljak, Zrinka. 2000. Violent Distortions: Bearing Witness to the Task of Wartime Translators. *TTR* 13 (1): 37–51.

Takeda, Kayoko. 2010. *Interpreting at the Tokyo War Crimes Tribunal: A Sociopolitical Analysis*. Ottawa: University of Ottawa Press.

Taylor, Philip H. 1948. Military Government Experience in Korea: Administrative and Operation of Military Government in Korea. In *American Experience in Military Government in World War II*, ed. Carl J. Friedrich et al., 355–380. New York: Rinehart Company.

Todorova, Marija. 2016. Interpreting conflict mediation in Kosovo and Macedonia. *Linguistica Antverpiensia* 15: 227–240.

Underwood, Richard. 2010. An Interview with Mr. Richard Underwood, Interpreter, Armistice Talks, Korean War. http://einfo.usembassy.or.kr/koreanwar/his2.html. Accessed 11 February 2013.

United Nations. 1950. *Yearbook of the United Nations*. Lake Success, New York: Department of Public Information, United Nations.

Wang, Binhua, and Minhui Xu. 2016. Interpreting Conflict and Conflicts in Interpreting: A Micro-historical Account of the Interpreting Activities in the Korean Armistice Negotiations. *Linguistica Antverpiensia* 15: 186–204.

Wolf, Michaela. 2007a. The Emergence of a Sociology of Translation. In *Constructing a Sociology of Translation*, ed. Michaela Wolf and Alexandra Fukari, 1–36. Amsterdam; Philadelphia: John Benjamins.

———. 2007b. The Location of the 'Translation Field': Negotiating Borderlines between Pierre Bourdieu and Homi Bhabha. In *Constructing a Sociology of Translation*, ed. Michaela Wolf and Alexandra Fukari, 109–119. Amsterdam; Philadelphia: John Benjamins.

5

Local Interpreters Versus Military Personnel: Perceptions and Expectations Regarding the Local Interpreter's Role and Agency Within the Afghan Conflict

María Gómez-Amich

1 Introduction

Being a relatively new concept when it comes to academic research and studies, the figure of the interpreter in conflict zones (ICZ) tends to be considered "as interesting as it is elusive to the rest of the profession and academia" (Ruiz Rosendo and Barea Muñoz 2017, 182), not only in Translation and Interpreting (T&I) Studies but also in War, Culture, Development, and Peacebuilding studies (Baker 2019; Tesseur and Footitt 2019). In recent years, however, we have witnessed an increase in the number of publications focused on ICZ's history, typology, perceptions, duties, role, challenges, strategies and relations with the users of their services (Stahuljak 1999; Monacelli and Punzo 2001; Thomas 2003; Hoedemaekers and Soeters 2009; Inghilleri 2010; Van Dijk et al. 2010; Salama-Carr 2011; Baker 2012; Footitt and Tobia 2013; Todorova 2016; Ruiz Rosendo and Barea Muñoz 2017; Gómez-Amich 2018; Ali et al. 2019; Kelly et al. 2019). This growing number of publications offers

M. Gómez-Amich, PhD (✉)
Independent Researcher, Dubai, United Arab Emirates

M. Todorova, L. Ruiz Rosendo (eds.), *Interpreting Conflict*, Palgrave Studies in Languages at War, https://doi.org/10.1007/978-3-030-66909-6_5

valuable details on how the ICZ plays a key role "in influencing both the conduct and the course of war and conflict" (Gallai 2019, 220), even though the literature published to date in this field is still incomparable to other interpreting settings such as Community and Conference interpreting.

Despite the fact that neither their existence nor their work has been properly recorded throughout the past centuries (Persaud 2016, 64), interpreters in various conflictive periods of history have been present, at least, since 3000 BC (Delisle and Woodsworth 1995, 246). Their ability to enable communication among speakers of diverse languages and cultures has always been put to a variety of uses throughout history. For instance, interpreters' skills and services were used in the administration of the Roman-conquered territories (Delisle and Woodsworth 1995), the expeditions to the New World (Valero Garcés 1996), the Opium Wars (Wang-chi Wong 2007), the First and Second World Wars (Footitt and Kelly 2012; Footitt and Tobia 2013; Gómez-Amich 2016), the Cold War (Baigorri Jalón and Manuela Fernández Sánchez 2010), the Former Yugoslavia conflict (Todorova 2016), the peace operations in the Balkans (Kelly and Baker 2013) and more recently the armed conflicts in Iraq and Afghanistan (Tipton 2011; Tălpaş 2016; Gómez-Amich 2017, 2018; Ruiz Rosendo 2019).

Interpreters in general, despite having "occupied center stage since the origins of cross-cultural communications" (Angelelli 2004, 1), are still facing real challenges when it comes to outlining their role and responsibilities, especially considering that in conflict zones the interpreter may be expected to cross certain limits traditionally imposed to their role, consequently becoming more visible. Nobody disputes that the conduit model based on Reddy's metaphor (1993 [1979]) was long ago debunked precisely because it aligned the concept of an empty conduit with the figure of the interpreter who was expected to simply act as a "transmission belt" (Berk-Seligson 2002 [1990]). On the contrary, it is now common knowledge that interpreters are human beings who "perceive reality through their own social lenses" (Angelelli 2004, 2) and as such there exists a series of key social factors to take into consideration when discussing their performance (cf. Wadensjö 1998; Inghilleri 2003; Angelelli 2012). Such societal factors include the experiences and perceptions that human beings have with regard to their own practices, behaviors and values that form our vision of this world. Consequently, our vision is the product resulting from our collection of experiences and knowledge acquired in social institutions such as family, religion, culture, education and the military. Accordingly, there will be infinite visions of our world because "the worlds in which different societies live are distinct worlds, not merely the same world with different labels" (Sapir 1949, 162).

All these societal factors will play a key role in any encounter in which interpreters' bridging services are required due to no common culture or language. In such scenarios, the interpreter will be expected to ensure communication between parties not only from a linguistic point of view but also through the "interpretation" of different and contrasting values, practices, and perceptions of society. The interpreter, therefore, is caught between a series of—potentially—divergent perception of societal factors as well as possibly different understandings on how all involved parties perceive their own roles within this world and in particular within the interpreted event at hand. Considering that "role" seems to be one of the most problematic concepts in Interpreting Studies, in any interpreted event there is always potential for role conflict, especially in dialogue interpreting where expectations may be quite idiosyncratic depending on clients, assignments and contexts (Takimoto 2006, 56).

2 Clients, Assignments and Contextual Features in Conflict Zones

The interacting rules that individuals follow and apply to communicative events depend on how communities, cultures and social institutions perceive and understand the world. Such perceptions—including our expectations on the main stakeholders of a social encounter—largely depend on the characteristics of the field in which we interact (Bourdieu 1977), that is, the institution in which the encounter unfolds. In the case of conflict zone interpreters working for the military,[1] both the parties

[1] See Inghilleri 2009, Allen 2012 and Ruiz Rosendo and Barea Muñoz 2017, for a general taxonomy of ICZ.

and the interpreter work within a very particular set of rules—*habitus*[2]—that are established by the military institution. The military field is characterized by a deeply rooted and solid hierarchical system based on the status differential that exists among the members of the institution. Such status (and power) differential governs relations and interaction in this type of contexts—and in particular in Afghanistan where foreign troops are considered to be an occupying force with considerable influence in certain aspects of the country.[3] As such, power and status asymmetries are key factors to take into consideration when studying interpreted events in conflict zones. In such a hierarchical institution, what role is it assigned to the local ICZ? Does the "normative role" (Goffman 1961) traditionally assigned to the interpreter fulfil the parties' needs in such contexts? How can the interpreter carry out the "execution" of his own role (Ibid.) in these scenarios? Does the interpreter have a say with regard to the "role distance" (Ibid) that may appear between his normative role and the execution of such when working for foreign troops deployed in a conflict zone? The above are the main research questions that have informed the present study and the analysis of its collected data.

In Gómez-Amich (2017)—a much larger research project where some of the data herein presented partially comes form—it was concluded that the concepts of "normative role," "role execution" and "distance of role" were three delicate aspects considering that the local ICZ's role, duties and responsibilities were nowhere specified in their contractual agreements signed with the Spanish troops. Their official contracts, in fact, were considerably vague focusing mainly on institutional rules and generally stating that the interpreters were expected "to offer their services in the broad sense [...] as demanded, according to instructions" (genuine contract). Evidently, with such liminality experienced by ICZ, the "role crystallization" (cf. Henriksen 2008, 53-54) seems to not have properly taken place yet, resulting in certain professional deficiencies such as the

[2] Bourdieu 1977. For an in-detail analysis of Bourdieu's theoretical framework applied to the figure of the ICZ, please see Gómez-Amich 2017.

[3] The ISAF (International Security Assistance Force) not only officially assisted to the Afghan Government with certain governmental reforms, but also advised, trained and supported the Afghan local security forces (Police and National Army) in building up influence, maintaining the peace and fighting the Taliban.

lack of clear guidelines on what each party can expect from the ICZ. Consequently, these five local ICZs seemed to have adapted their roles to the situation at hand. Such decisions, as stated by the ICZs themselves, allowed them to resort to creativity and originated from a series of risk and context analyses based on myriad aspects such as the main stakeholders, their culture and religion, the type of encounter and the subject matter.

These countless adjustments resulted in a series of strategies that allowed them to execute the role of "faithful renders of other utterances" (Hale 2008, 114) but always provided that their translations fully respected and firmly adhered to the strict rules of conduct that characterize the Afghan in-group culture (cf. Hoedemaekers and Soeters 2009, 348). In that way, the narratives collected in Gómez-Amich (2017)—which will be presented and discussed in upcoming pages—evidence how these five ICZ perceived their role as cultural experts at all times and gatekeepers when necessary. Based on such perception, the five study subjects carried out a series of strategies including, among others, omitting swear words, adding religious references, summarizing the original message, enhancing the use of respect terms and adding jokes of their own in order to nourish a friendly environment in which the parties would be comfortable, at ease and interested in communicating with one another.

Based on the collected data, these five local ICZs seem to have acted as advisors, mediators, lie detectors, intelligence sources, coordinators, guides and subject matter experts, which aligns with other case studies (Hoedemaekers and Soeters 2009; Spahic 2014; Ruiz Rosendo 2019) and essentially conforms to certain military expectations (Cummings 2012). According to Cummings—an US Military Officer—the ICZ is an "underutilized resource" (Ibid) and their services must be put to the most effective use for the benefit of each military mission. This aligns with the concept known as "utilitarian approach" (cf. Hsieh and Kramer 2012) according to which the interpreter in certain settings is expected to provide utility as per the users' institutional needs, which sometimes go beyond their language duties. This utilitarian approach seems to be—along with the narratives collected for this study—particularly significant when it comes to twenty-first-century military stratagem, based on which "winning the war has ceased to mean only the annihilation of the enemy, but also transforming civilians into allies in the theatre of war" (Cummings 2012). Consequently, in order to influence the local population, building up rapport with the local military personnel and civilians plays a key role for effective counter-insurgency and antiterrorism missions in certain irregular warfare scenarios such as Afghanistan (Hajjar 2016).

This approach, however, requires that efforts "go outside of the employment of purely military measures" (Jeppson et al. 2015, 28) and emphasizes how important it is for international troops to collaborate with local actors, especially considering that "the quality of relation between the international military and the host nation population may very well define the course of success for the whole military campaign" (Van Dijk et al. 2010, 923). For that, it is necessary that the foreign troops acquire cultural awareness—or at least have access to someone able to deploy it—that is, cross-cultural competence including "knowledge, attitudes, and behavioral repertoire and skill sets that military members require to accomplish all given tasks and missions" (Hajjar 2014, 652). Such cultural knowledge combined with the language proficiency required to successfully carry out this sort of military mission is precisely what forms the local ICZ's capital (Bourdieu 1977) so deeply valued and needed by the international troops, who have been increasingly enforcing local recruitment as a solution to scarce numbers and inadequate linguistic levels among their own military interpreters (Kelly and Baker 2013, 70; Tesseur and Footitt 2019, 271). The local ICZ's origin and identity, however, are both delicate aspects that tend to "trouble the military" (Van Dijk et al. 2010, 918) because "for many people anyone who speaks another language is a foreigner by definition, an outsider, an 'stranger', different from me, and someone different from me is a potential enemy" (Levi 1985, 109 my translation). Based on such, the local ICZ's "otherness" is undoubtedly enhanced by their insider and outsider's double nature, as not only do they not belong to the military institution, but might come from the enemy's group and/or community. The international troops, hence, need to hire a person from outside their institution and paradoxically give them access to critical operational information they would have never seen or heard under any other circumstances. Evidently, this situation accentuates the vulnerability of the foreign troops and emphasizes the dangers that may threaten their safety as well as the success of their military operations.

This ultracomplex "in-between" nature that characterize the local ICZ's work places them in sensitive situations prone to a series of "intra-role conflicts" (Takimoto 2006), that is, conflicts originating from the lack of parity among the main actors with regard to the expectations they have on each other's role, including the interpreter's role. Role perception can, therefore, vary depending on each individual, their identity, culture, ideology, opinions, values, attitude, principles and many other variables. Consequently, there may be scenarios in which different parts have different expectations on the ICZ (Monacelli and Punzo 2001), particularly in deeply challenging contexts such as the Afghan conflict. Some of such varied expectations may even be considerably divergent or even completely asymmetric, predominantly in multiparty encounters. Accordingly, the local population might expect the ICZ to act as their community advocate while the international troops may expect the ICZ to work in their favor as a gatekeeper, due to contractual obligations. This was, in fact, the common denominator among the military personnel who participated in this study. The results of their narrative interviews, intertwined with those of five Afghan ICZ (Gómez-Amich 2017), will be presented and discussed in the following pages.

3 Methodology

The data informing this qualitative, descriptive study was collected through a series of in-depth narrative interviews with five locally recruited interpreters from Afghanistan (Gómez-Amich 2017), in addition to ten military members of the Spanish troops deployed in this country as part of the NATO International Security Assistance Force (ISAF) mission between 2003 and 2015.[4] All interviews with the local interpreters were carried out in person in a large Spanish city where the Afghan subjects

[4] Spanish troops were initially deployed to Kabul in 2002. However, all interviewees for this study were deployed to the RC-West in 2003. Spanish troops withdrew from Afghanistan on the 31st of December 2014. Spain deployed a total of 35 Spanish Forces called ASPFOR (Afghanistan Spanish Force).

were living in 2014 under refugee status, whereas the sessions with military personnel were completed on an Internet-based calling platform.

All 15 sessions followed the narrative approach, which allows for the collection of spontaneous narratives with regard to the subject's perceptions on a particular topic, in this case how local interpreters and their employers perceived the ICZ's role. This case study never had any intention of reaching universal truths that could ever be used in the creation of prescriptive outlines. Rather, its aim was to analyze in detail a series of first-hand narratives framed within a rather unexplored field, for which small study samples can still provide very valuable data (Mason 2000; Torikai 2009), especially when it comes to in-depth narrative studies that take into consideration the subjects' perspective (Baker 2006; Salama-Carr 2011).

The interviews with the five Afghan interpreters were structured as per Wengraf's SQUIN method (2004), that is, Single Question to Induce Narrative. In accordance to this approach, all narrators were given the opportunity to freely speak about their perceptions and life stories. For this study, a series of semi-structured questions[5] were also used as a supporting tool, in order to ensure that key topics of particular interest to this study were covered. The second research stage that eventually gave form to this chapter consisted of ten interviews with Spanish military personnel that had been deployed to Afghanistan in one or more missions between 2003 and the end of 2014 and who had frequent (or daily) contact with the local population through locally recruited ICZ. These ten interviews were also inspired by the narrative approach, but on this occasion, the interviewer followed a script that had been previously assessed by experts on dialogue and conflict zone interpreting. At the end of each individual interview, the interviewees were given a series of local ICZ's narratives extracted from Gómez-Amich (2017). The military interviewees commented on such narratives and shared their opinions with regard to the content of such quotes, which mainly contained references to the strategies, performance and role perceptions of these five Afghan interpreters.

---

[5] The original interview script was piloted with a focal group.

The collected data for all 15 interviews was codified and subsequently analyzed on NVivo 11Plus following the "concept mapping" technique (Trochim and Linton 1986). A number of maps containing key ideas and concepts were generated and narrative patterns were codified in a series of thematic clusters that were named in accordance to certain concepts such as "ethnicity," "culture," "attitude," "trust," "relationship," "strategies," "loyalty," "neutrality" and "role perception." Upon completion of the codification process, narratives were first compared across each subject group, and in subsequent stages comparison focused on the full sample, that is, across ICZ and military personnel. This process led to a series of unexpected results and conclusions that will be presented and discussed in the following section.

4 The Role of the Local ICZ: Interpreters Versus Military Personnel

Daoud, Ghous, Karmal, Lemar and Maqsood[6] were between 19 and 29 years of age at the time of the interviews (2015). All of them were born in the Islamic Republic of Afghanistan, and although they came from different provinces and belonged to different ethnic groups, their lives have in common the continued dearth and struggle that the protracted conflict in Afghanistan has brought to the Afghan population for decades. Following the law of supply and demand that governs conflict zones, these five local interpreters were recruited by the Spanish troops based on their knowledge of the Spanish language, whose command varied significantly among them.

With regard to the military personnel that participated in this study (four females and six males), their ranks varied from Lieutenant Colonel (*Teniente Coronel)* to Private (*soldado)*, and their missions included (re) building roads, villages, schools, orphanages, water systems, and airports; mentoring the Afghan Police and Army; dealing with local providers; demobilizing; organizing the final withdrawal and attending international

[6] All interviewees have been anonymized, and fake names are being used to protect their identities. The military personnel have been given fake initials for the same reasons.

and local patients at a Role 2 Hospital. A total of 80% of the sample had previously completed other international missions before being deployed to Afghanistan, in locations such as Iraq, Lebanon, DRC, Pakistan, Kuwait, Kosovo, Nicaragua and Bosnia, to name a few. The average length of their stay in Afghanistan was three months at a time and the average number of missions in which they were deployed to that country was a total of three (most of them having been deployed twice and some of them up to five times making a total of 1.5 years in Afghan territory for some of them). All of them had close contact and worked hand-in-hand with local Afghan interpreters who carried out a number of interpretation tasks between local languages and Spanish.[7]

With regard to the local interpreter's recruitment process, according to the military respondents, the local ICZ were recruited with the support of the Spanish National Intelligence Centre (CNI). It is worth noting that only two of the five local ICZ were asked to pass some rudimentary tests (e.g., sight translation) even though all of them ended up carrying out the same sort of tasks. These two ICZ together with the other three—who had graduated in Spanish Language at the University of Kabul—were invited to interviews in the target language in order to explore their personal and family backgrounds, as well as to understand their motivations to become an interpreter for the Spanish troops. Despite the fact that no interpreting test was required, these ICZ performed considerably challenging social, political, ethical and communicative tasks such as interpreting during mine clearance classes, in joint military operations against the Taliban and at high-level meetings between Spanish and Afghan forces or tribal leaders. For such, they claimed to not have received any training or mentoring in this respect from the Spanish troops—which was confirmed by the Spanish military personnel interviewed for this study and also aligns with other conflicts around the world (cf. Salama-Carr 2011, 104). This is particularly alarming considering how complex the requested profile and skills are, and also due to the fact that adequate services in conflict zones can mean the difference between life and death.

[7] The Spanish troops would communicate directly in English with the other Allied Forces deployed in Afghanistan.

> In addition to properly interpreting in both directions, the ICZ should be able to alert us and to offer us extra information that may go beyond our understanding. He knows their customs, he can see things that we cannot, he can read between lines. (Captain S)
>
> It is his responsibility to translate everything that is said, but not literally. [...] The ICZ must not add his own opinions. If we wish to know them, we will ask him. He must not filter the message—it will be me who decides if I am interested in the content. [...] The ICZ know the customs, the ranks, the tribal communities, the cultural tricks, and he knows how to warn us of the bad boys. The ICZ not only understands the language but he also knows if Afghans are lying or if their words have a double meaning. (Captain M. S.)
>
> The ICZ must be a member of the troops he is working for. He must prove his obedience, follow the rules, adhere to the protocol, be clear and trustworthy to both parties, and he must be a good communicator. He must be clever, sharp and able to grasp and transmit meaning. [...] . If you can't trust your ICZ, their work is pointless. (Lieutenant Coronel Z)
>
> In addition to offering his best interpretations, the ICZ must create trust among parties, particularly when we deal with sensitive topics [...] (Major M. O)

The combination of challenging tasks and a complex profile required for this position combined with the lack of training offered to these five ICZ seem to have led them—as per their narratives—to carry out a series of on-the-spot risk analyses of each particular event, which allowed them to creatively tackle unavoidable challenges. Based on such analyses, they applied a series of strategies including additions, summaries, editions and omissions keeping in mind what they considered to be the parties' expectations with regard to their role as ICZs. Their self-perception as experts in Afghanistan and both its cultural and historical aspects seems to portray them as individuals who are particularly concerned about the social and cultural features of each interaction, because as stated elsewhere "it is not appropriate to say everything in any situation and sometimes a special way of stating something is required" (Hoedemaekers and Soeters 2009, 334). Such scenarios took these five local ICZ to execute considerably higher levels of agency and latitude compared to other settings of interpretation. Accordingly, the traditional narrative of the interpreter as an invisible and impartial facilitator of communication fades away in these contexts. This, however, is only partially aligned with the perception that the interviewed military personnel have the ICZ's role. In this regard, the collected data contained some thought-provoking narratives that shed new light on the perception of the interpreter's role. For example, Maqsood mentioned the following:

> Afghans speak too much. For example, they say four or five sentences but one is enough, so we were summarizing one sentence or two, that's all, because some sentences are no use. If someone speaks too much, you summarize in two or three sentences. You have to cut them short; we have to abbreviate. (Maqsood, interviewed interpreter)

It seems that to this Afghan ICZ, it is essential to safeguard the functional effectiveness of the language if he considers that the main actors may be unaware of the linguistic-cultural norms governing each party involved in the event. In this particular case, it is worth noting the central role played by Islam in Afghan culture. Being at its core, certain religious invocatory as well as protective and therapeutic expressions are constantly added to utterances originally shared by a Muslim speaker (Herrero Muñoz-Cobo 2000, 75). Consequently, the continued use of references to the Quran (Miri 2014, 7) as well as *hadith*, that is, deeds and statements of the Prophet Muhammed (Hoedemaekers and Soeters 2009, 347), may be considerably surprising for a person unfamiliar with such cultural-linguistic strategies. In addition to this, Afghan culture is strongly characterized by its deeply valued orality (Ruiz Benítez 2015) and the frequent use of metaphors and parables, which could make any listener from a less "imaginative culture" feel deeply perplexed (Feria García 1999, 100). The ICZ plays a key role in these contexts as the total unawareness of such political, cultural and religious-related linguistic features would lead the foreign troops to a dangerous ethnocentrism which may result in prejudices and a total lack of understanding. Based on this—and on what seems to be what Maqsood considered as the Spanish troops' expectations—this ICZ decided rather to summarize the original message, which can be a strategy welcomed by the parties as evidenced below or, alternatively, a technique that may jeopardize a whole operation (cf. Pym 2016).

> Summarizing was a common procedure because the original message from the Afghans used to be quite long. In those cases, our interpreter used to say, "Look, this is more or less what he has said, I am summarizing it for you". We had enough trust in the interpreters to believe them. (Private I)
>
> Who can assure you that the interpreter has understood the genuine idea in the original message? Even with a common language and with no interpreter there is always the risk of misunderstanding each other. Who does the interpreter think he is to interpret only whatever he thinks to be appropriate? (Major D)
>
> I think he did the right thing; in conflict zones we are in a rush because we are under fire and I believe it is a good idea to have the initiative to filter the message. (Captain B.S.)

The narratives above extracted from the interviews carried out with the Spanish military personnel evidence how intricate the ICZ's role is; must the interpreter adhere to faithfully interpreting the original content of the message regardless of the consequences? Must the ICZ alternatively advocate for the functionality in his performance? What about the contextual characteristics of each multicultural encounter? Is the ICZ expected to observe the institutional needs of each event? All these unanswered questions seem to have been particularly complex in this case study due to the fact that the ICZ's duties and tasks were not clearly specified in their contract. In addition to that, in accordance to collected narratives from the Spanish military personnel interviewed for this project, the locally recruited ICZ in Afghanistan did not receive any training and seldomly would they obtain any guidelines with regard to duties, role limits and performance expectations. Consequently, these ICZ's narratives portray them as individuals who—being deeply concerned about socially and culturally accepted translations within the Afghan context in which they navigate—seem to have executed higher levels of agency and latitude than those traditionally assigned to their "normative role" (Goffman 1961).

> Customs are very different [...] If the Spaniards said something weird, I did not translate it. Why? Because If I do, something bad is going to happen. [...]. (Lemar, interviewed interpreter)
>
> When one of the parties was upset and used swear words, I did not translate those words and they asked me, "Why did you not translate that part?" And I replied, "If I translate that, you will speak back and a conflict between the two of you will start, for which I will be responsible." (Ghous, interviewed interpreter)

In "highly-charged and highly-exposed situations" (Askew in Salama-Carr 2011, 105), framed within the complexity that characterizes conflict zones, any evident cultural disparities can tense up the interactions, making any differences among parties deeply contrasting and, at times, even conflicting. The ICZ is the funnel for all coalition's interactions with local civilian and military population at all levels (West 2011, 176), and he represents the only connection that the foreign troops have to the Afghans (Cummings 2012, 43) for whom the idea of honor is deeply rooted in their culture, and all threatening acts toward such are not taken lightly. Closely related to this, we find Goffman's "face" concept (Goffman 1967) which refers to the public image that any individual wishes to create, preserve and protect through the application of certain social and cultural filters as well as strategies depending on each context. Accordingly, in the above-mentioned narratives both ICZ seem to have applied a similar strategy to avoid face-threatening acts (cf. Brown and Levinson 1987) toward the Afghan party's honor in order to protect not only their own face but also the communication channels open between all speakers involved. Such editing and omitting strategies, however, make the ICZ become an obstacle because the parties remain unaware of the original message's content. The ICZ, therefore, acquires higher levels of power resulting in the main stakeholders losing control of the communication, the event itself and their legitimate rights to empowerment as main actors in the event.

> He must tell you because you need to know what the other party is saying so that you act accordingly. [...] The interpreter must translate the insults, but in a calm tone. No need to imitate the upset tone, for instance. The

interpreter should speak as if he were a priest with an emotionless voice. He must stay calm to provide reassurance to both parties. (Captain M.Q.)

The interpreter must check with the speaker and explain him the consequences, then let the speaker decide knowing what is unacceptable in the target culture. The interpreter must educate the speaker in those scenarios in which faithful translations should be avoided, but he should never decide by himself when to leave information out. (Private F)

Certain comments, such as insults given in the middle of a joke, are something that we Spaniards did not expect the interpreters to translate. Even though it may sound offensive, we think it is culturally ok, but actually if the interpreters translated that for the Afghans, we would have had a massive conflict because [for Afghans] honor is very important. (Major D.)

I think it is very professional the fact that the interpreter can detect aspects of our culture that must not be translated. [...] Speaking a language is more than just grammar and words; it means understanding how cultures work and how speakers use their language. I think they have been very professional by noticing this type of things. (Captain B. S.)

The parties are already immersed in negotiations and the ICZ shouldn't distort the reality. If something goes wrong, we will restart the negotiations, but the ICZ must not try to remedy anything [...] It may be the case that the ICZ is against violence and in his head translating certain messages may lead to violence, hence he tries to iron out the tension. This is laudable, but sometimes it is necessary to get upset in order to ensure the negotiations move forward. (Captain H.)

Below we can read another instance on how these ICZ seem to have performed as main actors who creatively resorted to high levels of agency in order to ensure the above-mentioned culturally appropriate translations. Evidentially, there exists certain role distance between their normative role and the ways in which they executed their role precisely because "the theoretical concepts of T&I Studies do not work in such situations" (Spahic 2014, 81, my translation).

Who controls the parties? The interpreter, he solves problems. [...] If they fight, it's the interpreter's fault. [...] I have seen with my own eyes the parties fighting and the interpreter translating the fight. No, no. You must

> not translate. [..] You must mediate. You must sort things out (Lemar, interviewed interpreter).

In conflict-affected societies, there exist social tactics and practices that individuals use in their daily interactions in order to preserve peace and minimize inter and intra-group confrontation and risk (Mac Ginty 2014, 556). Such practices include, among others, avoidance, ambiguity and ritualized politeness, all of which seem to be tactics applied by these five local ICZ when negotiating meanings between the locals and the international coalition. In this sort of scenario, where ICZ are required to make decisions that extend beyond translations, resorting to solutions that may promise the maximum effect with the minimum damage could be the answer. In other words, these ICZ, unbound by professional codes of conduct, seem to have opted for "self-legislation" (Inghilleri 2010, 192) based on "their own ethical codes" (Baker 2012, 21). Contextual and risk analyses of such situations could be the solution as mentioned in one of the above narratives by military staff. However, in high-pressure and dangerous situations such as conflict zones "you are thinking of your safety [first], and then your translation" (Ghous, interviewed interpreter). Nevertheless, these five Afghan ICZ claim to have felt—most of time—part of the Spanish team despite the "outsider" nature that characterizes the perception that international troops have on the locally recruited interpreters (Gómez-Amich 2018). According to the ICZ's narratives, this sense of belonging made their work easier, as a good military-interpreter relationship is essential in order to effectively work in certain military missions in foreign lands (Hajjar 2016). Could it be this sense of team membership and institutional belonging that encouraged these ICZ to intervene, mediate and extend their traditional role limits? Some military personnel, however, seem to mostly disagree with those self-assigned extra levels of agency and power.

> The interpreter must not mediate, the parties must sort things out between themselves. [...] I am sure there have been lots of encounters that were successful thanks to the interpreter's mediation, but that is only the fault of an unskilled military leader. Such responsibility should not be given to the interpreter. (Major C.)

> If you allow the interpreter to control anything, for instance, the speaking turns, you are giving the interpreter a degree of authority he must not have. The other party has to clearly understand that they are dealing with you, not with the interpreter. (Major D.)
>
> The interpreter is there only because I cannot speak the local language. He is a mere tool who works for me, not for both parties. (Captain L. P.)
>
> The interpreter's job is to help the parties to converse and understand each other. [...] Even though I think the interpreter's responsibilities should be limited, his job is not just to translate literally without considering the consequences. The interpreter's job is to help the parties understand each other and that may actually imply mediating between different personalities. (Private F.)
>
> The local ICZ is a link between the local population and the international troops [...] Evidently, when we are in contact with the local population the local IZ acts as a natural mediator. You cannot separate translation from mediation, because the ICZ is in between and knows both sides, the circumstances and the connotations of each scenario. Inevitably they work, unconsciously, as mediators not only through the language but also by ensuring understanding and mutual respect. The ICZ mediates without even trying. When they interpret, they offer cultural advice so that we can keep on interacting with each other in such scenarios. (Captain B. S)

In conflict zones there are, generally speaking, three types of interpreters, that is, locally recruited interpreters, nationally recruited interpreters and military interpreters who either belong to the military institution or see themselves as ranked military personnel (Snellman 2016). The loyalty of the military interpreter is effortlessly taken for granted, whereas the trust in the local ICZ is not intrinsic to his position due to the fact they belong geographically and culturally to the enemy's communities.[8] Notwithstanding such outsider nature, some of the interviewed ICZ as well as military personnel (cf. some narratives above) presuppose the loyalty of the local ICZ to their military cause as locally recruited interpreters "become *de facto* players in a conflict which they may not choose, but which they sustain both morally and instrumentally" (Inghilleri 2010, 185).

[8] For an analysis of positionality among national interpreters in conflict zones, see Ruiz Rosendo 2019.

> My goal is to do my work, which is to translate and win the trust and [...] to fulfil the aim of the commanders. (Ghous, interviewed interpreter)

Unsurprisingly, the Spanish military personnel agree with such a statement, as such self-perception that this ICZ has on his role is, evidently, useful for the Spanish troops who seem to prioritize a unidirectional flow of information favorable to them.

> Of course, the interpreters must be able to go further and to earn the trust of the other party in order to support us in attaining our objectives. (Captain R)
>
> It is true that the interpreter's job is to earn the Afghans' trust and to support the Spanish troops in reaching our targets, because he works for us. Our target is to obtain certain information and the interpreter must help us with the communication. (Private F.)
>
> It would be great if the interpreter can walk us through the right path and share with us key information. (Captain M.S)

In order to achieve such objectives, it is imperative for the Spanish troops to be aware of the interaction and cultural norms governing communicative events, which differ from country to country. These norms are not to be openly negotiated in interactions, but rather the parties are expected to be aware of them. That is not always the case in multicultural encounters where one or more participants are likely to be completely unaware of how to interact with one another, given that, as mentioned in previous pages, "the worlds in which different societies live are distinct worlds, not merely the same world with different labels" (Sapir 1949, 162). Feelings of discomfort and distrust may then flourish resulting from mismatching expectations and conflicting *skopos* (Inghilleri 2003), which leads to "culture bumps" (Archer 1986, 170) that can potentially make any act become a threat to our listeners (Herrero Muñoz-Cobo 2000, 70-71).

> Apart from translating, I also gave my opinion about how they should treat the Afghans in order to get on well with them. (Daoud, interviewed interpreter)

Locally recruited ICZ with the appropriate knowledge on culture, customs, traditions, history and other significant aspects that shape counties around the world play a key role in educating international troops who, in most cases, are deployed to rather assist and protect the local population, not to create further issues in a given geographical area. Local ICZ as cultural agents "can be seen to hold the key to the continuing success of the unit's work" (Tipton 2011, 28) and for that the international coalition generally recognizes how the ICZ's capital allows their military personnel to develop their soft skills (Ingold 2014; Hajjar 2016), a key component of the postmodern military culture (Gómez-Amich 2018). As a matter of fact, establishing trust-building relationships between the international coalition and the local population can provide means for obtaining intelligence (Eriksson 2000), a key factor to successfully completing advisory missions with Afghan Forces (Hajjar 2016) and anti-insurgency propaganda (Barrantes Olías 2015), which is particularly difficult in Afghanistan due to the high levels of illiteracy, the deeply rooted tribalism and the religious fanaticism that still govern most parts of the country.

> I totally agree with his statement and heartily thank them for their cultural guidelines. I think those are essential because the interpreters are our link to the local population. They are not only responsible for language interpretation but their role also implies bridging the cultural gap. (Captain B. S.)
>
> I think it is a good idea. The interpreters used to tell us how to behave during important dates such as Eid and Ramadan. We are there for quite long and it is important to melt with the locals in order to get along. We did not know how to behave in such important dates but thanks to the interpreters we tried to make the locals feel as comfortable as possible with our presence. And the other way around: when the Spanish national team was playing a soccer game on tv, the interpreters explained it to the locals and they were happy for us. It is very good if the interpreters can help us with these aspects because we are unaware of each other's customs. (Private I.)
>
> I am grateful if the interpreter offers cultural explanations but if I have a meeting with a tribal leader it is my responsibility indeed to know how to behave, what may offend them or what may please them. I must be

> informed and prepared for it. The interpreter's friendly reminders are welcome but that is not his responsibility. [...] If the interpreter offers cultural details, he should do it before the event [because] there are situations for which we do not get any training, for example weddings. We get trained on how to behave in meetings, discussions, formal gatherings ... But at a wedding I may create a massive conflict if I give two kisses to the bride. If the interpreter sees that I am doing something bad, he should tell me so that I can apologize and remedy my mistake. (Major D)

In spite of all the above, or maybe because of it, attitudes of trust toward the locally recruited ICZ seem to vary among the military personnel precisely due to the local interpreter's inherent "otherness" framed within such an antagonistic context.

K: Spaniards do not trust in anyone.
M: What about the Afghans?
K: Neither do they. The Afghans say I am paid, Spaniards also say I am paid for my job. None trust anyone. (Karmal, interviewed interpreter)

The figure of the local ICZ working for the international troops seems to generally inspire a pervasive sense of mistrust not only among international troops but also among the local population, who—sometimes based on ethnic and class affiliation—consider them informants and traitors because they represent the invading forces' objectives and values (Baker 2012, 202). Accordingly, local interpreters are usually identified with the foreign troops as confirmed elsewhere (Ruiz Rosendo 2019, 8), and consequently rejected and repressed by other locals—their families at times—for their "political neutralization" (Stahuljak 1999, 38) that allows them to work with infidels—which in Afghanistan is considered a treachery (Thomas 2003, 309). These are some of the reasons why some of them choose to cover their faces when interpreting between the international troops and the local population.

With regard to the military personnel's perception, it is worth noting that in the military context, preference is given to unquestioned institutional loyalty, and the very same capital that makes the local interpreter indispensable also transforms him into an outsider who is "professional deficient in that they lacked the desired military professionalism, encapsulated in the term 'security clearance', that is to say unquestioned and proven loyalty to their employer (the army), and insulation from the personal, social and emotional implications of the field of conflict" (Tesseur and Footitt 2019, 271). In contrast, the opposite seems to be true for the interpreters who work in development projects framed within post-conflict settings (Tesseur and Footitt 2019, 277) where the local insider nature of the ICZ is highly appreciated. In conflict zones, however, local interpreters "run the risk of being seen as belonging to no 'man's land'" (Ruiz Rosendo and Persaud 2018, 3), and in such a context characterized by pervasive danger and persistent threats to your life, achieving certain levels of trust seem to be more challenging, if not impossible.

> It is a conflict zone in one of the most dangerous countries on this planet. There are conflicts of interest. Do not trust anyone who didn't come with you on that plane [from Spain]. The objectives in theory are the same because we all work towards the wellbeing of the country. Nevertheless, you must not trust them because they may be your friend today but your enemy tomorrow. Maybe in a meeting the locals tell him, "We know where you are from, we know who your family is. If you do not help us prepare an ambush right now, we will all die here today". You can only trust your people. The interpreter is working with the Spaniards but he isn't one of us [...] (Private F.)
>
> The degree of trust is limited. He answers to his country, to his family. I understand it is hard for them but there is no doubt there will never be absolute trust. [...] In a Spaniard I trust 10/10, in a military interpreter I trust 8/10 and in a local interpreter I trust 4 or 5/10. (Major D.)
>
> In this life we cannot trust others 100%. A conflict zone is very complex, and military personnel are trained to avoid full trust. We follow instructions and we are trained to always have certain level of mistrust, because it is necessary. (Captain B. S.)
>
> Some of my Spanish military mates did not like the local interpreters and felt reluctant to work with them because they thought the local interpreters only worked for the money. But that was just a few of us. [...] Not only did I trust them, but some of us were also friends with them. [...]

> The local population nevertheless does not appreciate their figure, because they are working with foreigners. (Private I.)

5 Conclusions

It is believed that the figure of the interpreter in conflict zones—as well as other settings—has been present in Humankind's history from 3000 BC, even though, according to some scholars, their existence and work have been inappropriately recorded. The work of these individuals has occupied center stage throughout the past centuries, and their performance has allowed for cross-cultural communication to take place in a world characterized by a large number of societies living different realities that, at times, are diametrically opposed or conflicting.

Warfare in the twenty-first century is characterized by military stratagem that focuses on continued collaboration between local population and international coalition forces, aiming at transforming civilian population into troops' allies within the different theaters of war around the world. In the case of Afghanistan, building rapport and trustworthy relations between military personnel and local civilians has proved to be a crucial step for the success of military operations. For this, it is imperative to speak the local languages and dialects, as well as to be aware of the social norms governing everyday interactions. This valuable capital is kept in the hands of the locally recruited ICZ and allows him to appropriately navigate the social habitus typified in the host culture(s).

There exists, however, one more set of habitus to which the local ICZ is required to adhere, that is, the military habitus governing each international troop. For an outsider who does not belong to the military field, adjusting to such a particular habitus characterized by a deeply rooted and solid hierarchical system can be quite a complex process. In such cases, guidelines and norms are usually shared with the newcomers. This, however, was not the case with these five Afghan ICZ who, on the contrary, signed considerably abstract contracts lacking clear guidelines on how to execute their role. Consequently, they all seem to have resorted to creative ways of tackling unavoidable challenges, including strategies such as additions, summaries, editions and omissions. Yet, military personnel do not always agree with such gatekeeping strategies that generally lead the local ICZ to execute higher levels of latitude. Subsequently, the main stakeholders lose their legitimate rights to empowerment as main actors in the interpreted event.

In these lines, it is worth highlighting how the military respondents seem to disagree on certain crucial matters including when and how the ICZ should carry out summaries, what responsibilities should be given to the local ICZ, where the limit to his role should be set and to what extent the military personnel can trust the local ICZ's commitment to their cause. Yet, there was one key aspect that all military personnel interviewed for this case study agreed on, that is, the fact that the local ICZ is working for the international troops and, as such, he must act as their tool. Accordingly, the local ICZ is expected to prioritize the needs of the military staff focusing, for instance, on gaining the other party's trust for the benefit of the troops, supporting the troops in achieving their targets and ensuring a unidirectional flow of key information favorable to the employer. These results evidence how the features that characterize conflict zones actively challenge the normative role traditionally assigned to the interpreter as an invisible and impartial facilitator of communication.

References

Allen, Katharine. 2012. Interpreting in Conflict Zones. NAJIT. https://najit.org/interpreting-in-conflict-zones. Accessed 7 Jul 2019.

Ali, Holi Ibrahim, Awad Alhassan, and Ishaq Burma. 2019. An Investigation into the Interpreter's Challenges in Conflict Zones: The Case of Darfur Region in Sudan. *AWEJ for Translation & Literature Studies* 3 (3): 37–50.

Angelelli, Claudia V. 2004. *Revisiting the Interpreter's Role: A Study of Conference, Court, and Medical Interpreters in Canada, Mexico and United States*. Amsterdam-Philadelphia: John Benjamins.

———., ed. 2012. *The Sociological Turn in Translation and Interpreting Studies*. Amsterdam-Philadelphia: John Benjamins.

Archer, Carol. 1986. Culture Bump and Beyond. In *Culture Bound: Bridging the Cultural Gap in Language Teaching*, ed. J. Valdés, 170–178. Cambridge: Cambridge University Press.

Baigorri Jalón, Jesús, and M. Manuela Fernández Sánchez. 2010. Understanding High-Level Interpreting in the Cold War. *Forum* 8 (2): 1–29.

Baker, Catherine. 2012. Opening the Black Box: Oral Histories of how Soldiers and Civilians Learned to Translate and Interpret during Peace Support Operations in Bosnia-Herzegovina. *Oral History Forum* 32: 1–22.

———. 2019. Language Intermediaries and Local Agency: Peacebuilding, Translation/Interpreting and Political Disempowerment in "Mature" Post-Dayton Bosnia-Herzegovina. *Journal of War and Cultural Studies* 12: 236–250.

Baker, Mona. 2006. *Translation and Conflict: A Narrative Account*. New York-London: Routledge.

Barrantes Olías, Diana. 2015. David Petraeus: Auge y Caída de un Gran General. *Real Instituto Elcano,* January 15. https://blog.realinstitutoelcano.org/david-petraeus-auge-y-caida-de-un-gran-general/

Berk-Seligson, Susan. 2002 [1990]. *The Bilingual Courtroom: Court Interpreters in the Judicial Process*. Chicago: The University of Chicago Press.

Bourdieu, Pierre. 1977. *Outline of a Theory of Practice*. Cambridge: Cambridge University Press.

Brown, Penelope, and Stephen Levinson. 1987. *Politeness: Some Universals in Language Usage*. Cambridge: Cambridge University Press.

Cummings, Michael G. 2012. Influencing the Population: Using Interpreters, Conducting KLEs, and Executing IO in Afghanistan. *Global Security*. http://www.globalsecurity.org/military/library/report/call/call12—18ch06.htm. Accessed 27 Sep 2019.

Delisle, Jean, and Judith Woodsworth, eds. 1995. *Translators through History*. Amsterdam-Philadelphia: John Benjamins.

Eriksson, Pär. 2000. Civil-Military Co-ordination in Peace Support Operations: A Impossible Necessity? *The Journal of Humanitarian Assistance,* September, 14. https://sites.tufts.edu/jha/archives/1469.

Feria García, Manuel. 1999. El Traductor-Intérprete de la Administración de Justicia. In *Traducir para la justicia*, ed. M. Feria García, 87–108. Granada: Comares.

Footitt, Hilary, and Michael Kelly. 2012. *Languages and the Military. Alliances, Occupation and Peace Building*. Houndmills: Palgrave Macmillan.

Footitt, Hilary, and Simona Tobia. 2013. *War Talk: Foreign Languages and the British War Effort in Europe, 1940-47*. Basingstoke: Palgrave Macmillan.

Gallai, Fabrizio. 2019. Interpreting Ethics in Fragile Environments. *Journal or War and Culture Studies* 12 (3): 220–235.

Goffman, Erving. 1961. *Encounters: Two Studies in the Sociology of Interaction*. Indianapolis: Bobbs-Merrill Company, Inc.

———. 1967. *Interaction Ritual. Essays on Face-to-Face Behaviour*. New York: Pantheon Books.

Gómez-Amich, María. 2016. The Untold Story: June's Case Study. *Linguistica Antverpiensia* 15: 89–105.

———. 2017. Estudio Descriptivo de la Autopercepción de los Intérpretes en Zonas de Conflicto: Estudio de Caso en Afganistán. PhD diss., University of Granada https://hera.ugr.es/tesisugr/26758933.pdf. Accessed 14 Sep 2019.

———. 2018. Life in Conflict: A Series of Narratives by Locally-Recruited Interpreters from Afghanistan. *Close Encounters in War* 1: 22–44.

Hajjar, Remi M. 2014. Military Warriors as Peacekeeper-Diplomats: Building Productive Relationships with Foreign Counterparts in the Contemporary Military Advising Mission. *Armed Forces and Society* 40 (4): 647–672.

———. 2016. Effectively Working with Military Linguists: Vital Intercultural Intermediaries. *Armed Forces and Society* 43 (1): 92–114.

Hale, Sandra. 2008. Controversies over the Role of the Court Interpreter. In *Crossing Borders in Community Interpreting: Definitions and Dilemmas*, ed. Carmen Valero Garcés and Anne Martin, 99–121. Amsterdam-Philadelphia: John Benjamins.

Henriksen, Thomas D. 2008. Liquidating Roles and Crystallising Positions: Investigating the Road between Role and Positioning Theory. In *Global Conflict Resolution Through Positioning Analysis*, ed. F.M. Moghaddam, R. Harré, and N. Lee, 41–64. Dordrecht: Springer Science and Business Media B.V.

Herrero Muñoz-Cobo, Bárbara. 2000. La Enseñanza del Español a Inmigrantes Magrebíes. *Docencia e Investigación: Revista de la Escuela Universitaria de Magisterio de Toledo* 25 (10): 63–88.

Hoedemaekers, Ian, and Joseph Soeters. 2009. Interactions Rituals and Language Mediation during Peace Missions: Experiences from Afghanistan. In *Advances in Military Sociology: Essays in Honour of Charles C. Moskos, Vol. 12 Part 1*, ed. G. Caforio, 329–352. Bingley: Emerald Group.

Hsieh, Elaine, and Eric M. Kramer. 2012. Medical Interpreters as Tools: Dangers and Challenges in the Utilitarian Approach to Interpreters' Roles and Functions. *Patient Education and Counselling* 89 (1): 158–162.

Inghilleri, Moira. 2003. Habitus, Field and Discourse: Interpreting as a Socially Situated Activity. *Target* 15 (2): 243–268.

———. 2009. Translation in War Zones: Ethics under Fire in Iraq. In *Globalization, Political Violence and Translation*, ed. E. Bielsa and C. Hughes, 207–221. New York: Palgrave Macmillan.
———. 2010. "You Don't Make War without Knowing Why" The Decision to Interpret in Iraq. *The Translator* 16 (2): 175–196.
Ingold, Catherine. 2014. Cross-Cultural Competence Plus Language: Capturing the Essence of Intercultural Communication. In *Cross-cultural Competence for a Twenty- First-Century Military: Culture, the Flipside of COIN*, ed. R. Greene Sans and A. Greene-Sans, 303–316. Lanham, MA: Lexington Books.
Jeppson, Christian, Sampsa Heilala, Jan Weuts, and Giovanni Santo Arrigo. 2015. NATO's Approach to Irregular Warfare: Protecting Achilles' Hill. *Military Review September-October*: 27–39.
Kelly, Michael, and Catherine Baker. 2013. *Interpreting the Peace. Peace Operations, Conflict and Language in Bosnia-Herzegovina*. Basingstoke: Palgrave Macmillan.
Kelly, Michael, Hilary Footitt, and Myriam Salama-Carr, eds. 2019. *The Palgrave Handbook of Languages and Conflict*. Cham: Palgrave Macmillan.
Levi, Primo. 1985. *L'Altrui Mestiere*. Turin: Einaudi.
Mac Ginty, Roger. 2014. Everyday Peace: Bottom-Up and Local Agency in Conflict-Affected Societies. *Security Dialogue* 45 (6): 548–564.
Mason, Ian. 2000. Models and Methods in Dialogue Interpreting Research. In *Intercultural Faultlines*, ed. M. Olohan, 215–231. Manchester: St. Jerome.
Miri, Amir. 2014. Un Intérprete en Afganistán: Más Allá de la Traducción Lingüística. *Instituto Español de Estudios Estratégicos,* December 25. http://www.ieee.es/Galerias/fichero/docs_opinion/2014/DIEEEO149-2014_InterpreteAfganistan_Amir-Miri.pdf.
Monacelli, Claudia, and Roberto Punzo. 2001. Ethics in the Fuzzy Domain of Interpreting. A Military Perspective. *The Translator. The Return to Ethics: Special Issue* 7 (2): 265–282.
Persaud, María Clementina. 2016. Interpreting at War: A Case Study of EUFOR BIH ALTHEA. PhD diss., University of Pablo Olavide.
Pym, Anthony. 2016. Risk Analysis as a Heuristic Tool in the Historiography of Interpreters: For an Understanding of Worst Practices. In *New Insights in the History of Interpreting*, ed. Kayoko Takeda and Jesús Baigorri Jalón, 247–268. Amsterdam-Philadelphia: John Benjamins.
Reddy, Michael J. 1993 [1979]. The Conduit Metaphor: A Case of Frame Conflict in our Language about Language. In *Metaphor and Thought,* ed. A. Ortony, 164–201. Cambridge: Cambridge University Press.

Ruiz Benítez, Antonio. 2015. Sistema de lecciones aprendidas en conflictos en el ejército de tierra español. *GESI,* March, 9. http://www.seguridadinternacional.es/?q=es/content/sistemas-de-lecciones-aprendidas-en-conflictos-en-el-ej%C3%A9rcito-de-tierra-espa%C3%B1ol

Ruiz Rosendo, Lucía, and Manuel Barea Muñoz. 2017. Towards a Typology of Interpreters in War-Related Scenarios in the Middle East. *Translation Spaces* 6 (2): 182–208.

Ruiz Rosendo, Lucía, and Maria Clementina Persaud. 2018. On the Frontline: Mediating across Languages and Cultures in Peacekeeping Operations. *Armed Forces & Society* 1: 1–19.

Ruiz Rosendo, Lucía. 2019. Interpreting for the Afghanistan Spanish Force. *War & Society* 39 (1): 42–57.

Sapir, Edward. 1949. The Status of Linguistics as a Science. In *Selected Writings of Edward Sapir in Language, Culture and Personality*, ed. D. Mandelbaum, 160–166. Berkeley-Los Angeles: University of California Press.

Snellman, Pekka. 2016. Constraints on and Dimensions of Military Interpreter Neutrality. *Linguistica Antverpiensia* 15: 260–281.

Spahic, Edina. 2014. Interpretar en Situaciones Bélicas y Posbélicas. In *Traducción como Mediación entre Lenguas y Culturas—Translation as Mediation or How to Bridge Linguistic and Cultural Gaps*, ed. Carmen Valero Garcés, 79–84. Alcalá de Henares: Servicios de Publicaciones.

Salama-Carr, Myriam. 2011. Interview: Interpreters in Conflict: The View from Within. *Translation Studies* 4 (1): 103–108.

Stahuljak, Zrinka. 1999. The Violence of Neutrality: Translators in and of the War [Croatia, 1991-1992]. *College Literature* 26 (1): 34–51.

Takimoto, Masato. 2006. Interpreter's Role Perception in Business Dialogue Interpreting Situations. *Monash University Linguistics Papers* 5 (1): 47–57.

Tălpaş, M. 2016. Words Cut Two Ways: An Overview of the Situation of Afghan Interpreters at the Beginning of the 21st Century. *Linguistica Antverpiensia* 15: 241–259.

Tesseur, Wine, and Hilary Footitt. 2019. Professionalisms at War? Interpreting in Conflict and Post-Conflict Scenarios. *Journal of War and Culture Studies* 12 (3): 268–284.

Thomas, Roy. 2003. Follow-On Protection for Interpreters in Areas of Conflict. In *The Critical Link 3: Interpreting in the Community. The Complexity of the Profession*, ed. Louise Brunette, Georges L. Bastin, Isabelle Hemlin, and Heather Clarke, 307–317. Amsterdam/Philadelphia: John Benjamins.

Tipton, Rebecca. 2011. Relationships of Learning between Military Personnel and Interpreters in Situations of Violent Conflict. *The Interpreter and Translator Trainer* 5 (1): 15–40.

Todorova, Marija. 2016. Interpreting Conflict Mediation in Kosovo and Macedonia. *Linguistica Antverpiensia* 15: 227–240.

Torikai, Kumiko. 2009. *Voices of the Invisible Presence: Diplomatic Interpreters in Post-World War II Japan.* Amsterdam-Philadelphia: John Benjamins.

Trochim, William, and Rhoda Linton. 1986. Conceptualization for Planning and Evaluation. *Evaluation and Program Planning* 9: 289–308.

Valero Garcés, Carmen. 1996. Traductores e Intérpretes en los Primeros Encuentros Precolombinos. Un Nuevo Rumbo en el Propósito de la Conquista. *Hieronymus Complutensis* 3: 61–73.

Van Dijk, Andrea, Joseph Soeters, and Richard de Ridder. 2010. Smooth Translation? A Research Note on the Cooperation between Dutch Service Personnel and Local Interpreters in Afghanistan. *Armed Forces & Society* 36: 917–925.

Wadensjö, Cecilia. 1998. *Interpreting as Interaction.* New York: Pearson Education.

Wang-chi Wong, Lawrence. 2007. Translators and Interpreters during the Opium War between Britain and China (1839-1842). In *Translating and Interpreting Conflict,* ed. Myriam Salama-Carr, 41–57. Amsterdam-NewYork: Rodopi.

Wengraf, Tom. 2004. The Biographic-Narrative Interpretive Method, BNIM—Shortguide November 2004. Version 22 NCRM Eprints. eprints.ncrm.ac.uk/30/1/Biographic-NarrativeInterpretiveMethodShortGuide.doc. Accessed 15 May 2019.

West, Bing. 2011. *The Wrong War: Grit, Strategy and the Way Out of Afghanistan.* New York: Random House.

6

Negotiating Ideologies in Conflict Zones: The Case of the Interpreter in Lebanon

Yolanda Moreno-Bello

1 Case Study: Interpreting for the Spanish Army in Lebanon

This case study was carried out in Lebanon, a multicultural and multi-religious country, epicenter of geopolitical conflicts where the Spanish army has acquired a relevant position within United Nations Interim Force deployment. As of March 7, 2020, the Spanish Ministry of Defense listed on its website:

> The UN mission in Lebanon has among its tasks to monitor the cessation of hostilities between Hezbollah and Israel and to accompany and assist the LAF in the south of the country and along the separation between the two states, the so-called Blue Line. It also guarantees humanitarian access to civilian populations and the voluntary and safe return of displaced persons.[1]

[1] Available at: https://emad.defensa.gob.es/en/operaciones/21-ONU-UNIFIL-Libano/index.html?__locale=en.

Y. Moreno-Bello (✉)
CETAPS Universidade NOVA de Lisboa, Lisbon, Portugal

M. Todorova, L. Ruiz Rosendo (eds.), *Interpreting Conflict*, Palgrave Studies in Languages at War, https://doi.org/10.1007/978-3-030-66909-6_6

Various factors should be taken into consideration in this situation. The modern history of Lebanon is marked by war: The Lebanese Civil War (1975–1990), the conflict between Israel and Lebanon (1978), and the "First war" (1982) and "Second war" (2006) of Lebanon.

In this context, we must also look at the relation between politics and religion in both sides of the conflict. The Lebanese system of government is a Parliamentary democracy that distributes the executive duties among the main religious beliefs in the country: The president must be a Maronite Christian; the prime minister a Sunni Muslim and the speaker of the House must be a Shiite Muslim. In contrast, we find a military structure that is deemed secular according to the Spanish constitution (SC 1978),[2] based also on a hierarchical system but, above all, institutional and military.

In this deployment, military and freelance interpreters are involved, in order to facilitate the encounter between the Spanish army and the Lebanese civil population. This chapter aims to examine the role of interpreters beyond linguistic management, by delving into the ideological negotiation of both actors. In order to achieve this objective, an empirical research was carried out by conducting interviews with soldiers in Lebanon and context analysis of the subject of study.

The interviews were designed to examine the difficulties found while interpreting in conflict zones in terms of ideological differences and to determine what strategies are used by the interviewed interpreters. Using interpreters' accounts as qualitative data, we examined how ideologies are negotiated in conflict, by using frame analysis.

The methodology applied to delimit the ideological negotiation in conflict zones by translators and interpreters has two objectives:

- First, discourse technics used to build ideological frameworks within the conflict will be examined.
- Second, data extracted from interviews will be analyzed following the frame-analysis theory (see Table 6.1) applied by Baker (2006), focusing on the strategies used by interpreters, as well as their autonomy on its implementation, during the ideological negotiation.

[2] Spanish Constitution. Boletín Oficial del Estado, 29 de diciembre de 1978, 311, 29313–29424.

Table 6.1 Framing analysis proposed by Baker (2006):

Framing ambiguity	According to Goffman, "the special doubt that arises over the definition of the situation" (1974, 302). Frame ambiguity is a feature of everyday life and is often experienced by different parties to a conflict as a by-product of competing attempts to legitimize different versions of a given narrative
Temporal and spatial framing	One of the strategies discussed under "Framing narratives in translation" (this chapter). It involves selecting a particular text and embedding it in a temporal and spatial context that accentuates the narrative it depicts and encourages us to establish links between it and current narratives that touch our lives, even though the events of the source narrative may be set within a very different temporal and spatial framework. This obviates the need for further intervention in the text itself, although it does not necessarily rule out such intervention
Selective appropriation	One of the core features of narrativity in Somers (1992) and Somers and Gibson (1994). To elaborate a coherent narrative, it is inevitable that some elements of experience are excluded, and others privileged. Narratives are constructed according to evaluative criteria which enable and guide selective appropriation of a set of events or elements from the vast array of open-ended and overlapping events that constitute experience
Framing by Labelling	One of the strategies discussed under "Framing narratives in translation". Labelling refers to any discursive process that involves using a lexical item, term, or phrase to identify a person, place, group, event, or any other key element in a narrative
Repositioning	One of the strategies discussed under "Framing narratives in translation". Translators and interpreters can actively reframe the immediate narrative as well as the larger narratives in which it is embedded by careful realignment of participants in time and social/political space. Participants can be repositioned in relation to each other and to the reader or hearer through the linguistic management of time, space, deixis, dialect, register, use of epithets, and various means of self- and other identification

A semi-structured interview of ten open-ended questions was used to initiate the interviews. Follow-up questions were used in order to follow the natural path of a conversation. This flexibility led to questions and answers of diverse nature, although in this sample, only the excerpts that contained relevant information for our study were selected. To preserve the ethics of the research, interviewees have provided verbal agreement on being recorded even though their personal information has remained undisclosed.

In the study, excerpts corresponding to interviews with 12 local interpreters and 5 military interpreters from the Base Miguel de Cervantes (UNIFIL) were analyzed. From these 12 interpreters, 9 were freelance and 3 were military interpreters. The different interviews scrutinized for this chapter were conducted in Beirut and Marjayoun (UNIFIL military base). Restricting our sample to interpreters that have worked in Lebanon, the chapter discusses findings from the results of a broader project.

2 Interpreting and Frame-Analysis Theory

Many linguists (see Bruner 1991; Somers 1992, among others) have studied the discursive elaboration of "ideas". In words of Fairclough (1989, 15), "language connects with the social through being the primary domain of ideology, and through being both a site of, and a stake in, struggles for power".

Translation and interpretation, therefore, contributes to balance the negotiation between hegemonic and oppressed ideologies:

> Thus, through the medium of the structure of the linguistic field, conceived as a system of specifically linguistic relations of power based on the unequal distribution of linguistic capital [...], the structure of the space of expressive styles reproduces in its own terms the structure of the differences which objectively separate conditions of existence.

Angelelli (2003, 16) goes even further when she analyzes the role of the interpreter, stressing their visibility and their active role in the flow of narratives during their involvement:

> [According to her work, the interpreter is visible in all social and cultural elements that allow them to co-construct a definition of reality together with other co-participants of the interaction. The interpreter is present with his/her deeply rooted convictions about power, status, solidarity, gender, age, race, ethnicity, nationality, socio-economic status, as well as cultural norms and projections in which the interpreter is supposed to construct and interpret reality.

Likewise, Baker (2006, 105) points out that every translator and interpreter have to face basic ethical decisions by reproducing existing ideologies, or distance themselves from these ideologies, even refusing to translate a text in certain situations.

Baker (2006) proposes to implement the frame-analysis theory for linguistic and ideological negotiation in the field of translation and interpreting. Similarly, Goffman (1986), Lakoff (1991), Entman (1993) apply the frame-analysis theory for the comprehension of the context, those studies will be key to interpret the meaning and intention of the message.

Various definitions exist about the purpose and essence of the term "framework". For Goffman (1986, 10) "interpretation in every situation is constructed in accordance with guidelines which regulate occurrences [...] and our subjective vision within the situation."

Similarly, Entman (1993, 52) establishes that "framing" is used to select certain aspects of reality that we perceive and focus on them within communicative situations in a way that fosters a type of definition of the problem, casual interpretation, moral evaluation and/or recommendation of treatment.

Finally, paraphrasing Lakoff (1991), it is understood that the "framework" has to do with choosing the kind of language that fits with your vision of the world. However, it does not only have to do with language; first there are ideas. Language transmits and evokes these ideas.

In order to examine the role of the interpreter in negotiating ideologies in conflicts, the responses of the interpreters have been categorized according to the frame-analysis theory previously studied by Goffman (1974), Lakoff (1991) and Entman (1993), among others; and applied in *T/I* by Baker (2006).

3 Corpus Analysis: Framing Ideologies in Discourse

3.1 Framing Ambiguity

One of the main problems in interpretation is the ambiguity in the interventions. However, the accuracy of statements from conflict zones is of utmost importance given that citizen's freedom and safety depend upon these interventions. We must take into account that ambiguity is also used as a way to hide realities, modifying perceptions or the meaning of concepts.

Yule (2006, 98) also describes a similar concept called "structural ambiguity", which he defines as the situation in which an expression or sentence has two or more underlying structures or interpretations.

As Chilton (1997, 175) explains, violent conflicts are categorized following specific terminology, such as: war, civil war, guerrilla warfare, terrorist acts or even low-intensity conflicts. The categorization of these events reflects different conceptual and ideological associations understood by the speaker/listener. This framework reveals the ambiguity (Goffman 1986, 302) used in a conflict as an attempt to legitimize their ideology or view of the conflict.

As we observe, interview number 5 shows specific ideology through ambiguous language (see Table 6.2):

In table 6.2, the interviewee alludes to another type of scenario. In this case, it focuses on the terms: "camp" and "refugee resettlement". In the following excerpt, we observe how ambiguous language affects the understanding of sensitive concepts:

> E2 (5): "Tented settlements", is not a very common word [...]. or "Informal tented settlements", they don't call them "camps" anymore, I don't know why. UN stopped calling them "camps" [...] They are not "camps"; I forgot the reason. It's more accurate.

Table 6.2 Excerpt's analysis of framing by labeling

E5: (1) <<*Sensitive zone*>>/ << *complex situation*>>/ << *complications*>>/ << *not healthy environment*>>	E5 (2): << *Southern Lebanon*>>/ <<*border zone*>>/ << *bordering Israel*>>/ *UN presence*>>	E5: (5)<<*Series of assassinations: Rafiq al Hariri, all the martyrs...*>>/ <<*Palestinian issue*>>
Strategy:	Framing by labelling	
Negotiation:	The use of lexical items, specific terms, and phrases to describe the country/location indicates a particular narrative or point of view. The strong phrase "series of assassinations" shows a specific way of understanding events, as well as "Palestinian issue" is a euphemism to refer to the conflict. All terms and phrases implicitly adhere to a specific narrative.	

3.2 Framing Time and Space

According to Baker (2006), this framework consists on selecting a specific text and placing it within a particular space and time that highlights certain narrative/ideology. The sum of all of these possibilities constitutes what Goffman (in Baker 2006, 109) calls the 'spatial framework' of a participant.

In this case, interpreters interviewed, explained some of the elements of negotiation between civilians and the military. The following examples E2 and E6 coincide on the need to manage information depending upon the place where the conversation takes place, however; they understand autonomy differently:

> E2 (1): I mostly interpret for people of this region; I understand the culture also. [I would modify only] if they don't use the literary Arabic, if they use their own Arabic [...]
>
> E6 (1): I don't interpret everything literally, because I am aware that in Lebanon there are certain courtesy norms [...] If the person I am talking to, is expecting a baby, the first thing I do is asking about it.

The interpreter in E2 refers to common errors such as cultural differences and the need to elaborate due to misunderstanding or differences in dialects.

Nevertheless, their autonomy is limited. In this example, interpreters often lean toward a dialectal shift, avoiding intervention when possible.

In the following example, E6, the interpreter explains why she needs to mediate during the conversation. Therefore, she does not limit her autonomy in this negotiation:

> The conversation is between those two, [the officers] only want to know what has happened so that they give them the documents and see if they can help, but she has a story to tell you and you need to make her understand that you are sorry and that you are there for her…I feel that between them there is not that emotional connection, but between me and her there is […]. It is very cold between them; she speaks to me directly.

Furthermore, she also states that in some instances, the person being interviewed felt reluctant to open up because they don't feel connection with the speaker, "They have preconceived notions that he is not going to understand their situation" and adds: "they might say: 'I don't know if he is going to understand what I want to tell you'".

She insists that her main objective is to help understand one another at all possible levels: "With the linguistic information that is given, it's not enough"—explains E6—"Perhaps due to the cultural shock there are typical formulas. I would add 'I'm sorry' if someone has died, even before I interpret the information".

Furthermore, she admits that the terminology associated with God can be quite controversial: "There are certain verbs in Arabic that are only used with God as the 'creator from nothing', 'appear', or for example '*yihad*' which is in the Quran is the 'internal war', 'the temptations'".

As a matter of fact, in an article she explains:

> In our opinion, it would be convenient to translate expressions such as إنشاءالله (literally "God willing") with a simple "hopefully", which is an Arab expression that is closest in intention and meaning to the original use. In addition اللهمعكم (literally "God be with you") could best be translated with a simple "*adios*", or "good-bye" or to even omit phrases such as بسماللهالرحمنالرحيم (literally "the name of God"), which are used in an almost automatic and ritual way in order to distance them from the evil eye. (Iriarte-Díez 2015)

Further examples taken from E2, E9 and E11 indicate other forms of negotiation of the space and time framework of those in which interpreters have had to intervene (see Table 6.3):

This continuous climate of conflict has created two main lines of arguments based on dichotomous concepts such as, "ally/enemy", and "us/them". On one hand, the Lebanese "resist" against the potential foreign "invaders", in this case, influencing in the dichotomy "soldier/civilian". In interview 10, excerpt (2), the interpreter explains, "Soldiers are different than the civilians. Soldiers follow strict protocols. In the end, we deal with it, here people are used to it".

In our study, it was observed that the relationship between contextual elements and the negotiation between those two frameworks have been recurring in the conversations with interpreters who recognize the need to adapt to the context:

> E1 (2): Sometimes you know who you are going to meet. So you prepare accordingly if it's a religious man or a soldier, army personal or not.
>
> E2 (10): They'll be confused if they mention a holiday or Ramadan, or because the woman has to wear these religious clothes and I have to explain the whole context of the whole situation. So, sometimes you have to explain the culture behind what they are saying, because to me, it makes sense [but it may] not for someone else.

Table 6.3 Excerpt's analysis of temporal and spatial framing

E2: (2) "*You [need] training, how to go to the tents, how to act, to take off your shoes, they offer you tea, if you don't want the tea, you say: 'I'm fasting', or 'I've got diabetes', you don't say: 'it's disgusting', don't wear a mask not to show that they are dirty, don't get sanitizer with you, you can do it in the car*"	E9: (4) "*You have to communicate to the kid directly [...] The translator needs to be all the time in the class not to be strange for them and doing activities with the children, not to be just a translator*"	E11: (1) "When dealing with authorities we have to follow the protocol, however, in CIMIC missions we are freer to advice on how to ask, in the case of shaking hands with a woman and other costumes"
Strategy:	Temporal and spatial framing	
Negotiation:	Change of perspective of frame of temporal and spatial representations in the discourse.	

> E3 (2): You have to know what the political regime is, and what is the dress code, what are the recent events, that this country lived, how you have to speak to people, history.

The following example is an anecdote from an interpreter contracted locally by the Spanish contingency on the Cervantes Military Base. In this interview, both ideologies are shown in conflict; on the one hand, the Shiite community's religious symbols and on the other hand, the military mission:

> E10: (1) There was a religious man who was a bit tense. An Imam, a clergy of the Shiite community. I had to be in the interview to translate and I didn't bring a veil with me. We [referring to the Lebanese] normally know that if we have an interview with a religious man and I have to be there…as a woman, I have to wear a veil. No one forces me, not the Spanish Brigade, nor no one from abroad, but for respect. There are some that are sensitive, there are some that accept you, there are some who doesn't, some who would use whatever they can to make things tense […]. I went there and he didn't like me at all. Yes, he was angry as well at UNIFIL for the aerial violations by Israel […] Even though they didn't come to stop anything, they came here on a peacekeeping mission. So, they should not hold responsible for that.

This perception shows the negotiation between religious norms and at the same time, the impact that this can have on the encounter. In this case, the interpreter considers that a bad religious gesture in this context could have unleashed the Imam's political accusations. In turn, the interpreter seemed to be influenced by the narrative of the Spanish military, for which she works. This means that if we keep in mind that the Shiites, mainly in the south of Lebanon, support the armed group *Hezbollah* (the party of God) and that it has been the main participant in the fight against Israel, we understand that the Imam's main narrative is based upon a supposed inaction on the Spanish military's part. At the same time, the interpreter takes over the narrative from the Spanish military, justifying the inaction within the framework of their responsibilities.

3.3 Framing Selective Appropriation

Narratives are elaborated with patterns of omission and/or deliberated allusions, in order to accentuate specific aspects of the narrative. Therefore, these strategies should be identified by the interpreter and act accordingly. In this manner, interpreters explain the need to omit or add information, again, with the notion of autonomy being different in each interpreter:

> E2: (11) Sometimes, they ask a question and it doesn't make sense because he answered the same question and the guy didn't get it. I change it a little bit.
>
> E3: (5) Sometimes you have to go a little bit beyond the interpretation, but I always ask my client if I can do so [...]. By client I understand the person asking me to interpret for him, I will tell them what I will explain [...]. You have to make sure that the message is understood.

In the interpretation of offensive language, the interpreters acquire more autonomy and decide to avoid neutrality by suppressing controversial content (see Table 6.4):

Even still, there are interpreters that tend to consult with their contractor before modifying the content (see Table 6.5):

Table 6.4 Excerpt's analysis of selective appropriation I

E4: (2) << *I can't let the other guy feel that he said something wrong [...] I have to educate them, how to approach the subject*>>	E6: (2) << *There are things I can't translate but I can't share it because he is my superior and I don't feel comfortable telling him to be more polite*>>	E6: (7) <<*I can't translate everything that is said because I would morally destroy that person. You just skip it or smooth the content...*>>
Strategy:	Selective appropriation	
Negotiation:	Mitigation or omission of content to adapt it to the situation and avoid conflict.	

Table 6.5 Excerpt's analysis of selective appropriation II

E7: (1) << *If it's controversial, I'll say: "You sure you want to say this?" [...] If the language is too strong: "I would turn it don't myself" [...] You need to ask this in a different way or ask few questions before you go into that*>>	E10: (4) << *I let them know I'm changing the offensive language and sometimes they say: "Ok, but let him know that I caught him, and I know he is lying to me"*>>	E10: (5) << *If there is a word that it's going to impact too much, I try to avoid it. They respect me and trust my decisions*>>
Strategy:	Selective appropriation	
Negotiation:	Mitigation or omission of content to adapt it to the situation and avoid conflict.	

3.4 Framing by Labelling

Baker (2006) understands labelling as a logical process that includes the use of lexical elements, words or expressions to identify a person, place, group, event or any other key element in the narrative. Any label used to point out or identify a key element or participant of a narrative provides an interpretative framework that guides and limits our response to the narrative in question (Baker 2006, 122). As a result, labels are used to denominate certain events between those that share the same beliefs in an attempt to legitimize and discredit a narrative.

The following examples reference derogatory names:

> E2 explains: (9) "If someone said 'Mongolian' instead of 'down syndrome', I explained to them: 'He actually meant the person who has down syndrome'. I put it in context". The same way, E7 explains how in some situations he/she had to interpret: (4) "That guy is a cripple". In this case, the interpreter had to choose between being literal by using the offensive choice "cripple", or a more politically correct word "or you will say that he is handicapped, or physically challenged". The decision has to be made on the spot taking into consideration the context and the possible consequences.

Another type of resource to alleviate or aggravate the cognitive perception of an act through language are euphemisms. González (2009) talks about institutionalized euphemisms that gradually become technical jargon used by administrations in their statements and official interventions. Euphemisms such as "depressed populations" when they speak of "poverty", "collateral damage" when they speak of "crimes against civilian population", "migrants" to refer to "exiled", "neutralize" instead of "kill" or "operations stage" to refer to "war territory".

This can be observed in the following excerpts from interviews (see Tables 6.6 and 6.7):

In the study, a series of metaphorical relations that are typically used in politics are established. In this sense, the interpreter of E7 explains:

> E7: (5) When I conduct an interview with Hezbollah and we are talking about their fighters […], and [the soldier] says: Tell me how he was killed. I'm going to ask how he was martyred, because that's the language for them, and if I ask how he was killed, he is going to pull back in the interview […] If they don't feel that empathy, it's going to be like an interrogation, it's not going to be forthcoming.

In the following example, the variety of meanings can be observed in the word *Yihad* (جهاد). Contrary to the most common meanings in the Western world, such as, "holy war", "fight for Islam", the interpreters in Lebanon provided definitions with other meanings:

Table 6.6 Excerpt's analysis of framing by labeling I

E2 (3): << *Every camp has a chief, they call him "shaif" "shhawish"*>>	E2: (8) << *Neutralize*>>, *highlights << I will translate "kill them", there is no word in Arabic*>>	E2: (7) << *Someone anti regime, or against the refugees, [would say either: "Why did you betrayed your country". (If they are pro regime): "Why are your fighting against the government? You should be fighting for them now. You coward!"*>>
Strategy:	Framing by labelling	
Negotiation:	The use of the specific lexical item defines which narrative is the speaker adhering to. As well as certain terms can be used to show respect or authority. The use of certain phrases or terms can be also used to normalize stereotypes and that's why negotiation is key in the process of interpreting	

Table 6.7 Excerpt's analysis of framing by labeling II

E5: (3) << *Occupied territories>> <<Israeli Operation against Lebanon>> The use of <<occupied territories>> is of <<Israel>>*	E5: (4) <<*political figures or... civil society figures were assassinated>> This excerpt shows reframing of a previous statement to make the sentence more appealing to the listener, even if that includes syntax errors.*	*E6: (9) << There is a specific jargon in the Arab world such as: "occupied Gaza", to show which side they are in. So, when I am translating, I can't say: "Israel", I have to use their jargon>>*
Strategy:	Framing by labelling	
Negotiation:	Ideology is often reflected in the use of language, such as jargon and euphemisms	

'Fighting for honorable reasons', 'This word has a very different meaning depending in context. Originally it is a good word in Islamic culture', 'Crusade')

In this example, the translations for "collateral damage" from our interviews indicated a preference for literal translations in all the languages, even though the same dictionary specifies the dysphemism. The synonyms proposed for "subsequent damage" (ضررلاح), "troubles relations with", "incidental damage", "loss", "unintentional damage", "secondary damage", "unintended damage", "uncontrolled damage", "damage to intended targets", "accompanying", as well as the translations (all of which were literal) transmit the same ideology from the source language to the target language without questioning the context or the reason for using this expression. In only one case, the interpreter proposed the synonym, "civilian casualties", even though the meaning was not reflected in any of the translations. As we can see, the euphemistic terminology raises a meaningful barrier and therefore complicates even further its translation.

3.5 Repositioning of Participants

Elements such as time, space, deixis, dialects, register, the use of epithets and other ways of repositioning participants such as "I" and the "other" are tools to negotiate frames such as "here and there", "now and then", "them and us", "reader and narrator", "reader and translator", "listener and interpreter" (Baker 2006). In other words, speakers tend to distribute roles and social hierarchies by means of deictic terms with a specific purpose.

The following excerpts from interviews show negotiation in tone, formalities or categorical names (see Table 6.8):

Something similar occurs with roles established through hierarchies of power. In this case, the interpreter finds herself between two different types of jargon. The jargon used by the military tends to be more formal and of a higher register. Civilians, on the other hand, tend to use simpler language and a lower register. This way, the interpreter E6 recognizes the asymmetry that exists in this type of contexts.

> Against the asymmetry [I] simplify to the form in which he organizes the information or the words that he chooses, I, in Spanish, understand them perfectly, but, I am not going to complicate his life, even though I know

Table 6.8 Excerpt's analysis of repositioning of participants

E1: (1) << You adopt the same attitude of the person you are translating for or to>>	E2: (4) <<You have to introduce yourself, if the 'shhawish' doesn't like you, you'll have to leave the camp>>	E3: (1) To interpret to them you have to add terms of respect, because Jordan people like to be ... specially when they are a doctor, they want to look a bit different>>
Strategy:	Repositioning of participants	
Negotiation:	The switch of deictic elements allows the interpreter to negotiate ideologies, while when being forced to adopt the same attitude, it reduces the interpreter's agency.	

> the word in Classical Arabic [...] If he says that—we need a power of attorney—I explain to him what it is and how it is done, because if not, she may insist, "okay, okay" and has not really understood anything. So, I simplify without neither of the other two parties involved in the interpretation realizing.

As E6 states, language also reflects social class. She explains that there are official and personal titles that are not interchangeable between an ambassador or a minister: "The jargon represents levels of importance".

In the following examples, the interpreters portray situations in which negotiation between participants resulted in being crucial for the interpretation (see Table 6.9):

Normativity consists of the 'normalization' of events so that they seem an immovable event. Somers (1994, 609) defines normativity as the tool by which ideas or experiences of others can be suppressed, rejected and underestimated collectively.

In Osborne (2009, 161), we can find that the elements that conform normativity in war are also gender oriented:

> Wars, all wars, as well as the phenomena of militarism can be seen as one more way, albeit extreme, to divide work and roles which express beliefs opposite in nature between men and women: for men, war; for women, peace.

During conflicts women are considered passive subjects and men acquire a superior status taking control of the conflict. The notion of "heroism" (Osborne 2009, 162–171) also acquires a large regulatory burden, awarding greater status to those who risk their life to fight for a cause. Accordingly, the military system is organized following key hierarchies in its organization (see Bos and Soeters 2003).

As we have previously mentioned, military hierarchy and, therefore, other hierarchies like religious or political institutions need to negotiation at many levels, including, syntactically, semantically and kinetically.

Table 6.9 Excerpt's analysis of repositioning of participants II

Strategy:	Repositioning of participant
Negotiation:	Repositioning of participants can help preventing controversy, managing psychological aspects, age, cultural perceptions, and attitudes within the context.
Negotiating attitudes	E7: (2) << [If the language is too strong] I would turn it down myself>> (3) <<You need to ask this in a different way or ask few questions before you go into that>>
Negotiating age	Communication between adult and child: E9: (1) <<You need to talk to the kid the same way, talk the same language and the same way of talking [...] When they cry, I cry like them, I make the voice like them... Can you imagine if you are not talking the same language? [...] They might not know the words they are using; they are just expressing; they will look at you and talk even if you don't understand>> (2) << Children can't express so well in their own language>> (3) << You have to go on their level, talk the same way, smiling all the time>>
Negotiating culture	E10: (3) << I try to help with cultural aspects because Spanish people have a different way of building rapport [...] They would use offensive language to break the ice: "Era un cabrón">> << In Arabic is very offensive, especially when is coming from a young lady like me. If I am translating between a major and a soldier, they wouldn't understand that are not my words and therefore, I should show respect>>
Negotiating asymmetry	E2: (6) A lot of people go to the refugee camps and to the people with a superior mentality, especially Lebanese people. They are giving them attitudes [...] There is also, political grudges [...] because they see a lot of misery, and they want to detach from reality they can get a little mean. Sometimes they yell at them>>

4 Conclusions

By applying frame-analysis Baker (2006) to our corpus, we have observed how interpreters negotiate ideologies found in discourse. In other words, narratives in conflict are ideological representations of the world and as such, are tools to legitimize and discredit events, actions and even one's own discourse. This means that the interpreter plays a key role in the negotiation of conflict ideologies when interpreting a specific narrative.

Whether the interpreter maintains a literal message or, frames it within a new narrative, the interpreter is taking part, and in any case, neutrality disappears. Therefore, the interpreter is taking a decision, in every element of the narrative, in favor of it or not.

According to the methodology applied, the study has drawn the following conclusions:

4.1 Framing Ambiguity

Ambiguity has the intention to dilute the meaning of the events, facts or actions in order to favor the narrative in which the speaker is involved. According to our study, the interpreter could frame that intervention in a new narrative in a way in which communication is fluent and in order to avoid tensions or conflicts between participants. According to the responses obtained, we have observed that the difficulties that interpreters have in negotiating the terminological ambiguity are, in many cases, due to the fact that the meaning of that terminology is not questioned by the interpreter. Furthermore, it has been observed a lack of training in regards to specific terminology.

4.2 Framing Time and Space

The negotiation of the time and space can be observed in many linguistic strategies (terminological, semantic, syntactic, dialectal, pragmatic, proxemic, kinetically, etc.). Interpreters who were interviewed knew of the important cultural, social, and historic aspects, yet nevertheless in cases such as E2 or E11, interpreters considered that any change in intervention should be consulted first. This action limits their autonomy and at the same time, it undermines the fluency of the conversation.

4.3 Framing Selective Appropriation

In the excerpts displayed, the responses of the interpreters are heterogeneous. The autonomy of the interpreter was questioned in cases such as E3, E7 and E10 in contrast to the opinions of E4, E6 and E11. It is worth mentioning that the importance of this framework resides not only fundamental in knowing how to select what parts or elements can be omitted or added, but in detecting which selective appropriation strategy that the participants are using and what is the reason behind it.

4.4 Framing by Labelling

Metaphors, euphemisms and symbolisms are some of the strategies that labelling includes. Inevitably, language evokes a series of cognitive associations. Therefore, it is necessary for the interpreter to be able of understanding the ideological implications that the terminology used has on the message. Interpreters in E2, E5, E6 and E7 demonstrated having a deep understanding of political, religious and cultural implications of the message. Therefore, an increase in autonomy was also observed when reframing this narrative.

4.5 Repositioning of Participants

In this analysis, we found that interpreters enjoy a greater level of autonomy in deictic elements and procedures, but their autonomy diminished in such aspects as offensive language, tone or register.

4.6 General Conclusion

We observed that none of the interpreters see themselves as a completely neutral translation tool whose only role is to move words from one language to another. It was also observed that interpreters often consulted their contractor before making a noticeable change in language.

Interpreters lack autonomy in the reformulation of narratives framing elements such as 'selective appropriation', 'ambiguity' and 'repositioning of participants'. However, they feel more legitimized to reformulate or negotiate narratives framing elements such as space and time and labelling. While the interpreter tends to maintain literalness in elements of discourse that are more tangible (syntax, terminology, deixis…), they tend intervene more in elements related to cultural aspects.

Similarly, all the interpreters assert that negotiating is an interpreter's task; however, they show different levels of autonomy on doing so. Bearing in mind these results, we deduce that the new lines in translation and interpretation that have been centered on cultural mediation could be the reason of the autonomy in certain cultural elements. Therefore, new lines that open up negotiating possibilities of other elements could be useful in regard to empowering the interpreter to negotiate equally among all participants.

References

Angelelli, Claudia. 2003. The Interpersonal Role of the Interpreter in Cross-Cultural Communication. In *The Critical Link 3: Interpreting in the Community. The Complexity of the Profession*, ed. Louise Brunette, Georges L. Bastin, Isabelle Hemlin, and Heather Clarke, 289–302. Amsterdam and Philadelphia: John Benjamins.

Baker, Mona. 2006. *Translation and Conflict: A Narrative Account*. Londres: Routledge.

Bos, Miepke, and Joseph Soeters. 2003. Cross-Cultural Issues in Peacekeeping Operations. In *The Psychology of the Peacekeeper: Lessons from the Field*, ed. Thomas W. Britt and Amy B. Adler, 283–298. Londres: Praeger Publisher.

Bruner, Jerome. 1991. The Narrative Construction of Reality. *Critical Inquiry* 18 (1): 1–21.

Chilton, Paul. 1997. The Role of Language in Human Conflict: Prolegomena to the Investigation of Language as a Factor in Conflict Causation and Resolution. *Current Issues in Language & Society* 4 (3): 174–189.

Entman, Robert M. 1993. Framing: Toward Clarification of a Fractured Paradigm. *Journal of Communication* 43 (4): 51–58.

Fairclough, Norman. 1989. *Language and Power*. London and New York: Longman.

Goffman, Erving. 1986. *Frame Analysis: An Essay on the Organization of Experience*. Boston: Northeastern University Press.

———. (1986 [1974]). *Frame Analysis: An Essay on the Organization of Experience*. Boston: Northeastern University Press.

González, Victoria E. 2009. Palabras en la guerra. Comunicación, discurso y política. In *Comunicación y ciudadanía*, vol. 1, 74–81. Bogotá: Universidad Externado de Colombia.

Iriarte-Díez, Ana. 2015. Traducción: comunicación, concienciación, conciliación. La traducción literaria como puente entre culturas. In *Familias palestinas refugiadas en Líbano: Promoción de la convivencia pacífica*. ONG RESCATE Internacional.

Lakoff, George. 1991. Metaphor and War: The Metaphor System Used to Justify War in the Gulf. *Peace Research* 23: 25–32.

Osborne, Raquel. 2009. *Apuntes sobre violencia de género*. Barcelona: Bellaterra.

Somers, Margaret R. 1992. Narrativity, Narrative Identity, and Social Action: Rethinking English Working-Class Formation. *Social Science History* 16 (4): 591–630.

———. 1994. The Narrative Constitution of Identity: A Relational and Network Approach. *Theory and Society* 23 (5): 605–649.

Somers, Margaret R., and Gloria D. Gibson. 1994. Reclaiming the Epistemological 'Other': Narrative and the Social Construction of Identity. In *Social Theory and the Politics of Identity*, ed. Craig Calhoun, 37–99. Cambridge and Oxford: Blackwell.

Yule, George. 2006. *The Study of Language: Thoroughly Revised and Update*. Cambridge: Cambridge University Press.

7

The Spanish "Military Interpreter": A Practical Application in International Operations Arising from Armed Conflicts

Verónica Méndez Sánchez

1 Introduction

Interpreting and the Armed Forces have experienced a clear evolution in the last decades. The former is no longer seen as a simple linguistic reformulation, but it is approached from an interdisciplinary perspective, considering linguistic and extralinguistic factors, with a significant influence on the whole process and its final result. Therefore, it is a complex activity, constantly adapting to the new times and generating new needs to be covered by new strategies of analysis and resolution. Something similar happens with the Armed Forces' tasks, which are nowadays more numerous and diversified, developed in an interdisciplinary, multilingual, and multicultural context. Besides, global developments, technological

V. Méndez Sánchez (✉)
Independent Researcher, Salamanca, Spain
e-mail: vero_delfy@usal.es

M. Todorova, L. Ruiz Rosendo (eds.), *Interpreting Conflict*, Palgrave Studies in Languages at War, https://doi.org/10.1007/978-3-030-66909-6_7

progress, and globalization have promoted the transformation of the strategic landscape[1].

Over the last few years, many "military interpreting"[2] studies have been carried out highlighting the relevance of the interpreting in conflict zones (e.g. Baigorri Jalón 2003; Baker 2010; House 2014; Miri 2014; Snellman 2016). However, the "military interpreter" as a professional enrolled in the Armed Forces is a surprising and unknown denomination among other things because most researchers mainly focus on civilian mediators working for the Army, but not on enrolled soldiers performing as interpreters; something relevant, considering that, as explained in Ruiz Rosendo and Barea Muñoz (2017), different categories of interpreters can be identified. As we will see below, military interpreting is an arduous and complex task that requires a broad linguistic management, a high cultural awareness, and an interdisciplinary profile, not always recognized or properly regulated.

Finally, due to the importance of the context in which interpreting tasks are performed, we will present a brief overview of the linguistic and cultural scenario of Senegal. This will allow us to classify the potential risk factors that can affect the interpreter's activity and will help us on proving the complexity of the military interpreters' work, and the relevance of interpreting in the Armed Forces.

2 Interpreting and the Armed Forces: Opposed Fields in Continuous Relationship

Despite the evident evolution of interpreting and the Armed Forces, and the boosting of military interpretation studies, both professional fields continue to be unlinked disciplines.

[1] Further details on this matter can be found in the *Brahimi Report* of the High-level Independent Panel created to assess Peace Operations: https://reliefweb.int/sites/reliefweb.int/files/resources/N1518145.pdf.

[2] This category of interpreter will be further nuanced in Section 2.

Interpreting is a useful and necessary activity for society, a multicultural, ubiquitous, and universal science in constant evolution inspiring many studies and controversies. Similarly, the Armed Forces is an Institution with its own specific context, rules, and language, so that it can fulfill the same duty as any other professional scope. As a heterogeneous institution, it gathers high professional crossbreeding and a very wide-ranging thematic. This straightforwardly impacts on the volume and variety of discourses generated and, consequently, on the language brokering work. Hence, the relevance of studies such as this, which seek to highlight and clarify the regulatory deficiencies remaining in this field.

Furthermore, although it is true that the Armed Forces' main functions are linked to the Defence of the State and the practice of war, those duties are not the only ones. The Army also undergoes lengthy periods of non-involvement in any active conflict; therefore, it accomplishes other types of missions equally important and useful for any Nation, such as international humanitarian missions, surveillance, or support in natural disasters, among others. So, it is endowed with a social, political, and linguistic perspective, which is frequently unknown or ignored.

One of the reasons that could justify this lack of joint regulations, between the interpreting and the Armed Forces, is associated with the notable lack of interest and knowledge in Defence matters shown by the Spanish society[3]. The current reasons for this indifference are mainly founded on a lack of awareness about our current threats and a poor information dissemination on the work performed by the Army. This issue affects not only the military's value and reputation, but also the language brokering field.

Considering this wide unawareness about the military world, the previous knowledge handled by interpreters will impact the comprehension of the message transmitted in military contexts. In our view, it should not be ignored that in an area where many languages coexist, where thousands of soldiers work, where there is a need to interact, the military (and other civilian stakeholders) are able to communicate with other people,

[3] We are referring here to the so-called escasa cultura de Defensa (Poor Defense's Culture), designation largely studied by several researchers (e.g. Sanz Roldán 2000; Laguna Sanquirico 2014).

largely thanks to the job performed by interpreters, as explained by Páez Pérez and Batista (2013).

This is a professional field in which not only three different Armies converge[4], but also a large variety of professional specialties[5], so the interpreter's work must be approached from a kaleidoscopic perspective. Numerous skills and interrelated capacities are needed to achieve an accurate and professional work; linguistic, extralinguistic, educational, strategic, and instrumental qualities are sometimes very difficult to practice due to the remarkable secrecy often surrounding the Army, its specific language, and its distinctive hierarchy and discipline.

3 "Military Interpreting": Concept and Development

To understand the complex employment situation of military translators and interpreters in Spain, it is important to provide a brief overview of the functioning and development of the language brokering processes in this country.

3.1 The "Military Interpreter" in Spain

The "military" translator and interpreter, as a professional enrolled in the Armed Forces who translates discourses into different languages, is very common in countries such as Russia, where translation and interpreting are classified as risky activities and therefore "it was decided to avoid civilian translators recruited by the Armed Forces, and instead use military staff who must follow the orders provided and go to any place they are

[4] The Spanish Armed Forces are comprised of the Land Spanish Army ("Ejército de Tierra"), the Navy ("Armada Española") and the Air Forces ("Ejército del Aire").

[5] Each army of the Spanish Armed Forces has different professional specialties: infantry, engineering, mechanics, administration, catering, navigational systems, aeronautical support, air traffic control, military police, firefighters, musicians are just a few examples of the diverse professional expertise developed by the Spanish soldiers enrolled.

commanded"[6,7] (Pakhar in Alarcón Navío 2011, 330). This position is also implemented by France where there is a specific area of expertise devoted to it, the so-called Interpreter-translator of foreign language information[8].

On the contrary, the "military interpreter" is a surprising and almost unknown title in Spain. First, because the military staff have only recently been appointed for interpreting tasks (Ruiz Rosendo and Barea Muñoz 2017), and second, because the functioning and organization of the "military interpreting" procedures are included in the so-called institutional translation (the professional field of interpretation for the Public Services of the National State Administration). This means that there is not an official group of military interpreters in the Ministry of Defence nor in the Army, as stated in the *Translation and Institutional Interpretation white paper*[9]. Although the importance of this group of specialized translators and interpreters is highlighted, the confusion and lack of regulation that surrounds it seems obvious from the outset.

Thus, interpreters working for the Ministry of Defence do not have a title identifying them as such, instead they belong to the category of "Higher Technicians in Management and Common Services"[10], a professional collective covering several occupations and insufficiently defined. Available information about this group is limited, and its classification is at least confusing: "worker who, under the terms established for professional group 3 in Article 17 of the Unique Agreement, develops the activities of the Functional Area of Management and Common Services"[11]

[6] "Se optó por no recurrir a traductores civiles contratados por las Fuerzas Armadas, sino precisamente a militares que deben cumplir las órdenes que les den e ir a cualquier lugar que les manden".

[7] All translations of original quotes referenced in the footnotes belong to the author unless otherwise indicated.

[8] Original title: Intercepteur-traducteur des informations en langues étrangères. For further information on this specific topic, consult the official website of the French Air Forces: https://www.defense.gouv.fr/air.

[9] *Libro Blanco de la traducción y la interpretación institucional.* Drawn up by the members of the Network of Interpreters and Translators in Public Administration (RITAP in Spanish), in collaboration with the Ministry of Foreign Affairs and the European Commission.

[10] Original Title: Técnicos Superiores de Gestión y Servicios Comunes.

[11] "Es el trabajador que, dentro de lo establecido para el grupo profesional 3 en el artículo 17 del Convenio Único, desarrolla las actividades propias del Área funcional de Gestión y Servicios Comunes".

(BOE—"Official State Bulletin" 273/2009: Anexo II). They should be fluent in legal, financial, technological, aeronautical, and military terminology, as well as in the different sub-languages implied in each of these areas. Moreover, many discourses which must be translated for the Ministry of Defence are "classified", so the responsibility and compulsory discretion of those in charge of translating them is capital. When the interpreter is a military worker, this is magnified, as we will see below.

3.2 "Military Interpreter" in International Missions

Overall, this lack of regulation surrounding all interpreters related to the Spanish Armed Forces is also evident outside our borders, since as Baigorri points out "the norms governing the interpreting trade in situations of conflict are precisely the absence of solid rules that define interpreters' roles" (2011, 20). In addition, although the research on "military interpreting" has increased over the last few years, most of those studies are focused on the civilian interpreter assisting the Army, not on enrolled soldiers performing interpreting tasks. For that reason, our first question should be: what do we mean when we talk about a "military" interpreter? Is he or she truly "military" or a civilian working or assisting the Army? According to Ruiz Rosendo and Barea Muñoz (2017, 185), "there is no general taxonomy or classification of interpreters who work in armed conflicts in general", which is undoubtedly conducive to the existing confusion.

In this sense, "military" as an adjective to refer to all interpreters working in the Armed Forces does not seem very accurate. Mostly, when we speak about "military interpreters", we are referring to the natives from the operational zone, national interpreters recruited for their language skills with no specific training, or to other guild professionals deployed. In most of the cases, they are civilians offering their services to the different Armies, but they are not enrolled in those forces.

On the other hand, who are we talking about when we say military "interpreters"? Can they really be classified as "interpreters"? As already mentioned, in the Spanish Army there is not an official and specific corps of interpreters or any discipline devoted to it; so, when soldiers have to perform as interpreters, they normally do not hold any training on that field. In addition, the "military interpreter", as a member of the Army, he must obey orders and is subjected to the military discipline and hierarchy, thus the levels of responsibility, commitment, ethics, and prudence are further enhanced. These mediators are involved in at least three different contexts: the culture of their own Nation, the one of the countries where they are deployed, and the military culture (Snellman 2016). This is a crucial aspect mainly in the military field, since the lack of the proper training and knowledge of some of these contexts could be the cause of conflicts, some of them extremely serious[12]. Therefore, deployed military staff who perform interpreting tasks are "first and foremost soldiers" (Ruiz Rosendo and Barea Muñoz 2017, 189) with language skills but specialized in another field not related to language brokering, so the term "interpreter" seems not quite concise either.

Under these circumstances, how should we classify all these interpreters, civilian or military, who have to serve as mediators? For now, and until an official regulation exists allowing the proper classification of the different categories, the title "military interpreter" covers all the abovementioned mediators. In our opinion, this lack of consensus is not a simple contribution to the current confusion, but it represents the baseline problem. Bearing in mind that communication is the engine of interpreting and language is the fuel that makes it work, linguistic and terminological accuracy should not be treated as a trivial matter.

4 Interpreting in External Operations

Over the last few years, Spain's military participation in foreign operations has increased to such an extent that "has become another instrument of the Spanish Government's foreign policy"[13] (Melero Alonso 2012, 7). This demonstrates how important this matter is, not only in

[12] For more information about this topic, we recommend reading the study carried out by Matthieu Guidère (2008), entitled *Irak in translation. L'art de perdre une guerre sans connaitre la langue de son adversaire* (Official translation: "*Iraq in Translation: The Art of Losing a War without Knowing the Language of your Opponent*").

[13] "Se ha convertido en un instrumento más de la política exterior del Gobierno español".

social, political, and military matters, but also in other aspects related to the development and increase of language brokering processes within the Armed Forces.

When we speak about international military actions there are different operations, such as humanitarian assistance, peacekeeping, and cooperative missions[14]. In this chapter, we will not describe their conceptual and operational framework but, based on our own experience, we can assert that linguistic and cultural knowledge, as well as translation and interpreting tasks, are particularly crucial in all of them. Indeed, mission success depends on joint action, which is found in "mutual trust and understanding between military and civilian personnel, which can only be developed through a continuous dialogue and exchange of views"[15] (Miri 2014, 2).

As mentioned earlier, the new global landscape demanded a new and adapted strategic plan already contemplated in this kind of operations[16] based on linguistic interaction and personal relationships. The troops deployed, especially the "interpreters" (military with language skills but specialized in another field), frequently serve as dialogue interlocutors as well as mediators. This dialogue is considered as one of the most effective instruments for ensuring international stability. It is not only manifested between Army members of the different States; it is also presented in the daily communication with the civilian population, with the different organizations, with political representatives of governments and even with possible insurgent groups. This is extremely relevant for interpreters, but especially for those who are deployed abroad, since there are many "actors" involved and therefore "the cultural component of the language is essential to understanding the different idiosyncrasies"[17] (Martínez de Baños and Guerin 2008, 71). Furthermore, this new perspective no

[14] For more information, refer to the following link: https://www.defensa.gob.es/misiones/en_exterior/.

[15] "En la confianza mutua y el entendimiento entre el personal militar y civil que sólo se puede desarrollar a través de un continuo diálogo e intercambio de pareceres".

[16] Included in the aforementioned *Brahimi Report* and endorsed in the Spanish Defence Diplomacy Plan: https://www.defensa.gob.es/Galerias/misiones/diplomaciaDefensadoc/DGL-110506-Plan-Diplomacia.pdf.

[17] "El componente cultural de la lengua es fundamental para entender las distintas idiosincrasias".

longer contemplates combat tasks and strategies as priorities; instead, they are complemented by other types of sociocultural skills such as dialogue, empathy, flexibility, shared management, or integration, among others.

4.1 Cultural Awareness

Nowadays, the international success of a mission depends mainly on cultural awareness: regional knowledge, personal contact, respect for traditions, religions and different lifestyles, capacity for empathy, common sense, and so on. In short, it is necessary to implement the so-called *Cross-Cultural Awareness*, defined as: "a practical tool which helps consider culture as a key element within the decision making process in order to make effective decisions and to prevent or minimize damages to the personnel and to the goals of the mission" (Durán Cénit and Méndez 2010, 8). This process was designed to be implemented by all the deployed personnel, but it seems reasonable to assume that in the case of a "military interpreter" its application becomes even more important.

On international interpreting tasks, the outbreak of conflictive elements is much significant due to the direct contact established with different cultures, especially when the deployment area has such a different culture from ours, as is the African's case. That's why "the potential for translation difficulties increases exponentially. It is impossible to express the multitude of cultural variations found across this region of Africa" (House 2014, 9). However, these "obstacles" are present not only in the relationships with the local community, but also between troops of other Armies and civil institutions present in the area. To detect and prevent them, it is essential to carry out an analysis of the elements taking part in a significant way during external operations.

Based on research by Durán Cénit and Méndez (2016), it will be useful to establish a classification of the cultural dimensions, specifying which are the most important features:

- Political dimension: legal and political issues, infrastructure, educational system, public services, existing conflicts, Armed Forces, and their preparation and procedures.
- Social dimension: family, marriage conceptions, gender differences, ethnicities, stereotypes, deep-rooted traditions, religion, literacy level, among others.
- Economic dimension: capital, resources, poverty level, health conditions, employment, business conditions, or government aids.
- Historical dimension: political systems, religion, Army, common traditions and habits, general evolution of the State, local celebrations and festivities, and so on.

As shown, several elements are connected, so they can respond to common strategies. In any case, and in the light of the results obtained in Durán and Ávalos' research (2016), the most recurrent conflicts are caused by misunderstandings and through elements associated with language, corruption, discourse, gender, and honor. Thus, it seems unquestionable that intercultural and linguistic knowledge and interpreting are breaking down those barriers which can complicate and even damage the international missions.

5 The "Military Interpreter" in Senegal

Bearing in mind that interpreting hugely depends on the context, we will explain our personal and professional experience in Senegal to demonstrate the great relevance of this discipline in the Armed Forces. In this sense, "interpreting always consist of an adaptation to local needs. If the military system is made up of a complex network of subsystems, we can expect that interpreters were required to adapt to that complexity" (Baigorri Jalón 2011, 21). Therefore, it is essential to explain, even briefly, the social environment of development in the area where this study is based.

5.1 General Sociolinguistic Context

The linguistic and cultural diversity of the French language is not a new topic; all the particularities generated by the imbrication of the French language with other cultures have been approached in multiple studies (e.g. Gadet and Ludwig 2015). In this case, Africans are generally polyglot, but the Senegalese's case is particularly interesting[18]. It is a multilingual country; apart from French, it has six more official languages: Diola, Mandinka, Pulaar, Sérère, Soninké, and Wolof, as well as other regional dialects. All of them cohabit and alternate depending on different factors, such as the family, local area, speakers, and so on.

French is predominantly used in some more "elevated" domains, such as institutional or diplomatic environments, while the other national languages, mainly Wolof, are used in more traditional and ordinary contexts. Most of the Senegalese population proclaim their right to use their own regional languages, but it does not mean that they reject French. However, we do not deny the existence of power relations between different languages, since when one of them is adopted as a tool of communication for more "prestigious" matters, evaluative connotations emerge. In any case, Senegal's French language is adapted to its reality, it preserves most of the traditions that characterize it and build its identity.

5.2 Development and Conventions of the Military Interpreting

As a professional military of the Air Force, specialized in "fire-fighting"[19], we have been deployed in Senegal for five months, serving within the Spanish contingent in the A/M[20] Operation. More specifically, we were assistants to the Liaison Office (OFEN)[21], attached to the Framework for

[18] For more information, consult: Correard N'Diaye 1998; Cissé 2005; Blumenthal and Pfänder 2012; among others.

[19] Original Title: "Contra-Incendios" (C.I.).

[20] Original Title: "Apoyo a Mali" (Support to Mali).

[21] Original Title: "Oficina de enlace" (OFEN).

Cooperative Security Activities (SEGCOOP)[22], and coordinated by the Operations Command (MOPS)[23]. In this operation, the Spanish military provide advice and instruction to Senegalese soldiers to strengthen their training and military skills so that they not only are prepared to defend themselves and confront existing threats, but also acquire the necessary knowledge to instruct their own troops and become independent.

Since 2015, about 1000 Spanish military instructors have been deployed to this country. A country which, due to its geographical situation, is extremely vulnerable to illegal immigration mafias, piracy, terrorist attacks, and drug and arms trafficking. These instructors are joined by the members of the Liaison Office (OFEN), composed by an Officer, a Sub-officer, and a Troop soldier. This office is coordinating the activities; however, such coordination involves more than the development of language brokering processes.

The OFEN is permanently installed in Dakar, specifically in the *Escale Aérienne Senghor*[24], commanded by the French Army. Although their operations are different, both Armed Forces share the same facilities, so there is a continuous contact. This means that OFEN's members are in constant interaction with Senegalese, French, and, of course, Spanish Armed Forces. They have also contact with the civilian population and other institutions. Likewise, although the OFEN is installed in Dakar, the activities are developed throughout the country (Thiès or Saint-Louis, among other cities); as a consequence, OFEN's members have to travel frequently to supervise and support the Spanish instructors. In these trips, it is common to be in contact with the different ethnic groups. In this kind of operations, multiple "actors" endowed with diverse languages, cultures, and fields, and on whose relationships the success of the mission depends are involved.

This is not the only particularity of this job; the tasks to be carried out are multiple and very diverse. We highlight the administrative, training, and logistical tasks, and those involving direct and inverse translations, such as collecting information, analyzing documents, proofreading,

[22] Original Title: "Seguridad Cooperativa" (SEGCOOP).

[23] In Spanish "Mando de Operaciones" (MOPS).

[24] Military Base name.

direct and inverse interpretation of daily conversations, conferences, and meetings…

Taking into account that we are specialized in "military firefighter", the aforementioned do not seem to be easy tasks, since our professional field has nothing to do with these duties (although we must point out that due to our background studies on Philology and Translations, we had some advantages. In any case, this is not an isolated scenario faced by a "military interpreter", the temporary deployment to a position with a different specialty is quite common and as Camarena points out, "in the interpreting field for conflict situations the previous training of the person is not considered"[25] (2016, 7). In our case, the criterion to be assigned to this mission was the language knowledge, as having an intermediate level of French is a mandatory requirement to be temporarily deployed to Senegal.

In these operations, the language and culture complementarity are clearly highlighted, since, from our experience, knowing the language is not enough. In this sense, it should be noted that we have seen the constant development of one of the clichés associated with idiomatic knowledge, which also represents another difficulty faced by the "military interpreter". Most of the people assume that a good level of the source language allows to carry out translations or interpretations without difficulty, which is not true because "contrary to the belief of many, language skills alone do not guarantee interpreter success" (House 2014, 3).

Non-verbal language is also important. The interpreter must be able to decode body gestures that may help, but also hinder the interpretation if they are not well known. This is crucial in international operations, because by controlling it, "the outsider begins to understand certain unspoken and spoken intentions present in West African military dialog" (House 2014, 12).

Taking Senegal as the sample of this paper, it is important to have in mind the cultural clash, which is increased in this case because western and eastern societies are very different. In our opinion, even though Senegal is a welcoming country, where population stands out for its kindness and closeness, we cannot ignore that its social reality, its beliefs

[25] "En el ámbito de la interpretación en situaciones de conflicto no se tiene en cuenta la formación anterior de la persona".

and most of its traditions are different to ours. The so-called *rapport à la langue*[26] in French is not manifested or perceived in the same way in the African countries as it is in other continents, since the multilingualism of these States is a lifestyle. Senegalese population was born and grown up surrounded by different languages, religions, and ethnicities, so the *rapport à la langue* arises from the necessity of communication and understanding. Facing such a scenario, it seems obvious that cultural awareness is vital.

5.3 Conventions and Possible Risk Factors

As already mentioned, culture shock is a decisive factor in the framework of international missions, as it involves multiple elements which greatly influence the work performed by "military interpreters". These factors might have a noticeable impact on their "positionality, accountability, neutrality and ethics" (Ruiz Rosendo and Barea Muñoz 2017, 183), as well as increase the complexity of their tasks. For this reason, it is necessary to identify these aspects and analyze how they can affect the mediation in Senegal.

5.3.1 Linguistic and Cultural Diversity

The aforementioned linguistic and cultural coexistence can be tolerant and respectful, but also conflictive. Although plurilingualism and multiculturalism are the most common tendencies, they are not exempt from frictions or controversies, since they can often cause communication difficulties. Even if Senegal is a French-speaking country, this does not mean that the 100% of the population is fluent in French. In fact, a high percentage of the Senegalese, especially in rural areas, is not able to express themselves properly in that language. In addition, regional languages are important for Senegalese people, since they constitute their personal identity. Although they normally have no problem speaking in French, they are grateful when foreign speakers try to use them. Based on our

[26] The relationship, bond, or attitude maintained in terms of language.

own experience, we can assert that, although some colonization's actions are still latent in Senegal, the common tendency is the respect towards a language that also belongs to them, even though it was imposed.

5.3.2 Religion

Religion is a lifestyle in Senegal and has a major presence in the daily life; more than a 90% of the population is Muslim, while the remaining 10% is divided between Catholics and Animists. One of the most admirable aspects of this country is the religious harmony, characterized by the good relationships between people with different beliefs. Muslim faith is endowed with some aspects difficult to understand for western people, so interpreters should carry out a good documentation work showing their interest in the source culture, as well as an open mind. During our stay, the contact with the Muslim population was constant, so we had to put into practice our basic knowledge about this religion and an open mind toward matters that deserved our respect. Following their religion rules like waiting for the man to say "hello" first, postponing calls or visits to respect their prayer times or showing respect toward certain traditional habits (such as having three wives) contributed to the good development of our work.

5.3.3 Gender Inequalities

From our own experience and relying on the research carried out by the *Escola de Cultura de Pau* where Chapter 4 analyses the Gender Equity Index (GEI)[27], Senegal continues to be a country endowed with serious inequalities between men and women. This fact is more noticeable in the rural regions, as shown during our recognition's tasks and support to the Spanish instructors. For example, 95% of the students attending training courses were men because, although the number of Senegalese military

[27] For more information about this matter, see the following link: https://escolapau.uab.cat/?option=com_content&view=article&id=532%3Aanuarios-alerta&catid=46&Itemid=66&lang=es.

women has increased, their presence is confined to less active specialties[28]. During our conversations these inequalities were noticeable, since stereotypes like women being vulnerable, more emotional, less objective, more afraid, or more dependent... often appeared. It should also be mentioned that although gender parity is still far from being reached in this African country, personally, as woman, we never felt rejected or underestimated.

5.3.4 Social Reality

Senegal's social reality is very different from ours in terms of cultural, economic, political, health, and educational matters. This fact can affect professional development. The high poverty rate, the scarce budget for public services, the income disparity, the deficient organization of the educational system, the high-fertility rate, the independence conflicts, the illegal "traditions" still clandestinely practiced (such as ablation) or, the unsanitary and unhygienic conditions are only some of the delicate social aspects which deployed soldiers face.

5.3.5 The Interpreter's Personality

Finally, even if the interpreters have to be as loyal to the reality as possible, the interpreting will include some characteristics of them, since they also have their own identity and way of working. In this case, additional factors will be involved due to the military condition affecting the development and the result of the interpretation. First, and even though one of the guidelines imposed is not to distort the original message, "military interpreters" "must also be good diplomats, because they are often forced to mitigate the words of the person they are interpreting"[29] (Pakhar 2011, 335). This is especially relevant in international operations where different cultures coexist and are more susceptible to feel offended by the other's words or ideas. Second, these "interpreters" are primarily military

[28] For more information about this matter, see the following link: https://umoya.org/revista-umoya/.

[29] "Debe ser también un buen diplomático, porque a menudo se ve obligado a mitigar las palabras de la persona a quien traduce".

members with a greater degree of responsibility and a number of tasks and factors they must pay attention to: transmit a good impression, be alert, offer security, win the trust of the different actors, identify and minimize possible conflicts, be disciplined, and so on.

6 Conclusion

Interpreting and the Armed Forces are linked even though this relationship does not possess a fully structured regulation or organization. Despite complementing each other, the functioning of the language brokering processes in the Armed Forces is endowed with a complex structural system. The name of the professionals, the category in which they are classified, and their functions and working conditions are so hermetic and extensive that are also confusing. Therefore, we believe that to achieve greater visibility, structure, and development in this field, a revision and modification of the procedures and regulations that currently govern the interpreting in the military field is required.

Regarding "military interpreting" in international contexts, our personal and professional experience has allowed us to stablish our ideas and statements. This has been key for justifying that interpreting is such a necessary activity as it is considered an instrument of prevention and mitigation when facing possible conflicts. Nevertheless, it can also become the opposite. As Guidère (2008, 148) affirms "it is a new art of war, essential for the implementation of traditional war strategies and tactics"[30]. This is crucial in the military field, since serious conflicts have already happened due to the lack of interpreters in the areas or to incorrect interpretations. The interpreter is not only essential during conflicts but is also indispensable to avoid them.

On the other hand, interpreters cannot be experts in all the existing subject areas, especially in hermetic fields not benefiting from a wide dissemination of information. In this case, even if their main duty is not to interpret or translate, the presence of military interpreters is relevant

[30] "Il s'agit d'un nouvel art de la guerre, indispensable à la mise en œuvre des stratégies et des tactiques de la guerre traditionnelle".

among other things because they know and understand the profession and are more familiar with the different topics and with the specific language converging in the Armed Forces. As mentioned earlier, military interpreters' work has been proved to be complex and with a high level of responsibility. In case of deployment, the interpreter is a reader, researcher, linguist, and sociologist while carrying out military duties and facing some risks either cultural (because of possible frictions or misunderstandings), linguistic (due to the obligation to properly handle both source and target languages), social (because he/she is always in contact with other people), or professional (because of the military status). Although our participation in this international mission was a positive and professional experience, we believe that the work of the "military interpreting" deserves at least better training and more proper regulation.

References

Alarcón Navío, Esperanza. 2011. Entrevista a Alexey Pakhar: traductor y Coronel del Ejército ruso. *Sendebar* 22: 329–337.

Baigorri Jalón, Jesús. 2003. Guerras, extremos, intérpretes. In *Actas del I Congreso Internacional de la Asociación Ibérica de Estudios de Traducción e Interpretación*, ed. Ricardo Muñoz Martín, 159–176. Granada: AIETI.

———. 2011. Wars, Languages and the Role(s) of Interpreters. *Les liaisons dangereuses: langues, traduction, interprétation*, Dec 2010, Beyrouth, Lebanon, 173—204.

Baker, Mona. 2010. Interpreters and Translators in the War Zone. *The Translator* 16 (2): 197–222.

Blumenthal, Peter, and Stefan Pfänder. 2012. Le français en Afrique. In *Actes du colloque Convergences, divergences et la question de la norme en Afrique*, ed. Peter Blumenthal and Stefan Pfänder. France: Instituto de lingüística francesa.

Boletín Oficial del Estado (BOE). 2009. Resolución de 3 de noviembre de 2009, por la que se registra y publica el III *Convenio colectivo único para el personal laboral de la Administración General del Estado.* No. 273, de 12 de noviembre de 2009. Dirección General de Trabajo.

Camarena Gimeno, Inmaculada. 2016. *Estudio preliminar sobre la interpretación militar en España*. Unpublished MA thesis. Valencia. Universidad Jaume I.

Cissé, Mamadou. 2005. Langues, état et société au Sénégal. *Revue électronique internationale de sciences du langage Sudlangues* 1: 99–133.

Correard N'Diaye, Genevieve. 1998. Le français du Sénégal et le classement des particularités lexicales. In *Le régionalisme lexical*, ed. Michel Francard and Danièle Latin. Louvain-la-Neuve: Duculot.

Durán Cénit, Marién, and Antonio Ávalos Méndez. 2016. Detecting Conflictive Cultural Factors in Complex Scenarios: Military and Local Actors in Interaction. *Revista UNISCI* 41: 9–27.

———. 2010. Guidelines for Commanders and Staffs: How to Engage with Local Societies During Military Operations. *USJFCOM J9 Joint Concept Development and Experimentation.* Mando de Adiestramiento y Doctrina (MADOC).

———. 2011. La integración de la interculturalidad: Los factores culturales conflictivos. *Experimento multinacional n°6: conciencia intercultural. Revista del Ejército de Tierra* 845: 38–43.

Gadet, Françoise, and Ralph Ludwig. 2015. *Le français au contact d'autres langues.* Paris: Ophrys.

Guidère, Matthew. 2008. *Irak in Translation. L'art de perdre une guerre sans connaitre la langue de son adversaire.* Paris: Éditions Jacob-Duvernet.

House, Julie A. 2014. *Conference Interpretation in the Military Environment of Francophone West Africa.* Framework document. Instituto Español de Estudios Estratégicos (IEEE). Ministerio de Defensa.

Laguna Sanquirico, Francisco. 2014. *Reflexiones sobre el problema de la cultura de defensa. Documento de opinion 132.* Instituto Español de Estudios Estratégicos (IEEE): Ministerio de Defensa.

Martínez de Baños, Antonio, and Rachel Anne Guerin. 2008. *Aprendizaje de idiomas en las FAS. Una aproximación al inglés.* España: Ministerio de Defensa.

Melero Alonso, Eduardo. 2012. *Las operaciones militares de España en el exterior.* Barcelona: Institut Català Internacional per la Pau.

Miri, Amir. 2014. *Un intérprete en Afganistán: más allá de la traducción lingüística. Documento de opinión. Número 149.* Instituto Español de Estudios Estratégicos (IEEE): Ministerio de Defensa.

Páez Pérez, Vilma, and Salvador Escalante Batista. 2013. Traducción y comunicación. *Revista del Instituto Tecnológico de Costa Rica* 11 (2): 21.

Pakhar Alexei. (2011). In Entrevista a Alexey Pakhar: traductor y coronel del Ejército ruso. *Sendebar* 22: 329–337.

Red de intérpretes y traductores de la Administración Pública (RITAP). 2011. *Libro Blanco de la traducción y la interpretación institucional.* Madrid: Ministerio de Asuntos Exteriores y de Cooperación (MAEC).

Ruiz Rosendo, Lucía, and Manuel Barea Muñoz. 2017. Towards a Typology of Interpreters in War-Related Scenarios in the Middle East. *Translation Spaces* 6 (2): 182–208.
Sanz Roldán, Félix. 2000. La diplomacia de defensa: una aproximación desde España. *Arbor* 165 (651): 519–527.
Snellman, Pekka. 2016. Constraints on and Dimensions of Military Interpreter Neutrality. *Linguistica Antverpiensia 15*: 260–281.

8

Narrative Representations of the Interpreter in Wartime

Lucía Ruiz Rosendo

1 Introduction

Language and culture mediation has historically been an inherent part of armed conflicts due to the fact that, on the one hand, armed forces have traditionally been made up of troops who come from different countries and speak different languages and, on the other, conflict has brought forces who come from different cultures and speak different languages face to face (Ruiz Rosendo and Persaud 2016). Interpreters are, however, seldom mentioned by historians of the past and "condemned by their prescribed invisibility and neutrality, their side of the story remains untold" (Todorova 2014, 221). This trend began to be reversed in the 2000s, particularly after the invasions of Afghanistan and Iraq and the intervention of international military coalitions in these countries. At this point, the research interest in the role of interpreters in conflict zones

L. Ruiz Rosendo (✉)
Faculty of Translation and Interpreting, University of Geneva, Geneva, Switzerland
e-mail: Lucia.Ruiz@unige.ch

M. Todorova, L. Ruiz Rosendo (eds.), *Interpreting Conflict*, Palgrave Studies in Languages at War, https://doi.org/10.1007/978-3-030-66909-6_8

among linguists began to grow at a steady pace, due to the increasing visibility of and need for interpreters in international theaters of war. In fact, several scholars have agreed on the increasing need to explore the different factors shaping the work of the interpreter in different conflict regions (e.g., Palmer 2007; Inghilleri 2009; Stahuljak 2009; Footitt and Kelly 2012; Juvinall 2013; Ruiz Rosendo and Persaud 2019).

The literature explores the positionality and role of interpreters in different settings, the dangers and challenges they face when performing their activities and the ethical dilemmas that stem from their work. Most interpreters recruited in conflict zones are locally recruited civilians, and the narratives depicting them may be framed in terms of belonging to a specific ethnic group potentially considered as the enemy, and therefore distrusted by different actors involved in the conflict (Baker 2010; Packer 2007). The literature also deals with the controversial topic of visa refusal to interpreters who have worked for the military in Iraq and Afghanistan and who try to escape from post-conflict threats (Juvinall 2013). In fact, the local interpreters' positionality usually turns them into a target for the insurgents. Unlike the Western armed forces, for whom the risk ends with the end of the mission, these local interpreters have to assume further risks once these forces have left. There have also been discussions in the media (Bernabé 2009, 2012; MacAskill 2018), AIIC (International Association of Conference Interpreters) and in other organizations such as Red-T on the post-war protection of local interpreters, and some documentaries have been filmed, collecting the testimonies of interpreters who worked alongside NATO forces and have been left behind by the troops that they had served (Anderson 2014), this issue becoming an important topic of debate in a number of countries. Belonging to one culture and serving another, local interpreters are often mistrusted by both their employers and the local community (Baker 2010). The foreign military may regard local interpreters with suspicion since they are viewed as a potential threat, while the local population may see their compatriot interpreters to be "sleeping with the enemy" (Moerman 2005).

What still remains to be examined in greater depth is how contemporary war novels refer to the role of interpreters working in conflict zones in terms of the aforementioned topics, that is, the role of language intermediaries, and the various problems that arise relating to different cultures clashing, issues of trust and mistrust, and (im)possibilities of post-war protection. There are some studies that deal with the representation of translators and interpreters in fiction (Kaindl and Spitzl 2014). These authors create a term, "transfiction", to describe the "introduction and (increased) use of translation-related phenomena in fiction" (Kaindl and Spitzl 2014, 4). However, even if there are some studies that examine war autobiographical accounts (e.g., Todorova 2014), there is a paucity of works that explore the interpreter's role in war novels that have been created through the memoirs of those actors who were involved in the conflict.

In this chapter, I will focus on two war novels to examine the need for and the portrayal of the interpreter. As Lines (2017) argues, the novel is the "written form with the greatest potential to encapsulate the complex interrelationships of lived experience" (151) and convey different perspectives and meanings. This chapter considers two different texts that negotiate the lived experiences of Spanish soldiers who served in Iraq, both written by Spanish authors, to analyze how they depict the figure of the interpreter: Lorenzo Silva and Luis Miguel Francisco's *Y al final, la Guerra* [And Finally, War[1]] (2014) and Colomer's *Aunque caminen por el valle de la muerte* [Even Though They Walk Through the Valley of Death] (2017). Both narratives are set in the Battle of Najaf, a theater of war representative of an armed confrontation between Western troops and the Iraqi insurgency, but adopt different perspectives on their material. They have been chosen because they are based on real-life data obtained through interviews with military personnel, in other words, on the soldiers' memories. As Todorova (2014, 222) argues, the main particularity of a memoir is that it focuses on a "finite span of time within the subject's life" and on his memories, feelings and experiences. The novels examined in this chapter are based on multiple memoirs that are then analyzed by the authors to construct the narrative. They provide a rather realistic picture about the events and the military personnel's reactions toward and perceptions of these events.

For the purposes of the chapter, the novels are considered to be cultural artifacts that can be explored in order to analyze the role of the

[1] Author's translation, as for all subsequent translations.

interpreter in wartime. In both, the interpreters are depicted as locally recruited civilians who speak the local language(s) and the language of the foreign troops (i.e., Spanish) and are familiar with the local culture(s) because they belong to these cultures. They are ordinary individuals embedded in the conflict whose experiences prior to becoming interpreters have shaped their understanding of the war. This embeddedness is considered by scholars to influence the interpreters' positionality and, consequently, their neutrality and ethics. As the analysis will show, the interpreters are represented as outsiders not only to the military personnel, who show a certain level of mistrust toward them, but also to the local citizens, who are against their new role as interpreters for the "invaders". This is partly due to the fact that they perform in "non-places" (Kaindl 2014, 3), that is, in places that are "beyond territory and society". Consequently, the interpreters' fate is depicted as bleak, especially due to their being considered traitors by the insurgents. The analysis also highlights how the ideology[2] and the positionality of the interpreter condition his behavior toward the military personnel and his reactions to war incidents, and how the creation of empathy between the military personnel and the interpreters is a consequence of the former's behavior and respect for the local cultures. By analyzing these two novels, we find that foreign cultures and languages and the need for interpreters effectively arise as an integral part of the conflict.

2 Background

The operations led by the USA in Iraq after 9/11 were counterinsurgency efforts to deal with the new wars of the twenty-first century, characterized by asymmetric and hybrid warfare where non-state or private actors engage in guerrilla warfare, with insurgents targeting of both soft civilian and hard official targets. One of the insurgent groups was the Mahdi Army, relatively unknown until the Battle of Najaf and formed by Shiite

[2] Ideology is defined as "as a set of more or less systematic ideas that identify a constituency, the challenges the group confronts, the objectives to pursue on behalf of that group, and a (perhaps vague) program of action" (Gutiérrez Sanín and Wood 2014, 214).

cleric Muqtada al-Sadr in June 2003 in response to the US invasion of Iraq with the aim of expelling the US coalition from the country and establishing an Iraqi Shiite government. The consideration of the war as an asymmetrical and hybrid conflict is expressed in both narratives through the description of the militiamen loyal to the Mahdi Army as dispossessed non-state actors with a preference for insurgency and terrorism and not easily identifiable.

In these counterinsurgency operations, as well as in any other type of military operation carried out in a foreign country, interpreters were necessary to facilitate communication between the Western forces and the indigenous forces and local populations. If we follow Rétaillé's (2012) approach of the three spaces of globalized war (the space of war, the space of order and the space of contract) and his combination of cultural identity, geopolitical power, economic wealth, and the presence of the world in what he calls "*mondialité*", we could argue that interpreting is present in the three spaces, given the interrelationship between language, cultural identity, and globalization, and the important role of language in geopolitics and economy. As Baigorri Jalón (2015) states, the interpreting of languages and cultures acts as yet another factor in geopolitics and, given the crucial nature of language knowledge in communication, individuals capable of interpreting and facilitating communication represent a valuable asset in the situations described by Rétaillé, from trade exchanges to violent conflict. In the context of violent conflict, language becomes another weapon of war. It is my opinion that languages are even more powerful as weapons of war when they are languages not known by the Western forces, as is the case with those languages that include local dialects, such as Arabic in the Middle East. I argue that interpreters, as the only connoisseurs of both languages and cultures, use their positionality to develop a certain latitude in order to achieve certain goals. However, this very positionality is influenced by other more powerful agents involved in the communicative situation, these being principally the military personnel, but also those who, without being involved in the communication exchanges, constitute an invisible presence that haunts the interpreters, as is the case with the insurgents. The interpreters, as members of the local populations, are judge and jury: they are insiders to the conflict, and as such their positionality is conditioned by the narratives surrounding the conflict in terms of the role of the Western forces, that of the insurgents, and the interaction between the two groups. Conversely, their positionality influences how they are considered by the different stakeholders: the military personnel consider them to be first and foremost insiders to the community in conflict, and the Iraqi citizens, among them the insurgents, tend to out-group the interpreters from the moment they start to work for the Western forces; the interpreter, even if, to begin with, is part of the community, ceases to be so from the moment that he aligns with the foreign troops, and is subsequently considered to be a traitor. The interpreter then becomes the "other" to the local populations and remains an outsider to the military personnel. This argumentation reveals the complex positionality of locally recruited interpreters as individuals with a visible identity who carry out an unregulated activity and to whom M. Baker's (2010) opposite concepts of "villain" or "victim" and "friend" or "foe", or the perception of the interpreter as a "*homo sacer*" (Agamben 1998; Beebee 2010) apply.

Y al final, la guerra and *Aunque caminen por el valle de la muerte* are two war novels written in Spanish that describe the events of the Battle of Najaf, an armed confrontation that brought the Western troops and the Iraqi forces face to face with the Mahdi Army. The non-fiction novel, written by journalist Lorenzo Silva and military officer Luis Miguel Francisco, is based on interviews carried out in 2005 with more than a hundred Spanish soldiers who served in Iraq from April 2003 to May 2004 in the context of the US-led Operation Iraqi Freedom. The events and facts are narrated through the lens of the lived experiences of those who were deployed to the "Al Andalus" base and are supported by the consultation of official documents. It describes the battle with a concurrent subtextual analysis of the incident as the explosion of a conflict generated by US forces that dismantled the country without knowing how to rebuild it and underestimating the power of guerrilla warfare, and as an episode that involved the Spanish armed forces without the soldiers knowing how or why. The narrative is a documentary[3]-like story of the

[3] "Documentary" is defined in cinema as a "construction—a re-enactment of another time or place for a different audience—a graphing of history, in and through the cinematic image and sound"

work carried out by the Spanish troops in Iraq that uncovers war in the midst of the alleged and deceptive peace.

The second novel was written by Álvaro Colomer and describes the events that unfolded in the holy city of Najaf on 4th April 2004, focusing on the intervention of the Spanish Brigade Plus Ultra II. The text is based on more than 200 interviews with military personnel and civilians from Spain, the USA, El Salvador, Iraq, Germany, Great Britain, the Czech Republic, and Denmark. The author reconstructs the events in the light of the interviews, taking into account the subjective appreciations of the different actors involved and turning the text into a novel based on real events and real individuals who are included in the dramatis personae. It is, therefore, a recreation of the Battle of Najaf written as a piece of fiction. The author offers a critical and uncompromising portrait of the decisions taken by the Spanish military and the Spanish government, and poses a series of uncomfortable implicit questions that revolve around the indifference of the Spanish brigade's high command when confronted with this episode, the position of the Spanish transition government and the reasons that led the country to hide one of the most important battles in Spain's recent history. Following the dichotomy between the documentary drama and the drama-documentary used by Rayner (2017), I argue that Colomer's novel is a documentary drama in which the author "uses an invented sequence of events and fictional protagonists to illustrate the salient features of real historical occurrences" (342), while Silva and Francisco's text is a drama-documentary that recreates events from a real occurrence. Despite their differences, both narratives pursue, through a recapitulation of the testimonies gathered, the re-enactment of an episode of war.

Against this background, the research question of this study is what it is we learn from these novels that would enhance our understanding of the role of language intermediaries, and the various problems that arise relating to different cultures clashing, issues of trust and mistrust, and (im)possibilities of post-war protection. Methodologically, using Baker's (2006) narrative theory, I treat these two works as a compendium of

(Rabinowitz 1993, 120). In a war novel, the definition would be similar but without the reference to cinematographic allusions.

ontological narratives in which I identify and explore the passages that describe the interpreter. "Narrative" in this context is understood as a story that we live by and that helps us to understand the world, in this case specifically the role of interpreters through how they are described by others. The two narratives' commitment to recreating an identifiable episode of war based on primary sources who mention the interpreters involved underpins their importance in the portrayal of interpreters in wartime. It is this aspect of the narratives that confirms the significant role of written representations in showing and affirming how interpreters are viewed in war situations by those who surround them, in particular by the military personnel.

3 Depicting the Interpreter

Although the central focus of both war narratives is the Battle of Najaf, they each adopt a markedly different perspective. Silva and Lorenzo's *Y al final, la guerra* offers a more comprehensive analysis of the events that were unfolding in Iraq at the time and which led up to the Battle of Najaf than Colomer's *Aunque caminen por el valle de la muerte*. While the latter almost exclusively focuses on how the battle was waged, Silva and Francisco's text adopts a broader approach in order to describe not only the battle but also the circumstances surrounding it, as well as the work carried out by the armed forces in Iraq with the local populations and indigenous forces in the context of counterinsurgency operations. Silva and Lorenzo's account also offers a more comprehensive depiction of the interpreter: while Colomer tends to mainly resort to the interpreter in order to illustrate the dangerous situation in which he worked and the dark and depressing future that he faced after the withdrawal of the Western forces, Silva and Lorenzo offer a dual description of his role as, on the one hand, a civilian whose involvement in the Spanish mission was undeniable and whose reliability was unquestionable, and, on the other hand, an individual who betrayed the trust placed in him by the troops.

Along these lines, the first role is represented in Silva and Francisco's narrative by Nasser, the personal interpreter of one of the *comandantes*[4] who is so highly trusted by the military official that he is given a gun. Importantly, this trust is related to the positionality of Nasser as a Spanish citizen of Syrian origin and thus not coming from the community in conflict. This interpreter is described as someone who worships the *comandante*, whom he considers to be a hero. The *comandante*, for his part, is depicted as someone who trusts Nasser completely, seeing him as part of the group and repeatedly telling him, "Nasser, here you are my shadow" (p. 104). In one of the passages, the *comandante* is wounded, and Nasser expresses his dismay and gets personally involved in saving him. The following sentence summarizes the close relationship that develops between the *comandante* and Nasser: "Nasser, suppressing his emotion, told him, 'Mi comandante, we are at home.' Gonzalo still had time to squeeze his interpreter's hand" (p. 107).

The second role is represented in Silva and Francisco's narrative by Flayed Al Mayali, the confidant of a Spanish intelligence agent, who works as an interpreter with the agreement of the Iraqi secret services, who control him as a kind of double agent, and who is thought to have betrayed the Spanish troops. He is accused of passing on information that was used to plan an ambush against the Spanish forces because he is one of the few people who knew the route that the CNI (Spanish National Intelligence Centre) agents were going to take and the time of departure. The lack of trust in local interpreters is palpable in Silva and Francisco's narrative in another scene in which the Spanish forces bring down a group of armed Iraqis, one of whom is an Iraqi who insists that he is an interpreter for the Spanish contingent. In this scene, the Spanish officials doubt the truthfulness of the alleged interpreter's arguments and decide to wait for orders from the operations center before deciding how to proceed. In line with this consideration of the interpreter, Colomer refers to the mistrust of the Spanish officers toward the Iraqi civilians and forces, implicitly explaining that the mistrust toward the latter is related to the attacks perpetrated by the Iraqi forces against the coalition forces, the so-called insider attacks. Mistrust also stems from the terrorist attacks

---

[4] OF 3 according to the NATO code and the equivalent of *major* in British English.

perpetrated in Western countries. In the following excerpt, which takes place just after the 2004 Madrid train bombings, Spanish troops are following the news, which refer to the Islamists as those responsible for the attacks:

> Nothing is known there, but much is suspected here. You only have to look at the translators' attitude, with their shifty eyes and their sealed lips, to realise that they pretty much know who carried out the attack. In fact, as more information appears the interpreters start to disappear, as if they sensed that it isn't a good idea for them to be around the Spanish officers at a time like this, and they're not wrong, because in the coming days, and also in the coming weeks, they'll hear comments like "Fucking Arabs!" that they probably won't like. (Colomer, p. 59)

This excerpt illustrates how mistrust is mainly derived from the interpreters' belonging to the enemy's ethnic group and how the foreign forces' perception of them is influenced by the public narratives surrounding the "other" as an undifferentiated source of threat, these narratives constraining every form of interaction (Baker 2010). The reference to "fucking Arabs" illustrates the widely used and pejorative narrative of Muslims as a single and homogenous group that represents an undifferentiated menace (Packer 2007).

This negative view is partly and closely linked to the cultural clash between Western forces and local cultures. The cultural clash that the Spanish military personnel experienced in Iraq is present in both texts, particularly in Silva and Francisco's narrative, where one of the Navy officers describes the Western forces as witnesses of a country that is distinct in terms of cultural usages and traditions, where it hurts to see the treatment of women by the male population but where there are conventions that, although not understood, must be respected. Indeed, cultural awareness is put forward in Silva and Lorenzo's narrative as essential, and, in this context, the Spanish armed forces are seen to respect the local customs and traditions more than some of the other armed forces. In one of the passages, the authors describe how coffee is served during a meeting, according to Iraqi tradition in one glass, from which the highest-ranking officer drinks first, followed by the other personnel.

The US lieutenant-colonel refuses to drink, and this is commented on negatively by the Iraqis. The respect for the local culture and the empathy shown by the Spanish military personnel is described by Colomer as being highly valued by the local interpreters as members of Iraqi society. In the following passage, a group of interpreters help a member of the US military personnel, John de Witt, to sit up after he had fallen to the floor in fright upon hearing the opening machine gun fire of the Battle of Najaf:

> as John de Witt is one of the few Americans who respects the locals and who moreover tends to apologise when his army kills a group of civilians, the translators helped him to sit up, they slapped him on the back and they told him, 'Do not worry, my friend, because we have asked Allah to also protect you.' (p. 149)

In another scene, one of the Spanish officers, who wants to get on the right side of the Iraqis, asks the interpreters to translate his interventions in written form into Arabic so that he could read them out to the Iraqis directly with the aim of winning them over. This scene illustrates that in operations in culturally different countries, respect for and immersion in the local cultures, together with a combination of material and emotional resources and empathy for the local populations, are crucial elements for attaining the established goals. It is worth mentioning that the interpreter is a member of the indigenous population, and as such is in a good position to guide the military personnel through the local cultures and indicate whether the latter's behavior is appropriate in the given circumstances.

Thus, interpreters are considered to be an important and rare resource; rare because Iraqis who speak Spanish are difficult to find and recruit: both narratives recreate the claustrophobic environment in which the Western troops found themselves in Iraq and the problems they faced, such as the lack of infrastructure and public services, the heat, the dust, the sand, and the impossibility of communicating with the local populations without an interpreter; problems that are considered to be inescapable issues exceeding the worst predictions. Due to the need for and the lack of interpreters, the recruitment of well-trained linguists is seldom possible, and the interpreters are mainly young male Iraqi citizens who just happen to be there and speak the stakeholders' languages, there being no allusions made to recruitment, background, or competencies. Despite the explicit reference in both narratives to the need for interpreters, it is worth noting that they are not mentioned as present in all of the linguistic interactions, and the reader just has to assume that they actually are there because if not, communication would not be possible. In the chapter in which the Brigade Plus Ultra II is introduced, Silva and Francisco refer to Spanish General Coll and his meeting with the representatives of local institutions, religious leaders, tribal leaders, and political party representatives with no reference to the interpreter, even though the passage in question implies that relevant topics are discussed, namely the needs of the local populations. In other passages, interpreters explicitly accompany the military personnel to encounters with the local authorities or the local populations, or on patrolling operations:

> The patrol then moved to the area surrounding the Governor's house, where, it appeared, the target was located. They went into a shop where they had noticed an Iraqi uniform on display, and they engaged in a dialogue [with the shopkeeper] through the interpreter and Sergeant Santiesteban, who had taken the initiative. (Silva and Francisco, p.122)

Yet in other scenes, interpreters are explicitly described as not being present, and these are scenes in which misunderstanding and confusion are generated due to the lack of communication. Colomer describes how Plus Ultra II Infantry Sergeant Martín del Pozo orders the deployment of the troops and asks the Iraqi security officers to stand behind him when the infrared detects four men wearing green approaching. However, the Iraqi officers run toward the strangers shouting, which triggers a dispute that the Spanish officer does not understand but whose intensity leads him to recognize the gravity of the situation. In another scene, an Iraqi sheikh approaches the foreign troops with his arms raised in peace at the gates of the Al-Andalus base, marking a truce in the battle. However, the encounter reaches a dead end because there are no interpreters present and the outcome is unsatisfactory:

> there are no translators at the gates of Al-Andalus and a few kilometres away stand the ruins of that very Tower of Babel where language was first divided. The only lingua franca is now that spoken by the weapons and the meeting comes to a standstill, with neither adversary understanding the other, the only communication being through glances and gestures. A Spanish soldier becomes tired of so much sign language and grabs the sheikh by his tunic, pulls him inside and leaves him there in the base. (Colomer, p. 104)

In the above passage, it is understood that the interpreter is a figure whose presence is essential if communication is to take place and whose absence renders the meeting useless, since the attendees cannot communicate with each other. That said, the interpreter's efficiency is not highlighted to any real extent in Colomer's text, and the few references to the interpreter's work reveal a certain mistrust of what he is saying and how he is communicating the message. In one illustrative passage, a Spanish officer is attempting to calm a group of Iraqi protesters down by saying that he knows nothing about the kidnapping of religious leader Mustafa Al-Yacoubi, and the interpreter intervenes:

> The interpreter translates the message with excessive caution, taking too much time for so few words, and for a few seconds, while those present listen to what is being translated, the splashing of the rain in a puddle can be heard. Then, once the concepts have finally made their way over to the other language, there is an eruption of indignation. (Colomer, p. 89)

Despite this mistrust also being present in Silva and Francisco's narrative, at the same time they also depict the interpreter as a key player who uses his agency to convince the Iraqis and resolve disputes:

> They were moments of tension that were eventually relieved by an interpreter, who communicated to the demonstrators that it was neither the manner nor the place for that kind of action. The local population blamed the hospital for the death of a patient. The incident was brought under control there and then and did not escalate any further. (p. 48)

As mentioned previously, in both narratives the interpreters are approached tangentially and are not the focus of the story, with the exception of the passages that describe the danger faced by the interpreters because they worked for the Western forces. In fact, the post-war protection of local interpreters has been a recurrent topic in the literature and in the news (see Anderson 2014; Fitchett 2012, 2019; Juvinall 2013), both of which reflect the dangerous situation that interpreters have been left in after the withdrawal of the Western forces. The Iraqi interpreters' positionality turned them into a target for the insurgents and were therefore exposed not only to the danger that accompanies warfare itself, but also to the danger that had to be faced once the coalition forces had withdrawn: the insurgents, along with the local forces that were loyal to them, considered the Western forces to be infidels to their culture and values, and those working with them were considered to be traitors. In one passage, Colomer describes a scene in which the interpreters express their fears regarding the potential victory of the Mahdi Army, because if the insurgents take the barracks and hoist the green flag, the interpreters will be stoned to death due to their being considered traitors who work for the enemy, something that cannot ever be forgiven. The American Deputy Ambassador calms their fears by saying that if the base has to be evacuated, they will not be abandoned, although he is not sure about this:

> The Deputy Ambassador has assured them that his government will never turn its back on them, that George W. Bush does not forget the friends of democracy, that their lives are not at risk under the figure of the bald eagle, but the truth is that he would not swear on the Bible in defence of his own words, he has heard about similar situations in other conflicts in which nobody lifted a finger to help the locals, in fact he would not even bet 50 cents on those who all but wear a sign around their necks saying 'Traitor'. (Colomer, p. 167)

Even though, in another chapter, interpreters are described by Colomer as having no future prospects and, therefore, no fear of being hit by a projectile during intense crossfire, in contrast to the American soldier who falls to the floor in fright upon hearing machine gun fire, in the following excerpt it can be seen that the interpreters are actually afraid of the potential victory of the Mahdi Army. In addition to the Iraqi interpreters' potentially bleak fate, the passage also refers to the empty promises made to them by the military personnel. Colomer illustrates this reality by providing a scene in which a sergeant is distressed after discovering that the promise to naturalize the interpreters hired by the Ministry of Defence will not be kept:

> Those Iraqis were hoping to leave with the Spanish troops the moment that they begin to withdraw, but the government has hung them out to dry without giving a second thought to how both the interpreters and their families are going to die at the hands of the followers of Muqtada al-Sadr. Tomorrow the rebels will raid their homes, drag them to a public square and cut their throats as punishment for helping the invader, and when some journalist asks the politicians in Madrid about the collaborators who were left behind in Diwaniya and Najaf, the politicians will shrug their shoulders as if to say that they were only a bunch of traitors to their country after all. (p. 226)

4 Conclusion

As this study has shown, rather than being invisible at war, interpreters are taken for granted, in that the existence of other languages and cultures in such scenarios is assumed by military personnel and are not given the same importance that linguists attach to them. When interpreters are described as a collateral component of intercultural and interlinguistic encounters and their liminality is made explicit, their positionality emerges as complex and unique vis-à-vis the parties in the conflict. Paradoxically, without being the focus of the story, interpreters are actually essential to the troops not only because of the fundamental role that they play in international theaters and the peculiarities of their wartime role, but also because they are a means of exploring issues such as cultural awareness and acceptance of the other in conflicts in the Middle East. The interpreter's role goes beyond translating the linguistic message to including cultural mediation, which is essential in military operations taking place in a country with a diametrically distinct culture.

The analysis shows that the question of the interpreter's identity is a central theme and that the interpreters appearing in the two novels exemplify the problematic issue of the lack of protection for interpreters who have served for Western armed forces in the Middle East. Also, along the lines of Kaindl and Spitzl's (2014, 9) reflection, the represented interpreters embody existential conflicts and contradictions: their invisibility and ubiquity, their power and subordination, their faithful and dubious nature, the fact that they can be oppressed and uncontrollable and that they can "enable or prevent communication". As the authors say, "they are changeable, oscillating beings that are hard to grasp because they are constantly in motion and have so many layers to them" (ibid.).

The narratives use, each in a different fashion, deliberate recreations of the role of the interpreter to authenticate their descriptions of military operations taking place in a culturally different country and to convey a sense of "local flavour". The similarity of their portrayals of the interpreter helps to establish and reinforce the idea that interpreters in war zones and scenarios are usually, but not always, locally-recruited interpreters who are paradoxically considered to be an ambivalent resource: on the one hand, they are indispensable for communication but, on the other, they belong to the community in conflict and therefore arouse the mistrust of the military. How the interpreter is viewed by the military forces therefore depends on his ethnicity: the more different his culture, the less he is trusted. It is generally assumed by military personnel that local interpreters have developed an ideology that may have modified certain emotions; a consequence of conditions that place extreme demands on civilians and lead to the promotion of particular ideas (Schubiger and Zelina 2017) about the conflict, its stakeholders and the operations. As Halperin (2014) suggests, these emotions lead to individual attitudes toward outgroup members and condition how experiences are perceived. In the context of insurgency in Iraq, it is worth noting the external intrusiveness of the insurgents' ideological prescripts, that is, the penetration of the insurgents' ideological content into social structures and the high institutionalization of the ideology. The interpreters, as civilians, are surrounded by this ideology in their everyday life, and this is one of several factors which make them unreliable for the Western forces. Interpreters are also unreliable for members of local communities, including the insurgents, and this leaves them in an uncertain and dangerous position after the withdrawal of the armed forces. In fact, the topic of post-war protection is referred to in both narratives on several occasions as one of the main topics brought up in the interviews. Ultimately, in spite of the cultural clash with and the mistrust towards indigenous populations and forces, empathy for the local populations, including the interpreters, through respect for the local culture, is considered in both narratives to be essential in modern counterinsurgency operations taking place in countries which are culturally extremely different.

References

Agamben, Giorgio. 1998. *Homo Sacer. Sovereign Power and Bare Life* (trans. Daniel Heller-Roazen). Stanford: Stanford University Press.

Anderson, Ben. 2014. *The Afghan Interpreters.* https://www.youtube.com/watch?v=k7k1XJcDpV4. Accessed 15 January 2018.

Baigorri Jalón, Jesús. 2015. Máximo Rodríguez, un intérprete español del siglo XVIII en Tahití. In *Traducción y representaciones del conflicto desde España y América*, ed. Icíar Alonso Araguás, Alba Páez Rodríguez, and Mario Samaniego Sastre, 107–123. Salamanca: Ediciones Universidad de Salamanca.

Baker, Mona. 2006. *Translation and Conflict: A Narrative Account.* London; New York: Routledge.

Baker, Mona. 2010. Interpreters and Translators in The War Zone. *The Translator* 16 (2): 197–222.

Beebee, Thomas O. 2010. Shoot the Transtraitor! *The Translator* 16 (2): 295–313.

Bernabé, Mónica. 2009. Un niño entre militares. *El mundo.* http://www.elmundo.es/elmundo/2009/04/22/blog01/1240396242.html. Accessed 20 April, 2018.

———. 2012. Por favor, que los españoles no se vayan. *El mundo.* http://www.elmundo.es/elmundo/2012/12/09/espana/1355028595.html. Accessed 20 April 2018.

Colomer, Álvaro. 2017. *Aunque caminen por el valle de la muerte.* Barcelona: Literatura Random House.

Fitchett, Linda. 2012. The AIIC Project to Help Interpreters in Conflict Areas. In *Languages and the Military. Alliances, Occupation and Peace Building*, ed. Hillary Footitt and Michael Kelly, 175–185. London: Palgrave Macmillan.

———. 2019. Interpreting in Peace and Conflict: Origins, Developing Practices, and Ethics. In *The Palgrave Handbook of Languages and Conflict*, ed. Michael Kelly, Hillary Footitt, and Myriam Salama-Carr, 183–204. London: Palgrave Macmillan.

Footitt, Hilary, and Michael Kelly, eds. 2012. *Languages at War*. Basingstoke: Palgrave Macmillan.

Gutiérrez Sanín, Francisco, and Elisabeth J. Wood. 2014. Ideology in Civil War: Instrumental Adoption and Beyond. *Journal of Peace Research* 51 (2): 213–226.

Halperin, Eran. 2014. Emotion, Emotion Regulation, and Conflict Resolution. *Emotion Review* 6 (1): 68–76.

Inghilleri, Moira. 2009. Translators in War Zones: Ethics under Fire in Iraq. In *Globalisation, Political Violence and Translation*, ed. Esperanza Bielsa and Christopher W. Hughes, 207–221. London: Palgrave Macmillan.

Juvinall, Ben. 2013. Heaven or Hell? The Plight of Former Wartime Interpreters of the Iraq and Afghanistan Conflicts Living in the U.S. *Michigan State Journal of International Law* 21: 205–227.

Kaindl, Klaus. 2014. Going Fictional! Translators and Interpreters in Literature and Film. In *Transfiction. Research into the Realities of Translation Fiction*, ed. Klaus Kaindl and Karlheinz Spitzl, 1–26. Amsterdam; Philadelphia: John Benjamins.

Kaindl, Klaus, and Karlheinz Spitzl, eds. 2014. *Transfiction. Research into the Realities of Translation Fiction*. Amsterdam/Philadelphia: John Benjamins.

Lines, Lisa. 2017. Representations of the Spanish Civil War in Twenty-First Century Anglophone Novels (2000–14). *Journal of War & Culture Studies* 10 (2): 150–164.

MacAskill, Ewen. 2018. Afghan Interpreters Working for UK Army 'Failed' by Government. *The Guardian*. https://www.theguardian.com/politics/2018/may/26/afghan-interpreters-uk-army-failed-british-government-commons-report. Accessed 12 June 2018.

Moerman, Ellen R. 2005. Interpreters under Fire. *Translation Ireland* 16 (1): 12-15.

Packer, George. 2007. Betrayed: The Iraqis who Trusted America the Most. *The New Yorker*. http://www.newyorker.com/magazine/2007/03/26/betrayed-2. Accessed 15 April 2018.

Palmer, Jerry. 2007. Interpreting and Translation for Western Media in Iraq. In *Translating and Interpreting Conflict*, ed. Myriam Salama-Carr, 13–28. Amsterdam: Rodopi.

Rabinowitz, Paula. 1993. Wreckage upon Wreckage: History, Documentary and the Ruins of Memory. *History and Theory* 32 (2): 119–137.

Rayner, Jonathan. 2017. Naval Narratives of Re-enactment: *In Which We serve* and *Sea of Fire*. *Journal of War & Culture Studies* 10 (4): 340–355.

Rétaillé, Denis. 2012. *Les lieux de la mondialisation*. France: Editions Le Cavalier Bleu.

Ruiz Rosendo, Lucía, and Clementina Persaud. 2016. Interpreters and Interpreting in Conflict Zones and Scenarios: A Historical Perspective. *Linguistica Antverpiensia, Special Volume, New Series, Themes in Translation Studies* 15: 1–35.

———. 2019. On the Front Line: Mediating Across Languages and Cultures in Peacekeeping Operations. *Armed Forces & Society* 45 (3): 472–490.

Schubiger, Livia I., and Matthew Zelina. 2017. Ideology in Armed Groups. *Political Science & Politics* 50 (4): 948–952.

Silva, Lorenzo, and Luis Miguel Francisco. 2014. *Y al final, la guerra*. Barcelona: Planeta.

Stahuljak, Zrinka. 2009. War, Translation, Transnationalism: Interpreters in and of the War (Croatia, 1991–1992). *Translation Studies* III: 345–374.

Todorova, Marija. 2014. Interpreting Conflict. Memories of an Interpreter. In *Transfiction. Research into the Realities of Translation Fiction*, ed. Klaus Kaindl and Karlheinz Spitzl, 221–232. Amsterdam; Philadelphia: John Benjamins.

[illegible] "Interpreting and Translation [illegible] Western [illegible] in [illegible]." [illegible]

[illegible] Words [illegible] War [illegible] History [illegible]

[illegible]

[illegible]

9

After the Towers Fell: The Fate of Two Arabic Linguists

Maya Hess

1 Introduction

After the catastrophic attacks of 9/11, the United States government embarked on a search for the culprit armed with a massive toolbox containing expanded executive powers, unlimited funds and anger righteously minted from the knowledge that America had been wronged. But it all went terribly awry: The nation marched off to a wrong war (Peña 2003), men were tossed into a legal no-man's land on Cuban soil and detained indefinitely without charges (Weaver 2006), and innocent linguists were prosecuted and branded terrorists and spies in U.S. military and federal courts (U.S. Air Force 2003; *U.S. v. Sattar* et al. 2005).

The accomplices in the search were many and everywhere. They cherry-picked intelligence (Stein and Dickinson 2006) while operatives in the know turned a blind eye. They guarded prisoners while kicking and soiling their holy books (Watson 2005). They wandered the halls of the Justice Department fabricating indictments and drafting euphemistically

M. Hess (✉)
Red T, New York, NY, USA
e-mail: mhess@red-t.org

M. Todorova, L. Ruiz Rosendo (eds.), *Interpreting Conflict*, Palgrave Studies in Languages at War, https://doi.org/10.1007/978-3-030-66909-6_9

worded torture guidelines devoid of morality (Cole 2009). They used their Fourth Estate platform to propagate false pro-war information (Taibbi 2015). And they leaned forward in jury boxes unjustly pointing fingers of guilt (*U.S. v. Sattar* et al. 2005). Surely all were not evil; some must have been well-meaning men and women intent on keeping their home and hearth safe. But how could they have gone so wrong in their quest to hold someone accountable?

To understand some of the psychological processes that lay behind their choices, this chapter examines the narrative of distrust fomented and exploited by the Bush administration in its war on terror. Specifically, it looks at the role distrust played in the prosecutions of two Arabic linguists who provided translation and interpretation services at the Guantánamo Bay detention camp and in a U.S. federal prison, respectively. Employing archival evidence and ethnography, Part One provides case summaries and positions the linguists within the overall landscape of distrust. For the Gitmo translator, the material is drawn from open sources and court documents, while the prison interpreter data is based on trial records and participant observation. Part Two analyzes the social and psychological dimensions of this distrust, applying theoretical concepts found in social (in)justice literature to the two cases, and the Conclusion offers thoughts on the redefined scope of justice (Opotow 1995) within which linguists in these settings are forced to operate.

2 Part One: The Fate of Two Linguists

The rubble of the World Trade Center has proved to be a fertile breeding ground for various manifestations of distrust. Pre-9/11, an Arabic linguist's job included interpreting at attorney-client meetings with alleged and convicted terrorists and translating inmate mail; post-9/11, those activities were construed in some instances as spying and providing material support to terrorism, as will be shown below.

Two prosecutions in particular stand out: the court-martial of Ahmad Al Halabi, an Air Force linguist at the Guantánamo Bay detention camp who found himself accused of being part of a major spy ring (U.S. Air Force 2003), and *U.S. v. Ahmed Abdel Sattar* et al. (2005), the conspiracy trial of Mohamed Yousry, a prison translator/interpreter who was convicted of aiding and abetting a foreign terrorist organization. The Al Halabi ordeal illustrates how the government tapped into the general climate of distrust in which Muslim linguists were operating, while the Yousry verdict redefined the role of interpreters in the United States in a way that has taken this distrust to perilous new heights.

(1) **Ahmad I. Al Halabi**: In November 2002, Senior Airman Al Halabi was working as a supply clerk at Travis Air Force Base in California when he was called upon to serve as a translator/interpreter at the Guantánamo detention camp, a military prison located within the U.S. naval base in Guantánamo Bay, Cuba. A naturalized U.S. citizen of Syrian descent, his primary assignment was to translate detainee mail into English, while other tasks ranged from accompanying prison guards to cell blocks and facilitating their conversations with detainees to handing out library books (Parker 2004a). In July 2003, when he was set to leave for Syria for his wedding, Al Halabi was arrested and charged with 30 offenses, the most serious of which carried the death penalty. Among the accusations leveled at him were aiding the enemy, espionage and attempted espionage, false official statements, and failure to obey an order or regulation (U.S. Air Force 2003). In the course of a year, most of which he spent in solitary confinement in a naval brig, the case effectively collapsed, and in September 2004, he pled guilty to four counts of violating the Uniform Code of Military Justice (UCMJ). These counts charged him with disobeying orders by taking unauthorized photographs of camp facilities and moving classified material, giving a false statement to investigators about taking the photographs, and retaining classified documents (U.S. Air Force 2004). It should be noted that with respect to the picture-taking charge, the military conceded that many soldiers were caught doing the same, but Al Halabi—who snapped the photos of the guard towers as souvenirs and told the judge that he made the false statement because he was scared—was the only one targeted for an espionage investigation (Leung 2004). Incidentally, the news media were allowed to shoot at the camp, and pictures of the guard towers were circulating online (ibid.). In terms of moving classified material, this involved Al Halabi taking a copy of his orders to his housing unit without placing it in the proper container, while the misconduct charge of retaining

classified documents stemmed from the fact that he had kept unauthorized documents as a memento (he described himself as a packrat, and only one document turned out to be classified) (Parker 2004b). Of interest and to contextualize, linguists had not received any training whatsoever in how to handle classified information (Gaudiano 2004). At the conclusion of the trial, the court sentenced Al Halabi to the 295 days already served and ordered that he receive a reduction in rank and a bad-conduct discharge (U.S. Air Force 2004).

To convey the absurd nature of the dropped charges, two examples are provided:

> Charge III, UCMJ Article 2: Did, at Jacksonville Naval Air Station, Florida, on or about 23 July 2003, with intent or reason to believe it would be used to the injury of the United States or to the advantage of Syria, a foreign nation, attempt to deliver over 180 electronic versions of written notes from detainees held at Camp Delta, Guantánamo Bay, Cuba, writings relating to national defense, which directly concerned intelligence gathering and planning for the United States' war against terrorists, to a citizen of a foreign government by emailing such notes via an unsecured internet. (U.S. Air Force 2003)

These detainee notes were indeed on Al Halabi's laptop for the simple reason that the prison was experiencing a shortage of computers, and translators had been asked by their command to use their personal computers until additional devices arrived. On the basis of this request, Al Halabi worked on his own computer for three months (Leung 2004). As regards the content of the notes, Donald G. Rehkopf and James E. Key, two of Al Halabi's lawyers, brought to light that these notes neither related to national defense nor were they secret as charged but rather consisted of, say, correspondence between a mother and her son (ibid.). Compounding this governmental misrepresentation, it turned out that Al Halabi never emailed anything as alleged. In fact, Key explained that although the military's initial computer expert concluded that emails had been sent, another expert had informed the prosecution shortly thereafter that this was not the case. However, the latter withheld this exculpatory information for several months, failing to communicate it to the Court or the defense (ibid.). Considering that sending sensitive information supported the death sentence and Al Halabi languished in solitary confinement, it was surprising that the Court did not consider this prosecutorial misconduct. Charge I, UCMJ Article 92, Specification 10: "[...] conducting unauthorized communications with detainees by furnishing and delivering unauthorized food, to wit: baklava pastries" (U.S. Air Force 2003) related to Al Halabi's alleged distribution of pastries. However, the evidence revealed that the baked goods arrived at the base while he was on a mission out of the country and were eaten by fellow linguists prior to his return (Torriero 2004).

The irony is that, in fact, some of the charges should have been brought against the government. In his pre-trial motions, Rehkopf detailed a range of governmental misconduct, including improper handling of evidence by failing to use gloves, withholding exculpatory evidence in that the authorities were aware of translation errors made by government linguists in text that formed the basis of some of the espionage charges, and attempting to cover up sloppy investigatory and linguistic handiwork (Military 2004). As a result, one of the prosecutors, Captain Dennis Kay, had an ethics complaint filed against him and resigned from the military (Martin 2004).

This flawed Article 32 pre-trial investigation may help explain why the convening authority ordered the proceedings closed to the public for reasons of national security even though, to the extent possible, such hearings are open to spectators. Al Halabi's lawyers promptly challenged this order by filing a petition with the Air Force Court of Military Appeals for extraordinary relief in the form of a writ of mandamus to remedy the abuse of discretion, in this case excessive secrecy, by the investigating officer (*In re Al Halabi* 2003, September 15). They requested open proceedings except when classified material was to be presented and petitioned for a stay until the Court issued a decision on the matter. The Court ruled the national security argument by the prosecution insufficient and quashed the blanket order (*In re Al Halabi* 2003, September 16). This ruling was a ray of transparency, especially since under the order the arrest of Al Halabi had been kept a secret. Now, representatives of the national press were given access to the proceedings, although many meetings among the Court, prosecution and defense counsel were held behind closed doors.

Despite extant restrictions, the media was instrumental in exposing the investigation. They not only reported on the proceedings but also adduced evidence from various sources documenting the atmosphere in which Muslim linguists at Guantánamo were required to work. By all accounts, it was an atmosphere rife with Islamophobia[1] coupled with profession-specific distrust, that is, the Translator-Traitor Mentality (TTM),[2] which forced these individuals to navigate between two hostile camps.

During his 90-minute court presentation, Al Halabi testified that some non-Muslim soldiers considered Muslim translators sympathetic to the Al-Qaeda and Taliban operatives in the camp and called them "detainee-lovers," with one sergeant even going so far as to suggest that Al Halabi's name should be "Airman Al Qaeda" (Bailey 2004). In media interviews, he recounted similar name-calling and related that the inmates saw him and his colleagues as "traitors" because they wore American uniforms and spoke English (Leung 2004) and that they threw urine and feces at them (Parker 2004a), while non-Muslim guards hurled choice epithets (Golden 2004) and were suspicious because they spoke the same language as the inmates (Gaudiano 2004). He indicated that guards viewed many of his actions as sinister, for example, when he pointed out what he considered poor treatment of detainees (Leung 2004). Overall, Al Halabi painted a picture of a camp drenched in Islamophobia where prisoners and Muslim soldiers alike were targets. Kim London, another one of his lawyers, concisely summed it up: "The root cause of all this stemmed from his different religion, his funny name, because he was from a different homeland" (Martin 2004).

[1] The U.K. think tank on race equality, The Runnymede Trust (2017), defines Islamophobia as "unfounded hostility towards Islam" or "anti-Muslim racism" (1) that may take the form of discrimination, exclusion, prejudice, or violence against Muslims, while Gottschalk and Greenberg (2008) consider Islamophobia an "anxiety of Islam" and more expansively identify it as "a social anxiety toward Islam and Muslim cultures that is largely unexamined by, yet deeply ingrained in, Americans (5)."

[2] For a discussion of the concept, see "Translator-Traitor: A Critical Ethnography of a U.S. Terrorism Trial" (Hess 2014, 148–149).

This atmosphere was confirmed by officials, who stated that the case fed on "antipathy between Muslim and non-Muslim troops at Guantánamo, rivalries between Christian and Muslim translators," and an assortment of "petty personal conflicts" (Golden 2004). In fact, testimony during the court martial revealed that the command had ordered a "climate assessment" due to the simmering religious tensions, but the results were excluded. Other evidence plainly attesting to Islamophobia that the defense sought to enter, such as an anti-Muslim image that had been disseminated by email at the camp, was also not admitted (Gaudiano 2004).

What is equally noteworthy is that Al Halabi's treatment vastly differed from that of Col. Jack Farr, a non-Muslim Army intelligence officer and chief of interrogations at Gitmo, who faced similar charges of mishandling intelligence and lying about it. His case, however, was settled administratively and resulted in no prison time (Torriero 2004); moreover, it was largely kept out of the public eye and Farr was allowed to work during the investigation (Army Intelligence Officer 2003). This disparity came to the attention of Muslim groups, which accused the Pentagon of discrimination that the latter, as expected, denied (Torriero 2004).

What was also significant was that the Department of Justice (DOJ) frequently got involved despite the fact that it was a military matter. Due to this interference or "review," the trial experienced several delays (Marshall 2004); as Rehkopf succinctly pointed out, "It is the political season, and there is no legal basis" (ibid.). Thus, it would seem that the DOJ was overly eager to ensure that Bush's post-9/11 script was adhered to, notwithstanding Al Halabi's right to a speedy trial.

So while Al Halabi was subjected to a judicial rollercoaster that went from his potentially facing the death penalty to having the vast majority of charges dissolve into thin air, Yousry was less fortunate and was convicted to serve 20 months in federal prison.

(2) **Mohamed Yousry**: In 2005, a Manhattan jury found Yousry and his two codefendants, Lynne Stewart, a defense lawyer, and Ahmed Abdel Sattar, a paralegal, guilty of all charges (*U.S. v. Sattar* et al. 2005). Yousry,

who served as a translator and interpreter for Omar Abdel Rahman's[3] defense team, had been charged with three counts. The first count accused him and his co-defendants of conspiring to defraud the United States by hindering the Bureau of Prisons and the DOJ in the administration and enforcement of the Special Administrative Measures (SAM)[4] that had been imposed on inmate Rahman (Comey 2003).[5] The second count charged Stewart and Yousry with conspiring to provide and conceal material support to terrorist activity, and the third count pertained to providing and concealing material support to terrorist activity by enabling Rahman to communicate with his followers (ibid.).

Thus, for the first time in U.S. history, a translator/interpreter was held responsible for the legal strategy of an attorney as well as for the actual content of the conversations he translated. Stewart, who considered Rahman to be a key figure on the world stage (Ties to Terror 2002), had decided on a particular legal strategy that included keeping his case as high profile as possible. To that end, she called a Reuters correspondent in Egypt and issued a press release that conveyed her client's views on a specific political issue. And it was this telephone call (which was in English with no interpreter present) that violated the SAM and gave rise to the indictment.

Yousry, in his role as linguist, encountered distrust from all sides—from Rahman himself, from the government, from the defense, and, as evidenced by the verdict, from the jury. Rahman, for example, didn't trust him because he did not adhere to Islam's core beliefs and practices and, as a result, no longer wanted Yousry to work on his case (M. Yousry, personal communication, n.d.).

---

[3] Rahman, also known as the blind sheikh, was considered to be the spiritual leader of the Islamic Group, or *Gama'ah al-Islamiyya*, an extremist Egyptian social movement designated a foreign terrorist organization by the U.S. government (U.S. Department of State 2001). He was serving a life sentence for his role in the 1993 plot to bomb New York City landmarks and died in prison in 2017.

[4] The Special Administrative Measures are rules promulgated by the Department of Justice to prevent prisoners loyal to a power other than the United States from communicating with their associates either through phone calls or contact visits and from engaging in criminal activities on behalf of that power (U.S. Department of Justice 1997).

[5] To perpetrate this fraud, the government claimed that Yousry and Stewart had enabled communication between Rahman and persons/entities with whom the latter had been barred from communicating.

Throughout the nine-month trial, Michael Tigar, the lawyer for Yousry's co-defendant Stewart, stirred distrust of Yousry by employing various TTM tactics. One of these was to designate the entire Arabic language as TTM territory by continually invoking the "I don't speak Arabic" argument, which carried the implication that the crimes laid out in the indictment took place in Arabic. Specifically, since Stewart "doesn't speak the language" (*U.S. v. Sattar* et al., 2184),[6] she could not have participated in the sinister "things that happen in Arabic" (2186). In fact, Tigar emphasized the point that Stewart neither spoke nor read Arabic so often that it essentially became a refrain when he questioned her on the stand (7515, 7578, 7696).

The government's distrust came in many shapes and forms and went so far as to criminalize the very job description of interpreter. In his opening statement, the prosecutor declared: "Mr. Yousry was Abdel Rahman's translator. You will learn that Abdel Rahman speaks primarily Arabic. He is also blind. As a result of those two facts, and because of the prison restrictions, Yousry was one of the only people in the world who could communicate directly with Abdel Rahman" (2125). Aside from the fact that Yousry was not Rahman's translator but the translator/interpreter for Rahman's attorneys, an inaccuracy designed to group Yousry with Rahman, the message to the jury was that if Yousry had not provided the language link, Rahman would not have been able to communicate his radical views to the outside world and none of the alleged criminal activities would have taken place. The government thus accorded Yousry strategic importance by implying that his role constituted the linchpin in the conspiracy. To emphasize his position, the prosecutor reversed the attorney-interpreter hierarchy by stating that, for example, "Yousry was accompanied by a third Abdel Rahman attorney" (2139); as the evidence showed, however, Yousry played a subordinate role to all of Rahman's attorneys (9077). Through such inaccuracies, the government reframed Yousry's work as an interpreter at attorney-client meetings as the actions of an independent terrorist agent. Put differently, they construed interpreting as smuggling messages. This was reflected in the cloak-and-dagger language that permeated the trial—the content of attorney-inmate

[6] This refers to the trial transcript page number.

conversations was referred to as "messages" (8261; passim) or "terroristic messages" (11110); Yousry's performing his duties was seen as "smuggling messages" (2155; passim), "pass[ing] messages" (2141; passim) and functioning as a "message pipeline" (2136); or the government claimed that the defendants "shuttled secret messages" (2135).

Thus, the prosecution masterfully strung together pieces of information that formed a powerful TTM chain of distrust. Nothing was beyond (over)reach, anything and everything was distorted to fit the narrative: Yousry's mother tongue became an unfortunate handicap evoking 9/11 and interpreting turned into smuggling messages. All combined, it formed a perfect TTM storm reinforced by Islamophobia, in that the prosecution cynically exploited the West's generalized distrust of all things Islam and Muslim (Panagopoulos 2006, 608).

In line with this strategy, the prosecution constantly emphasized the link between Islam and violence by inundating the jury with the extremist speech of others, much of it drawn from Rahman's conspiracy trial (*United States v. Rahman* 1993). Dissertation research seized from Yousry's apartment also provided Islamophobic fodder. For instance, the prosecutor took the jury on a long terrorist journey through the Middle East, covering the history of the Islamic Group and providing a veritable who's who of terrorists that included Ayman Al-Zawahiri and Osama bin Laden (6839–6862). Strategically downplaying that they were reading an interview from *Political Islam*, a book assigned to college-level students across America, the prosecutor's dramatic performance suggested that Yousry not only possessed virulent terrorist polemic, but that this polemic had fueled his conspiratorial mind.

While a great deal of evidence was introduced that portrayed Islam and the Muslim culture in a negative light, material contextualizing Islam beyond its association with terrorism was not admitted (8448). As a result, the prosecution excelled at shrouding Yousry in its simplistic Islam-equals-violence theme. The defense, by contrast, pursued a strategy that amounted to a subtle form of Islamophobia. At every turn, Yousry's lawyers distanced their client from the religion of Islam out of the well-intended concern that some jury members might harbor Islamophobic sentiments. David Ruhnke set the tone at the outset when he told the jury in his opening statement: "Mr. Yousry, as the evidence will show [...]

is not a particularly religious person. He is not a practicing Muslim at all. Indeed, as he will tell you when he testifies, he has never even been in a mosque, not once, not in his entire life" (2207).

Ruhnke thus presented not being a practicing Muslim and never visiting a mosque as worthy goals. Of course, disavowing any connection to Islam/being Muslim implies that there is something wrong with it. In fact, his assessment that Yousry is "just an overall nice guy who is not, as we say, a radical Muslim, any kind of Muslim at all" (2208) suggested that being a nice guy and being Muslim are somehow mutually exclusive. In their attempt to negate Yousry's Muslim background, the defense even asked a witness who happened to be a former U.S. Attorney General and who was part of Rahman's legal team if he ever saw Yousry pray ("I don't remember Yousry ever praying, no" (8749).) and if Yousry drank ("In the evening I would have a glass of wine and Mohammed [sic] would have a glass of wine" (8749).).

Thus, misled by the government, which reinforced the notion that Islam is synonymous with terror by playing Rahman's fire-and-brimstone sermons for days on end and waving dissertation research as if it were a jihadi manifesto, and confused by a defense team that stripped Yousry of all Muslimhood, the jurors lost the ability to distinguish. As a result, they chose to suspend reason and align themselves with the prosecutorial storyline. The analysis that follows is an attempt to isolate some of the socio-psychological aspects of the extreme distrust that lay at the root of both the Yousry and Al Halabi cases and allowed for the leap to brand these linguists terrorist agent and spy, respectively.

3 Part Two: Distrust

Lewicki et al. (1998) define distrust as "confident negative expectations regarding another's conduct," which refers to "fear of, a propensity to attribute sinister intentions to, and a desire to buffer oneself from the effects of another's conduct" (439). Distrust of linguists working in Middle Eastern languages runs the gamut. It may manifest simply as apprehension based on unfamiliarity with the foreign sounds of another speech community and its associated culture or as something much more extreme, as evidenced in the two cases at hand.

Distrust, in part, stems from the "difficulty of imagining others" and appreciating their "full weight and solidity" (Scarry 2000, 40). This difficulty increases exponentially when it pertains to individuals who (1) are of a different ethnic origin, (2) practice another religion, (3) speak another language, (4) engage in a profession that historically has been viewed with suspicion, and, last but not least, (5) hail from the part of the world that gave birth to the 9/11-terrorists. And the greater the difficulty, the easier it becomes to inflict harm. To avoid inflicting harm as a function of the inability to imagine, Scarry notes that many ways of addressing the issue of the "other" have been suggested and implemented, and she divides them into two categories. One category comprises spontaneous, routine solutions that are based on generosity of spirit and require and trust the ability to imagine, whereas the other category does not rely on our better selves and assume "imaginability" but attempts to eliminate "the inherently aversive structural position of 'foreignness'" (40) through constitutional design.[7] She believes that, ideally, one should apply both solutions, but if the constitutional measures are in place, spontaneous solutions have a better chance of taking hold.

It is patently clear that the participants in the legal proceedings discussed above fell short of imagining the other, that is, the Arabic linguists. What's more, the constitutional design left much to be desired and compounded the perceptual deficiencies. For instance, the military prosecutors, backed by the DOJ, exploited the legal system to attribute traitorous intentions to Al Halabi; they drummed up a multitude of sins that tapped wholesale into the distrust with which translators are viewed and, since Al Halabi was Muslim, into the omnipresent Islamophobic climate. Scarry writes that otherness is "an elaborate sequence of additions and subtractions" (48), and depending on the representational strategy, the person is either depicted as a monster or becomes invisible. The military's representational strategy involved voiding Al Halabi's persona of all its essential, human aspects, magnifying his Middle Eastern ethnicity and

[7] Scarry primarily discusses citizenship law; however, here "constitutional design" applies to the United States Code and the Uniform Military Code of Justice.

characterizing him as a spy who betrayed the country that welcomed him with open arms. In doing so, they succeeded in projecting him as someone deserving of capital punishment. While "justice" ultimately prevailed for Al Halabi, the overreach is cause for serious concern, as is the fact that the legal safeguards were slow to materialize.

In contrast, in the Yousry case, all constitutional stops were pulled out and a great deal of procedural justice was heaped onto the defendant by a meticulously methodical court. This procedural avalanche, though giving the impression of fairness, in reality allowed the government to stage a nine-month-long performance of the prosecution's blood-and-mayhem narrative, which was ample time to ferment and solidify any pre-existing distrust. Rather than provide a proper framework that would allow for fairly imagining the other, for instance, by allowing into evidence teacher evaluations attesting to Yousry's non-partisan political views (which was denied),[8] the constitutional design was hijacked to further the government's agenda. And this agenda was executed to the fullest. When Bush (2002), in his infamous axis-of-evil State of the Union Address four months after 9/11, divided the world into us versus them, he undertook what Apfelbaum (1979) terms "grouping" (197). In that particular situation, the evil or out-groups were North Korea, Iran and Iraq; however, an unfortunate byproduct was that the president's exclusionary differentiation threw all things Arab and Middle Eastern into the same pot. And since humans are often less-than-nuanced in their thinking, whether on historical, geographic or other dimensions, Al Halabi and Yousry suffered the same fate. Apfelbaum notes that in the grouping process, not only is the collectivity labeled with the same identifying features but each individual is marked as such and "stripped of the surplus meaning it may have acquired over the years" (197). Following suit, the military and federal prosecutors as well as the 12 members of the Yousry jury emptied the two men of any and all redeeming qualities. In this way, they wholly complied with Bush's fear-mongering directive and reduced Al Halabi and Yousry to spy and terrorist agent, respectively.

[8] Yousry was an adjunct professor of Middle Eastern history at York College, City University of New York.

The fact that Al Halabi was ultimately released, albeit with a tarnished reputation, was in no small measure due to the military prosecution's overall bumbling. In contrast, Yousry's case was far more insidious, since the trial was conducted under the "cover of legitimacy" (202). This means that while all the i's may have been dotted from a legal perspective, the truth was a casualty from the start and the trial simply served to implement the dictates of the powers that be. In other words, the entire legal system supported the group in power through their implicit consensus that the system is legitimate, which according to Apfelbaum is in itself "a consequence of the power processes" (202).

The actors in the two cases were numerous, and their complicity in bolstering the legitimacy of the system can also be explained, in part, by system justification theory. This theoretical framework deals with the "social and psychological needs to imbue the status quo with legitimacy and to see it as good, fair, natural, desirable, and even inevitable" (Jost et al. 2004, 887). In the contexts at hand, the Gitmo officers and the members of Yousry's jury may well have felt an increased need to protect the system against terrorist threats after 9/11. Jost and Hunyady (2002) hypothesized that "people will defend and justify the social system in response to threat by using stereotypes to differentiate between high- and low-status groups to a greater degree" (121), and there is some empirical support for their thesis. For example, Goodwin and Devos (2002) found that in the wake of 9/11, there was increased stereotyping of Arab Americans, which means that Al Halabi and Yousry were not only distrusted because of the nature of their profession but as a function of aggressive religious and cultural stereotyping.

4 Conclusion: A Narrower Scope of Justice

While the toxic amalgam of distrust outlined above—the Translator-Traitor Mentality, a failure to imagine the other, Islamophobic grouping and stereotyping—as well as the need to view the system as legitimate set off the scapegoating of Al Halabi and Yousry, it took a societal toll that far exceeded the fate of these two men.

Opotow (1995) defines scope of justice or moral community as the psychological boundary within which justice and moral rules are perceived to be relevant. She points out that a narrower scope "constricts the set of situations in which justice concerns are applicable" and that for "social categories outside the scope of justice, the concepts of deserving and fair treatment do not apply" (347). Both Al Halabi and Yousry, convenient pawns in the government's agenda, were deemed expendable and expelled from this scope. Whether as representatives of a profession whose default handicap is distrust and/or as Arab Americans, a group particularly distrusted and victimized post-9/11, they were denied not only fair treatment but justice itself.

In the end, the harm done to these two linguists befell all of America. Although the military and federal prosecutors and jurors were the overt actors, they simply stood in for a society that, for the most part, stood idly by. And the reflecting pools marking the site where the World Trade Center once towered not only memorialize the 9/11 victims but also symbolize the bloody footprints of a narrower scope of justice.

References

Apfelbaum, Erika. 1979. Relations of Domination and Movements for Liberation: An Analysis of Power Between Groups. In *The Social Psychology of Intergroup Relations*, ed. William G. Austin and Stephen Worchel, 188–204. Belmont, CA: Wadsworth.

Army Intelligence Officer Charged With Violating Security at Guantanamo. 2003. *OUDAILY*, December 1. http://www.oudaily.com/army-intelligence-officer-charged-with-violating-security-at-guantanamo/article_df1b160e-d92e-52cb-aa53-1e194b9e4b81.html. Accessed 2 September 2019.

Bailey, Eric. 2004. More Jail Time Wanted for Interpreter in Spying Case. *The Los Angeles Times*, September 24. https://www.latimes.com/archives/la-xpm-2004-sep-24-me-halabi24-story.html. Accessed 7 September 2019.

Bush, George W. 2002. State-of-the-Union Address. *CNN*, January 29. https://www.washingtonpost.com/wp-srv/onpolitics/transcripts/sou012902.htmindex.html. Accessed 3 September 2019.

Cole, David. 2009. *The Torture Memos*. New York and London: The New Press.

Comey, James B. 2003. United States v. Sattar et al., 02 Cr. 395 (JGK). Superseding Indictment. New York, NY: U.S. Department of Justice, U.S. Attorney, U.S. District Court, Southern District of New York, November 19.

Gaudiano, Nicole. 2004. Al Halabi Spy Charges Dropped. *Air Force Times*, October 4. http://www.airforcetimes.com/legacy/new/0-AIRPAPER-371122.php. Accessed 17 March 2009.

Golden, Tim. 2004. Loyalties and Suspicions: The Muslim Servicemen; How Dubious Evidence Spurred Relentless Guantánamo Spy Hunt. *The New York Times*, December 19. https://www.nytimes.com/2004/12/19/washington/us/loyalties-and-suspicions-the-muslim-servicemen-how-dubious.html. Accessed 2 September 2019.

Goodwin, Stephanie, and Thierry Devos. 2002. *American Identity Under Siege: National and Racial Identities in the Wake of the September 11th Attack*. Paper presented at the annual meeting of the Society for Experimental Social Psychology, Columbus, OH, October.

Gottschalk, Peter, and Gabriel Greenberg. 2008. *Islamophobia: Making Muslims the Enemy*. Lanham, MA: Rowman and Littlefield Publishers, Inc.

Hess, Maya. 2014. *Translator-Traitor: A Critical Ethnography of a U.S. Terrorism Trial*. Unpublished PhD thesis, City University of New York.

In re Senior Airman (E4) Ahmad I. Al Halabi. Misc. Dkt. No. 2003-7. Petition for Extraordinary Relief in the Nature of a Writ of Mandamus; Stay of Article 32 Proceedings. U.S. Air Force Court of Criminal Appeals. September 15.

In re Senior Airman (E4) Ahmad I. Al Halabi. Misc. Dkt. No. 2003-7. Order. U.S. Air Force Court of Criminal Appeals. September 16.

Jost, John T., and Orsolya Hunyady. 2002. The Psychology of System Justification and the Palliative Function of Ideology. *European Review of Social Psychology* 13: 111–153.

Jost, John T., Mahzarin R. Banaji, and Brian A. Nosek. 2004. A Decade of System Justification Theory: Accumulated Evidence of Conscious and Unconscious Bolstering of the Status Quo. *Political Psychology* 25 (6): 881–919.

Leung, Rebecca. 2004. Spy Ring at Gitmo? *CBS News*, November 28. http://www.cbsnews.com/stories/2004/11/24/60minutes/main657704.shtml. Accessed 1 September 2019.

Lewicki, Roy J., Daniel J. McAllister, and Robert J. Blies. 1998. Trust and Distrust: New Relationships and Realities. *Academy of Management Review* 23 (3): 438–458.

Marshall, Scott. 2004. Talk of Interference, Closed Testimony Shake Al Halabi Spy Trial. *Contra Costa Times*, September 21. https://www.pegc.us/archive/Press/Others/misc_digest_2004_9.txt. Accessed 2 September 2019.

Martin, Patrick. 2004. Another Guantanamo 'Spying' Frame-up Collapses. *World Socialist Website*, September 25. https://www.wsws.org/en/articles/2004/09/guan-s25.html. Accessed 7 September 2019.

Military May Be Bungling Yet Another Guantánamo Espionage Trial. 2004. *JAGCENTRAL.org*, June 16. http://jagcentral.org/2004_06_13_archive.html. Accessed 22 May 2008.

Opotow, Susan. 1995. Drawing the Line: Social Categorization, Moral Exclusion, and the Scope of Justice. In *Conflict, Cooperation, and Justice: Essays Inspired by the Work of Morton Deutsch*, ed. Barbara Benedict Bunker and Jeffrey Z. Rubin, 347–369. San Francisco, CA: Jossey-Bass.

Panagopoulos, Costas. 2006. The Polls – Trends: Arab and Muslim Americans and Islam in the Aftermath of 9/11. *Public Opinion Quarterly* 70 (4): 608–624.

Parker, Laura. 2004a. Spy Case Was a 'Life-Altering' Experience for Airman. *USA Today*, October 17. https://usatoday30.usatoday.com/news/nation/2004-10-17-halabi_x.htm. Accessed 7 September 2019.

———. 2004b. Airman's Spying Charges Dropped. *USA Today*, September 22. https://usatoday30.usatoday.com/news/nation/2004-09-22-gitmo-deal_x.htm. Accessed 1 September 2019.

Peña, Charles V. 2003. Iraq: The Wrong War. *CATO Institute Policy Analysis No. 502*, December 15. https://www.cato.org/publications/policy-analysis/iraq-wrong-war. Accessed 22 December 2019.

Scarry, Elaine. 2000. The Difficulty of Imagining Other Persons. In *The Handbook of Interethnic Coexistence*, ed. Eugene Weiner, 40–58. New York: Continuum.

Stein, Jonathan, and Tim Dickinson. 2006. Lie by Lie: A Timeline of How We Got into Iraq. *Mother Jones*, September/October. https://www.motherjones.com/politics/2011/12/leadup-iraq-war-timeline. Accessed 1 September 2019.

Taibbi, Matt. 2015. Judith Miller's Comeback. *Rolling Stone*, May 29. https://www.rollingstone.com/politics/politics-news/judith-millers-comeback-62957. Accessed 1 September 2019.

The Runnymede Trust. 2017. *Islamophobia: Still a Challenge for Us All*. Report. https://www.runnymedetrust.org/uploads/Islamophobia%20Report%202018%20FINAL.pdf. Accessed 2 September 2019.

Ties to Terror. *On the Record with Greta Van Susteren*. Fox. Washington. 6 May 2002. Television.

Torriero, Ernie A. 2004. Muslims Allege Double Standard in Spy Charges. *Chicago Tribune*, October 18. https://www.chicagotribune.com/news/ct-xpm-2004-10-18-0410180165-story.html. Accessed 2 September 2019.

U.S. Air Force. 2003. Charge Sheet Ahmed I. Al Halabi. *FindLaw.com*, August 27. https://www.pegc.us/archive/JTF-GTMO_Cases/Al-Halabi_charges.pdf. Accessed 31 August 2019.

———. 2004. Trial Ends for Air Force Translator. *AF. mil*, September 27. https://www.af.mil/News/Article-Display/Article/135974/trial-ends-for-air-force-translator. Accessed 1 September 2019.

U.S. Department of Justice. 1997. 9-24.000 Requests for Special Confinement Conditions. Washington, D.C. http://www.usdoj.gov/usao/eousa/foia_reading_room/uSAMs/title9.24mcrm.htm. Accessed 17 March 2005.

U.S. Department of State. 2001. *2001 Report on Foreign Terrorist Organizations*. Washington, DC: Office of the Coordinator for Counterterrorism, October 5. http://www.state.gov/s/ct/rls/rpt/fto/2001/5258.htm. Accessed 16 December 2005.

United States v. Rahman, 93 Cr. 181 (MBM) (S.D.N.Y. 1993).

United States v. Sattar et al., S1 02 Cr. 395 (JGK) (S.D.N.Y. 2004–2005).

Watson, Roland. 2005. US Admits Guard Soiled Koran at Guantanamo. *The Sunday Times*, June 4. https://www.thetimes.co.uk/article/us-admits-guard-soiled-koran-at-guantanamo-g8dmbnn3x73. Accessed 1 September 2019.

Weaver, Robert C. Jr. 2006. No Man's Land. *Commonweal Magazine*, October 6.

Part III

Humanitarian Interpreting

10

Psychological Aspects of Interpreting Violence: A Narrative from the Israeli-Palestinian Conflict

Manuel Barea Muñoz

1 Introduction

Recent academic research has evidenced a growing interest in interpreting in conflict-related scenarios. Most of the works within this literature focus on the role of the interpreter in complex transnational contexts such as humanitarian crises (Delgado Luchner 2015; Delgado Luchner and Kherbiche 2018; Todorova 2019), the inclusion of linguistic mediators in environments highly conditioned by trust and power relations dynamics—as in the case of interpreting for the military—(Hajjar 2017; Snellman 2016; Talpas 2016), peacekeeping interpreting (Bos and Soeters 2006; Edwards 2002; Ruiz Rosendo and Persaud 2019), and issues of protection, particularly regarding the ad hoc interpreters employed by journalists and the military within the framework of the War on Terror (Fitchett 2012; Packer 2007).

M. Barea Muñoz (✉)
University of Geneva, Geneva, Switzerland
e-mail: Manuel.Barea@unige.ch

M. Todorova, L. Ruiz Rosendo (eds.), *Interpreting Conflict*, Palgrave Studies in Languages at War, https://doi.org/10.1007/978-3-030-66909-6_10

The previous research shows that given the inherent complexity of any armed conflict, as well as the oftentimes non-professional nature of the job of the interpreter in conflict-related scenarios, it is difficult to gather strong, verifiable data on interpreting practices implemented as a consequence of a conflict situation. Hence, certain works concerning the interpreter's fieldwork mainly cover the language requirements within international peacekeeping operations held in the framework of the Bosnian War (Baker 2010; Persaud 2016), and the post-9/11 asymmetrical conflicts comprising international military operations, largely Afghanistan and Iraq (Gómez Amich 2017; Jones and Askew 2014).

Against this background, our study addresses how the civilian interpreter perceives, from a psychological standpoint, her own position inside the interpreting setting, the related working conditions, her performance, and her response to what in some cases are traumatic experiences resulting from her work in a protracted conflict. Furthermore, it is imperative to consider this very specific topic within an equally specific context and, therefore, profile: the interpreter working in on-the-ground missions in the Israeli-Palestinian conflict.

Considering this backdrop, our study can be broken down into the following research questions: what are the working conditions of an interpreter working in on-the-ground missions in the Israeli-Palestinian conflict? Do these working conditions change depending on the setting? What are the psychological aspects derived from these working conditions? Do these psychological aspects affect the interpreter's performance?

In order to answer our research questions, we conducted semi-structured interviews with interpreters who work in on-the-ground missions in the Israeli-Palestinian conflict. Raw data was managed in the conceptual framework of a qualitative study conducted in the Faculty of Translation and Interpreting at the University of Geneva. Accordingly, this chapter aims at presenting the results of said qualitative study in the form of a paradigmatic narrative with the purpose of shedding light on the working conditions and psychological impacts of interpreting in the Israeli-Palestinian conflict.

2 Contextualization

Unfortunately, researching in conflict-related scenarios leaves little room for generalization; as well as in most other settings, the conflict-derived situation where the interpreting practice is developed shapes said development (Inghilleri 2003; Ruiz Rosendo and Persaud 2019). Consequently, it is safe to say that the interpreting practice would somehow vary from one environment to another, that is, from one conflict to another, and even from one setting to another, despite taking place within the same conflict. For this reason, we believe that it is paramount to contextualize the conceptual framework of our research.

Thus, our study must be considered within the Israeli-Palestinian conflict, a protracted conflict, nowadays asymmetric, located in the Middle East. Although we will be focusing on its essence as a protracted conflict arising from occupation, we find it necessary to define what makes it a conflict. Along these lines, we consider the definition of "absolute war" by Clausewitz (2006 [1874]) in the sense that it aims at nullifying the enemy by destroying all of its resources. However, at the same time, we apply the term "conflict" to the Israeli-Palestinian situation following the definition provided by the Uppsala Conflict Data Program, that is, two territories, one of them necessarily being a state, which confront each other with the use of armed force resulting in at least 25 battle-related deaths (Gleditsch et al. 2002). In the same vein, the phrase "conflict-related scenario," as used in this text, refers to every communicative situation originated in the context of the conflict, including conference settings.

Moreover, the analysis of a protracted conflict gives us the opportunity to examine the role of the interpreter depending on its current situation and historical development. In this case, given that the conflict is in a stalemate, most interpreting is implemented in a post-conflict scenario. This results in many interpreting assignments being commissions of inquiry, fact-finding missions, and conferences on law, economics, and policymaking strategies. For that reason, and considering the inherent difficulties of establishing a typology of interpreters in conflict-related scenarios, we could argue that the population under study belongs to a category that would have more in common with the practice of humanitarian interpreting (as they are civilians participating in missions in the field) than with interpreting for the military.

Besides, these missions imply a direct contact with the local population and authorities, municipalities, NGOs, and victims' associations. Therefore, in this context, the main data collection device for the subsequent report is conducting interviews with witnesses and victims of human rights violations, thus setting the need for language and cultural mediation. In this regard, and given that the fieldwork involves Arabic speakers, the very nature of the mission explains the professional profile of the population under study, that is, Arab interpreters with training and professional experience working in the field in the Israeli-Palestinian conflict.

3 Methodological Approach

As mentioned, this chapter originates from a qualitative study based on semi-structured interviews with 11 interpreters. The interviews were conducted with local trained interpreters and staffers, both working in the field for international organizations[1] in the framework of the Israeli-Palestinian conflict.

The research, based on an inductive and iterative method (Babbie 2001) distinctive of the Constructivist Grounded Theory (c.f. Charmaz 2006), was designed as a case study with a phenomenological approach from the researcher's perspective. Drawing similarities and through saturation, raw data was codified in order to build a paradigmatic narrative (cf. Delgado Luchner and Kherbiche 2018) aimed at preserving the anonymity and confidentiality of such a sensitive population. Building a paradigmatic narrative does not imply, however, the generalization of findings and theory within the data or the aspiration to cover all the details presented by each participant in their own personal narratives; it aims to convey the perception of a given phenomenon (in this case,

[1] Due to confidentiality reasons, we cannot specify the name of these organizations.

interpreting in the Israeli-Palestinian conflict) as experienced by the very participants of this study.

In terms of the limitations of the method, we will mention our inability (mainly logistical) to conduct fieldwork and to gather data from Hebrew interpreters. Nevertheless, it is worth noting that having international missions on the ground in the Israeli-Palestinian conflict implies communication with Arabic speakers, hence the predominance of Arabic interpreters in the population under study.

In addition, our methodological approach also aims at delving into what differentiates a conflict-related scenario from a conference setting with the purpose of analyzing the theoretical neutrality of the interpreter and her relationship with the conflict in terms of positionality. In this sense, the question would be whether the professional code of ethics that affects quality assessment and performance, as well as working practices traditionally associated with conference interpreting, could be found (at least intact) in the figure of the interpreter who works on the ground in armed conflicts (Guo 2015).

4 Interpreting in the Israeli-Palestinian Conflict: A Paradigmatic Narrative

The results of our study are shaped in the form of a paradigmatic narrative that, according to quantitative data also gathered via elicitation, is experienced by a Palestinian woman in her 50s (hereafter named Aya) with training in interpreting and plenty of professional experience both in conference interpreting and in conflict-related scenarios. Additionally, the description of the psychological aspects of on-the-ground interpreting in the context of the Israeli-Palestinian conflict, which are drawn from the analysis of the results of our qualitative study under the form of a paradigmatic profile that outlines how the participants experience the phenomenon in which they are involved, can be broken down to five main areas of discussion, namely: (1) relation and response to the conflict, (2) setting and performance, (3) coping mechanisms on the ground,

(4) emotional impact in the aftermath of the mission, and (5) self-representation.

4.1 Relation and Response to the Conflict

In terms of her response and relation to the conflict itself, a prominent feature of her personal and professional profile is that, since we are talking about a protracted conflict, Aya was born into the Israeli-Palestinian conflict. Therefore, her personal history being attached to that of the conflict, she is familiar with its current situation and historical development, as she has also participated in several of its phases. She is even, to a certain degree, used to it; both the related violence and the status quo originated from it, specifically the occupation. This connection with the conflict is manifested through a high degree of empathy toward the locals and the interviewees that came into contact with the delegations and investigators coordinating and carrying out missions in the field, for whom Aya is interpreting. This is due to the fact that encountering some of these people reminds her of her own family and neighbors, an image often repeated by means of the idea that each of them could very well be an acquaintance. In this sense, it is also worth noting that, as she is a mother, when interpreting with child victims, it is not unusual for her to be reminded of her own children.

As a Palestinian herself, her own sense of belonging is not only expressed at an emotional level but also at a professional one; the mobility associated with the on-the-ground work of the interpreter in conflict-related scenarios is oftentimes a noteworthy issue, if not directly a handicap, due to her Palestinian nationality. In terms of setting and transportation arrangements, it would be occasionally necessary to travel from the West Bank into Israeli territories and also into Gaza through Israel or Egypt, which is a journey that may be time-consuming for a Palestinian national, as well as highly bureaucratic and scrutinized, frequently requiring a UN laissez-passer, or an international special permit issued by the European Union (should the mission be deployed by the Parliament or the Commission).

With regard to local interpreters, especially freelancers, this mobility problem is of capital importance, not only in terms of being professional (schedule-wise) but also in terms of employability, with the case of the Kalandia checkpoint being the most idiosyncratic. There, the interpreter may be held for an undefined amount of time in order to cross, which, in regard to the development of a certain workday, must be taken into account by the members of the delegation. At the same time, this circumstance may entail the possibility that the interpreter is finally not granted access to cross the checkpoint, which ultimately would deprive the mission of an interpreting service, then perhaps involving the possibility of cancelling the entire day's schedule or at least modifying it in a significant way. The prospect of such a situation, which would understandably affect the implementation of the mission, is often in the minds of the entities and stakeholders who must provide linguistic mediators to on-the-ground missions, and thus, the employment process is obliged to consider the potential drawbacks of hiring a Palestinian interpreter depending on the planned field visits and itinerary. Because of this, some employers, should they need to contract on-the-ground local interpreters, prefer the services of other Arabic-speaking professionals, for example, Moroccans.

Continuing with the question of the on-the-ground interpreting setting, most of the mission fieldwork rests on gathering direct information from witnesses or victims, which is the reason why most of the settings are interviews with such individuals. Sometimes those interviews are conducted in hospitals and prisons, and often they are held in hotels, usually the same hotel in which the mission is based.

Along the lines of the aforementioned fieldwork, it is worth noting that Aya interprets on visits to places where she, being a Palestinian, would not go. They are normally hot spots, territories where the characteristics and consequences of the conflict are more pronounced and where the manifestations of the occupation are more evident, Hebron being one of the most salient examples. In Hebron, the settlements are built in the old town (downtown Hebron), which is an unusual situation; that means that some streets are forbidden to Palestinians. In this regard, the employment of a Palestinian interpreter is also an important matter, in the sense that if the interpreter is not allowed to enter certain streets, it indirectly entails that the whole delegation would not go there either (as, without her, effective communication would not be fully guaranteed), thus affecting the course of the visit.

4.2 Setting and Performance

In regard to her performance—specifically when conveying the content of certain communicative exchanges, namely victims' testimonies—it is not unusual for Aya to choke on her words or even cry while interpreting. As we are talking about interviews mostly conducted in a hotel conference room arranged for such a purpose, a conference setting modality is put into practice with the technical support of a mobile booth or a "*bidule*." Because of this, she is thankful for being able to work in pairs, with a colleague, with the possibility of switching interpreters (e.g., in case one of them suddenly bursts into tears and therefore cannot continue). This would not always solve the problem, as it sometimes happens that both interpreters are overcome with emotion at the same time, due to the nature of the content which they must interpret. Eventually, they find a way to keep interpreting and still perform professionally, even if they are choking on their words or sobbing. However, should the interpreter be unable to get herself together, it is not infrequent to momentarily pause the session. Aya relates this assumed inability to reach a constant emotional level of machine-like interpreting to the interpreting technique itself, by which she has to deliver the message to the B language via a first-person narrative. This way, she would internalize the content of the message, which deals with practices of human rights violations, and whose main ideas, after two or three days on the mission, would have been repeatedly explained. This is particularly wearing from a psychological standpoint in interviews concerning victims of torture, some of them children. In relation to this, due to the intensity of the sessions content-wise, these tend to be short, a maximum of 30–45 minutes. Still, working days are long, as delegations seek to condense as many procedures and tasks into one day, also due to the fact that missions usually last two to five days.

4.3 Coping Mechanisms on the Ground

As mentioned before, on-the-ground interpreting in these types of missions and settings tends to be psychologically stressful and demanding. Since this is the case for Aya, she has been, throughout her career as an interpreter in the Israeli-Palestinian conflict, prone to develop certain coping mechanisms to be displayed in the field. Some of them are directly put into practice during debriefing sessions that take place right after the interpreting session, where she would talk and exchange impressions with her interpreter colleague and other members of the mission about the interviews. She would also be welcomed to express her feelings and to cry as a means to get rid of any possible accumulated tension or stress. Although these debriefing sessions are common practice, they are nevertheless not conceived as a method to deal psychologically with the situation and information that the interpreter is exposed to, as they tend to be addressed from a research and investigative standpoint. In some cases, for instance, if the person who conducts the interviews with the victims and witnesses happens to be a psychologist, the debriefing session with the interpreter would likely be approached from a psychological perspective. Also, it is possible that should she work for an international organization, the interpreter may be provided with psychological and therapy services once she has returned home, but in the same manner as in a debriefing session, which is a one-time service, and does not take the form of ongoing regular therapy.

Therefore, perhaps the most interesting coping mechanisms applied by Aya to face the emotional and psychological challenges of interpreting on the ground in this very specific context are the ones developed by herself. Not only after the interpreting session, but also right before, she would concentrate on her favorite piece of music, running it through her mind, listening to it on headphones or humming it to herself. On other occasions, she would also say a prayer. Moreover, it is useful to talk to other people not directly involved in the mission or not-therapists, such as other colleagues, friends and family—people who can sympathize with her experience and feelings.

This, however, would be useful just right after the fact; that is why Aya has developed a coping mechanism to be put into practice *during* her performance in order for it not to be hindered, which would be a choice from within the range of machine-like interpreting possibilities: conveying the content of the communicative exchange focusing exclusively on its form, without personally (mentally) attributing any meaning whatsoever to the words being uttered. This procedure of detaching herself from the communicative situation and the facts being addressed through the linguistic exchange is achieved by concentrating exclusively on words, not emotions nor meaning. Nevertheless, interpreting in such a sensitive context calls not only for professionalism on the part of the interpreter but also for her capacity to build rapport and trust with the victims, which is achieved through human connection, that is to say empathy. On certain occasions, mainly when there is a direct contact between the interviewee and the interpreter, building rapport and trust with said interviewee makes the information and communication output flow easier, and it may even guarantee a proactive attitude on the interviewee's part, who would be willing to share more data with empathetic investigators and members of the delegation, whereas a cold machine-like behavior may prompt shorter answers and a lesser tendency to share information.

4.4 Emotional Impact in the Aftermath of the Mission

Hence, according to Aya's experience, the main on-the-ground coping mechanism to deal with the emotional intensity of the work is actually a high commitment to said work while she is performing it. This would entail that as the psychological complexity is momentarily set aside during the mission in favor of its success, the emotional burden frequently manifests itself in the aftermath of the mission, that is to say when she is finished with the work, when she has time to deeply think about the information received (and conveyed through her). As a result, Aya displays multiple signs of trauma and occupational burnout syndrome that may be related to possible post-traumatic stress disorder. Most of these signs include anxiety (shakiness), insomnia, nightmares, nervous breakdowns, inability to speak for hours or even days, daydreaming (with flashbacks where she relives certain experiences), and depression. For her, the most usual response to her recounting of the on-the-ground events and testimonies is staying in bed, crying, and an unwillingness to speak. At night, she may not be able to sleep, and if she does manage to sleep, she can experience night terrors. Aya does not seek therapy to mitigate or manage this; in fact, when she started working in the conflict, after the First Intifada and in the following years, neither her nor her colleagues knew that there was something called "post-traumatic stress disorder" or that they were exposed at work to some form of trauma. Therefore, the main coping mechanism put in place to face these emotional states were one-time debriefing sessions that, hopefully, were conducted by a psychologist, as well as sharing feelings with other colleagues with similar experiences. Aya sums this up as "crying on each other's shoulder." It is also worth noting that this type of personal implication directly linked to a professional occupation would sometimes encourage the interpreter to decline certain assignments or specific missions and even to quit her job.

4.5 Self-representation

In the same vein, the idea of the interpreter's self-representation within this background could be introduced as an umbrella that would cover the concepts previously addressed, as well as another relevant point of the psychological aspects of on-the-ground interpreting in the Israeli-Palestinian conflict. Because of her sense of belonging in many ways to the conflict, Aya does not perceive herself as a neutral part who operates in the margins of the mission; when she is working for the delegation, she is *in the delegation*. Circumstances like the reception in Hebron or the complexity of navigating the Kalandia checkpoint crossing not only directly affect her work and employability, but also affect the work of the rest of the delegation and the development of the workday and the mission as a whole. On top of this, she also considers herself to be involved in the conflict as a born Palestinian; she is emotionally invested, her family and neighbors and her sense of homeland being the main source of the psychological side of her interpreting work and inner conflict between ethical professionalism (the traditionally deontological position of the interpreter as a neutral conduit between the communicating parties) and humanity, which is based on her displays of empathy toward the local population and specifically the interviewees, victims of human rights violations in the Occupied Territories. Thus, both as a Palestinian and as a professional working in the field in the conflict, her self-awareness also often translates in self-questioning, as she considers herself to be a direct witness to what she views as the futility, helplessness, and resignation that for the last years have generally defined the Israeli-Palestinian conflict from the Palestinian point of view.

5 Discussion

The insight into the phenomenon of on-the-ground interpreting in the Israeli-Palestinian conflict given by the participants of our study provides us with interesting answers to our research questions as well as complex notions that need to be examined in future research.

5.1 Working Conditions and the Interpreter's Positionality

From a professional perspective, it is worth noting that these interpreters have training and ample working experience in conference interpreting that is positively useful in certain conflict-related scenarios, as interviews with victims of human rights violations are oftentimes developed in what is virtually a conference setting, with the use of "bidule" or voice-over in a simultaneous performance. It is also remarkable that, in the context of the conflict, the majority of the work takes place in the booth as compared to directly in the field and that the access to on-the-ground work is frequently through conference interpreting, blurring the lines that theoretically would separate the traditional conference setting from a conflict-related scenario.

However, although the working conditions in a conference setting and a conflict-related scenario would not necessarily diverge, the content of the mediated event and the surrounding circumstances in a conflict-related scenario would have an impact on the interpreter's work, as long as we bear in mind the interpreter's degree of positionality. In this case, the interpreter's positionality comes from her direct relation to the conflict, not just as a local, but also as part of a delegation that aims to shed light on the current situation in the field. At the same time, this sense of belonging is perceived by the interpreter in her high level of empathy toward one of the parties involved in the mediated event, that is, the victims of human rights violations, who oftentimes remind her of her own family and neighbors. Indeed, the conflict itself permeates and affects every practice derived from it, including interpreting, which is, at the end of the day, not just a professional occupation but also a human practice driven by context (Inghilleri 2003). Thus, the interpreter's motivation to work on the ground can be described in both financial and occupational terms (Ruiz Rosendo and Barea Muñoz 2017), as well as in a sense of duty toward her family and homeland.

Moreover, in terms of the interpreter's positionality, it is worth noting her key feature as someone being born to the conflict, therefore belonging to one side and thus opposed by the other, and at the same time as an active actor who participates in a mission that is not always well regarded by either side—the Israelis arguing that the investigations exclusively focus on the alleged Israeli violations of the International Humanitarian Law and the Palestinians expressing their now habitual disenchantment toward these international initiatives (cf. Bermejo García and Pozo Serrano 2011; Shlaim 2011 [2003]), proving her role as both an insider and an outsider (Ruiz Rosendo and Persaud 2019). This characteristic would once again confront the idea of the interpreter as a neutral conduit who achieves full impartiality (Gómez Amich 2017; Snellman 2016), emphasizing the presence of a gap between how an interpreter *should* operate and how she *actually* operates in conflict-related scenarios. Furthermore, from a semantic and deontological standpoint, this question hints at the possibility of re-examining the accuracy of referring to these interpreters as indeed "interpreters."

In addition, this idea comes into focus when comparing the presumed tasks of a conference interpreter and the tasks carried out by a liaison interpreter. The former limits herself to interpreting, whereas the latter performs interpreter duties as well as serving as a facilitator between the delegation and the local population, going to greater lengths to grant communication and adjustment, such as asking people in the vicinity for addresses or explaining the menu at a restaurant. Thus, our on-the-ground interpreter performs the job proper to a professional conference interpreter while simultaneously acting as a fixer (c.f. Palmer 2007). This is due to the fact that she is an active part of a civilian non-military mission sent to the conflict but also part of said conflict, a local at all events, and therefore her double status as an eventual future beneficiary of the investigation and as a participant in that same investigation defines her position.

5.2 Working Conditions and the Interpreter's Emotional Response

Along these lines, it is relevant to take into account the interpreter's emotional response to this particular situation while also bearing in mind our research questions. Since we have already alluded to the working conditions and psychological aspects of the fieldwork, we proceed now with examining whether those working conditions change depending on the setting and if those psychological aspects affect the interpreter's performance. As we presented in the paradigmatic narrative, the working conditions would vary depending on the mission, especially if this involves a journey that includes crossing borders or checkpoints. In this case, the level of risk would not vary depending on the client, as this stressful atmosphere of visiting settlements and crossing checkpoints would be predictable and unchanging from a Palestinian perspective. Nonetheless, the level of risk and stress would vary depending on the mission, because schedules and allowances would differ should the mission entail crossing borders or visiting hot spots. In this case, the interpreter must be aware of and obtain any possible paperwork that the authorities require be filled out, as well as extra working time in order for her to proceed safely from the Occupied Territories to Israel and vice versa, which would eventually influence her employability.

5.3 Working Conditions and the Interpreter's Performance

Concerning the interpreter's performance, it is usually not compromised, besides acute displays of empathy throughout the course of certain mediated events. Still, it is in the aftermath of said events when the emotional impact is felt. This would not vary necessarily from one mission to another, as the psychological aspects of interpreting in this type of context in the Israeli-Palestinian conflict are presented to the interpreter in a rather homogeneous way, hence the similar consistency in the appearance of defense and coping mechanisms.

In this regard, if, on the one hand, the interpreter's performance is just slightly affected, on the other hand, her emotional integrity is usually highly affected. As we are dealing with a non-military context, closer to a humanitarian environment, and short-length missions, the interpreter tends to bring these feelings back home and lean on debriefing sessions and non-professional shared therapy with colleagues who have undergone similar experiences. However, freelancers and staffers would perceive this impact in a different fashion: while freelancers usually live in Palestine and are therefore more accustomed to the conflict situation (they also have a more accurate account of historic events) and are more likely to be preoccupied by their professional circumstances and the labor market, the staffers, residing abroad, are more prone to self-awareness and self-questioning, as they feel immersed in a reiterative experience based on going to the field for a few days and thereafter returning home to then deal with its effects.

6 Conclusion

Future research will be required in order to further examine the emotional impact of interpreting in scenarios related to the Israeli-Palestinian conflict from a psychological approach, namely human response to diverse forms of trauma. At the same time, it is vital to continue expanding on noteworthy concepts like the positionality of the interpreter in conflict-related scenarios, which also has relevant psychological implications.

It is also worth mentioning that the professionalism and ethical self-awareness of the interpreter (a born Palestinian) in the Israeli-Palestinian conflict does not fully withdraw her sense of belonging to the conflict when she is embedded in an international mission. She conducts the tasks of an interpreter, for example, in conflict-related conference settings and meetings, but also, when on the ground, that of a cultural mediator and facilitator. This would pose the question of the accuracy of the term "interpreter in conflicts" for its apparent simplicity. In this respect, we should consider the interpreter's belonging to the conflict as a core side to her positionality, thus casting doubt on the concept of neutrality usually associated with the interpreting practice, a notion reflected in the emergence of a strong feeling of empathy during the mediated event that could eventually affect the interpreter's performance and that, in the aftermath, could entail a significant psychological impact with personal and professional repercussions.

Therefore, the challenging complexity of the communicative situations and interpreting settings in the fieldwork of missions in the Israeli-Palestinian conflict is expressed not only through the coping mechanisms built on the ground, or thereafter during debriefing sessions, but also through the emotional reactions of the interpreters and their response to psychological conditions that may subsequently linger due to repeated exposure. This circumstance exemplifies the complex reality of the interpreter in the Israeli-Palestinian conflict. Training programs should consider this, as well as the substantial necessity of psychological training, and eventual ongoing therapy sessions. Additionally, they should recognize the need for coping mechanisms to be put in place for effectively facing the emotional challenges which are taken for granted, yet which are often overlooked in favor of focusing on other aspects of interpreting in conflict-related scenarios.

References

Babbie, Earl. 2001. *The Practice of Social Research*. Wadsworth, OH: Thomson Learning.

Baker, Catherine. 2010. It's not Their Job to Soldier: Distinguishing Civilian and Military in Soldiers' and Interpreters' Accounts of Peacekeeping in 1990's Bosnia-Herzegovina. *Journal of War and Culture Studies* 3 (1): 137–150.

Bermejo García, Romualdo, and Pilar Pozo Serrano. 2011. *Una tierra, dos Estados: Análisis jurídico-político del conflicto árabe-israelí*. Pamplona: EUNSA. Ediciones de la Universidad de Navarra, S. A.

Bos, Geesje, and Joseph Soeters. 2006. Interpreters at Work: Experiences from Dutch and Belgian Peace Operations. *International Peacekeeping* 13 (2): 261–268.

Charmaz, Kathy C. 2006. *Constructing Grounded Theory: A Practical Guide Through Qualitative Analysis*. Thousand Oaks, CA: Sage.

Clausewitz, Carl von. 2006 [1874]. *On War* (Vol. I). http://www.gutenberg.org/files/1946/1946-h/1946-h.htm. Accessed 5 October 2020.

Delgado Luchner, Carmen. 2015. *Setting up a Master's Programme in Conference Interpreting at the University of Nairobi: An Interdisciplinary Case Study of a Development Project Involving Universities and International Organisations*. PhD diss., University of Geneva.

Delgado Luchner, Carmen, and Leila Kherbiche. 2018. Without Fear or Favour? The Positionality of ICRC and UNHCR Interpreters in the Humanitarian Field. *Target* 30 (3): 408–429.

Edwards, Victoria. 2002. The Role of Communication in Peace and Relief Mission Negotiations. *The Translation Journal* 6 (2). http://www.translation-journal.net/journal/20interpr.htm. Accessed 5 October 2020.

Fitchett, Linda. 2012. The AIIC Project to Help Interpreters in Conflict Areas. In *Languages and the Military. Alliances, Occupation and Peace Building*, ed. Hilary Footitt and Michael Kelly, 175–184. Palgrave Macmillan.

Gleditsch, Nils Petter, Peter Wallensteen, Mikael Eriksson, Margareta Sollenberg, and Havard Strand. 2002. Armed Conflict 1946–2001: A New Dataset. *Journal of Peace Research* 39 (5): 615–637.

Gómez Amich, María. 2017. *Estudio descriptivo de la autopercepción de los intérpretes en zonas de conflicto: estudio de caso en Afganistán*. PhD diss., University of Granada.

Guo, Ting. 2015. Interpreting for the Enemy: Chinese Interpreters in the Second Sino-Japanese War (1931–1945). *Translation Studies* 8 (1): 1–15.

Hajjar, Remi. 2017. Effectively Working with Military Linguists: Vital Intercultural Intermediaries. *Armed Forces and Society* 43 (1): 92–114.

Inghilleri, Moira. 2003. Habitus, Field and Discourse. Interpreting as a Socially Situated Activity. *Target* 15 (2): 243–268.

Jones, Ian, and Louise Askew. 2014. *Meeting the Language Challenges of NATO Operations*. Palgrave Macmillan.

Packer, George. 2007. Bretrayed: The Iraqis Who Trusted America the Most. *The New Yorker*, March 26. https://www.newyorker.com/magazine/2007/03/26/betrayed-2. Accessed 5 October 2020.

Palmer, Jerry. 2007. Interpreting and Translation for Western Media in Iraq. In *Translating and Interpreting Conflict*, ed. Myriam Salama-Carr, 13–28. Amsterdam/New York: Rodopi.

Persaud, Clementina. 2016. *Interpreting at War: A Case Study on EUFOR BiH ALTHEA*. PhD diss., University Pablo de Olavide.

Ruiz Rosendo, Lucia, and Manuel Barea Muñoz. 2017. Towards a Typology of Interpreters in War-Related Scenarios in the Middle East. *Translation Spaces* 6 (2): 182–208.

Ruiz Rosendo, Lucia, and Clementina Persaud. 2019. On the Frontline: Mediating Across Languages and Cultures in Peacekeeping Operations. *Armed Forces and Society*: 1–19.

Shlaim, Avi. 2011 [2003]. *El muro de hierro. Israel y el mundo árabe*. Granada: Almed.

Snellman, Pekka. 2016. Constraints on and Dimensions of Military Interpreter Neutrality. *Linguistica Antverpiensia* 15: 260–281.

Talpas, Mihaela. 2016. Words Cut Two Ways: An Overview of the Situation of Afghan Interpreters at the Beginning of the 21st Century. *Linguistica Antverpiensia* 15: 241–259.

Todorova, Marija. 2019. Interpreting for Refugees: Empathy and Activism. In *Intercultural Crisis Communication. Translation, Interpreting, and Languages in Local Crisis*, ed. Federico M. Federici and Christophe Declercq, 153–173. London: Bloomsbury.

11

United Nations Interpreters in the Arab Spring

Cherine Haidar Ahmad

1 Introduction

United Nations interpreters are sometimes called upon to work in zones marked by military or political conflict. In such cases, they are asked to fulfill their interpretation duties far from what is commonly called the "comfort zone" represented by conference rooms in United Nations headquarters.

The start of the Arab Spring in late 2010 led to a long series of uprisings that spread across the whole Arab region. It had a domino effect in North Africa and the Middle East. Waves of demonstrations and protests were met in different ways in different countries. The unrest led to changes in regime, sectarian violence, harsh repression and even civil war. United Nations involvement took different forms in different instances—for example, commissions of inquiry such as the Independent International Commission of Inquiry on the Syrian Arab Republic—but one of its main features was the presence of United Nations interpreters in the field.

C. Haidar Ahmad (✉)
University of Geneva, Geneva, Switzerland

M. Todorova, L. Ruiz Rosendo (eds.), *Interpreting Conflict*, Palgrave Studies in Languages at War, https://doi.org/10.1007/978-3-030-66909-6_11

Since most of the countries involved were Arabic-speaking, the selected interpreters were all nationals of Arab States who worked for the Arabic booth. It is true that the interpreters in question were all United Nations staff, but it is also true that all of them may be presumed to have had their own political views and all undoubtedly had some degree of emotional engagement in the topic. Moreover, some of them were sent, if not to their own countries, to a neighboring country with which they potentially had some level of historical or personal connection. Based on a factual description of the deployment and the cultural backgrounds of interpreters who participated in these field missions, and on their own first-hand accounts of their experiences, this chapter aims to show how the positionality of United Nations Interpreters can be defined as being both external and internal.

2 Brief Overview: Interpreters in the Field and Positionality

Interpretation in conflict zones is by no means a new phenomenon. Conflicts between peoples or between nations, or even within the same country where belligerents did not necessarily speak the same language, have always required a certain form of linguistic mediation (Rosendo and Persaud 2016). Interpreters would provide their services to established States or religions or participate in expeditions or military campaigns. They formed an integral part of military or diplomatic corps (Delisle and Woodsworth 2012). Nonetheless, despite their active role, the presence of interpreters is rarely mentioned in historical accounts (Baigorri Jalón 2004) and, when it is, it is only brought up as a corollary to the events that took place.

The presence of interpreters in conflict and humanitarian settings, the complexity of their role and their positionality has started to attract the attention of scholars only recently (Askew and Salama-Carr 2011). This may be partly attributable to the extensive airtime the media has devoted to wars and conflicts in recent years. That live television cover-age has served to arouse the curiosity and interest of researchers and, thus, interpreters have also become the object of studies and theories (Baker, M. 2010; Moser-Mercer and Bali 2008; Palmer 2007; Inghilleri 2010).

Nonetheless, researchers have shown that interpreters working in the field in modern times are not always categorized according to their professional competencies. In other words, they are not always recruited because of their effective mastery of specific interpretation skills or their knowledge of the conflict in which they are deployed. This means that the deployment of interpreters in the field does not necessarily take account of what was defined by Ruiz Rosendo and Barea Munoz (2017) as the conflict "typology". Interpreters' presence in the field is often a random event. This has been demonstrated by Catherine Baker who has recorded how soldiers and civilians in the Balkans came to act as interpreters in the field by pure chance (2012). The categorization of these individuals as interpreters often took place at a later stage, after they had been employed, and it was often vague, with no clear job description on the part of recruiters and a hesitating perception on the part of interpreters as to what their role actually was, especially in case of local and untrained interpreters (Askew and Salama-Carr 2011). We may safely say, then, that there is no clear categorization of interpreters working in conflict zones today (Ruiz Rosendo and Persaud 2016). In such contexts, interpreters can play several roles at a time: they can be linguistic mediators or fixers, or they may even have military functions. This seems to be a recurring characteristic in modern conflicts (Baker, C. 2010) and leads to different perceptions of interpreters by the users of their services according to the functions that the recruiters assign to them (Palmer 2007).

The complexity and diversity of the functions that interpreters are asked to cover in the field in modern times raise the question of the positionality and the visibility of the interpreters themselves, especially in conflict zones where highly sensitive issues are at stake (Baker, C. 2010). Positionality in this chapter is interpreted in the strictest sense, that is to say the interpreters' cultural and educational backgrounds, their age, sex, and political affiliations and, finally, their status as insiders or outsiders. However, perception of the role of interpreters—and thus of their positionality—differs considerably according to different narratives. By analyzing narratives of the Balkans war in which interpreters were protagonists, Catherine Baker (2010) has shown that interpreters were not perceived in the same way by all parties. They were considered by civilians—that is, by local communities—to be "friends" or "enemies", and this fact exacerbated the positionality issue. The same author considers that, notwithstanding this dual perception, the narratives of the interpreters themselves helped to forge the story of the conflict (2010, 141).

Recent studies seem to focus more on local interpreters who work in conflict zones or in the field and who were recruited by military or humanitarian organizations (Delgado Luchner and Kherbiche 2018) and on their role in humanitarian emergency situations in the context of violent conflicts (Todorova 2020). However, a whole category of interpreters has apparently been neglected: United Nations interpreters operating in the field, specifically in the Middle East. The only exception we have been able to find is an article written by Ruiz Rosendo and Barea Muñoz (2017) where the authors scrutinize an aspect often ignored in other sources; namely, the typology of the conflict per se and the category of staff interpreters working in the field for international organizations such as the United Nations. It is difficult to maintain that oaths or codes of conduct may resolve the positionality question, even if United Nations interpreters respect impartiality and neutrality as two core principles of their work. In fact, such codes, as stated by Delgado Luchner and Kherbiche (2018, 4) describe "how the interpreter *should* position herself/himself, and not necessarily how she/he *does* position herself/himself in practice". Clearly, the same thing applies to United Nations interpreters, having a clear idea of the institutional position that they have when fulfilling their role does not necessarily mean that interpreters always abide by these parameters.

3 The Organizational and Historic Context of the Research

The Office of the United Nations in Geneva, which constitutes the framework of the present analysis, hosts, inter alia, the Human Rights Council, which is the engine of United Nations human rights machinery.

United Nations interpreters may be staff members or freelancers but, in highly sensitive missions, it is the organization's practice to send staff members. They are considered to be less subject to intimidation or reprisals as they form an integral part of the United Nations mission, and they enjoy the same immunities in the performance of their duties as any other United Nations staff member. This undeniably contributes to the interpreters' perception of their role and utility, and it reinforces their sense of belonging to the United Nations. Like all other United Nations staff, they take an oath when they join in which they promise to serve the organization, its values and objectives. This would seem, then, to leave no room for personal questioning by United Nations interpreters as to how they position themselves in the field.

The specific historical framework chosen for this chapter on United Nations interpreters working in the field is the "Arab Spring". In fact, while it is easy to identify the beginning of the "Spring" with the protests in Tunisia in 2010, it is more difficult to determine when it ended. Nor is it easy to pinpoint the beginning of the "Arab Winter", a designation used by some authors to indicate the revival of authoritarianism, the rise of Islamic extremism and the emergence of large-scale conflicts in several Arab countries (Birnbaum 2017).

Events associated with the "Arab Spring" generated a higher than normal number of field missions for the United Nations. Since the uprisings took place in Arabic speaking countries or regions, United Nations interpreters having Arabic as mother tongue and French or English as second language were sent as part of these missions. Most of them, with some rare exceptions, were from the United Nations Office in Geneva. Field missions from the United Nations Office in Geneva fall into a number of different categories; however, for the purpose of this chapter and on the basis of the specific historical framework, only fact-finding missions, commissions of inquiry and ad hoc missions will be considered.

This research is confined to considering the positionality of United Nations interpreters in the context of the Arab Spring, on the basis of their own accounts. The main research questions raised in the chapter are: (1) does the positionality of United Nations interpreters change when working in her/his country of origin in a conflict setting, and (2) that are the main challenges that interpreters face in this context.

4 United Nations Interpreters During Field Missions

Researchers wishing to explore this subject face a number of major obstacles, first and foremost that of access. Conducting an ethnographic study as an embedded researcher in a United Nations field mission, in order to provide a detailed account of interpreters' work in the field, is not authorized. Understandable reasons of security mean that such an approach is not possible and that researchers must rely exclusively on the narratives of the interpreters themselves. The second obstacle consists in ensuring that the nature, date, and place of the mission, the different interlocutors involved and the totality of the information they exchange are not revealed. United Nations interpreters work under oath, and confidentiality is of paramount importance for them, just as it is for interpreters in general. Their personal behavior while on duty reflects the image of the organization, and disclosing any information obtained during the course of their duties would amount to a sanctionable act of professional misconduct. These are red lines and they are not to be crossed, as is reflected in the accounts of the interviewees. The main features of the missions that emerge from those accounts are sensitiveness, confidentiality, and danger.

I should add that my own insider position as a United Nations interpreter—and, more specifically, an Arabic interpreter—made it easier for me to select the interviewees as I possessed information about the missions, the interpreters who served on them and, to some degree, the complexity of the work involved. An outside researcher could not have had access to such a wealth of information. Nonetheless, I was also conscious of the problems raised by my insider status (Labaree 2002). Conveying my colleagues' accounts conferred a profound responsibility on me, as I had to decide, irrespective of confidentiality, what information I was willing or unwilling to reveal about my colleagues and my organization (Humphrey 2012). This meant that I had a dual identity (Shaw 2011) as my familiarity with the topic and with the interviewees themselves entailed the potential disadvantage of me assuming a biased posture (Drake 2010) holding information that are of public domain and that cannot be qualified as confidential. Moreover, the fact that I shared similar experiences with the respondents also represented a risk: the interviewees could hold back important information considering it obvious or superfluous to a fellow interpreter and staff member. I took every care during the interviews to ask detailed and exhaustive questions in the hope that the respondents give lengthy and complete answers.

5 Selection of the Participants and Methodology

To answer the research questions, a highly ad hoc mission with enquiry duties was selected: a United Nations team formed of military and non-military personnel sent to an Arabic speaking country and accompanied by four United Nations interpreters. The difficulty was related to the long working hours for a variety of users, the complex language combination and the extensive use of dialects. Two of the participating interpreters were selected to participate in this study: a male and a female, one a national of the country concerned, the other a non-national but perfectly conversant with the local dialect. The national interpreter had been on field missions in the country of the non-national while the non-national had also been on field missions in her/his own country. This made it possible to make a more precise comparison. The gender choice was random as the selected mission was not gender sensitive, and the main criterion was to choose interpreters with similar profiles. In this case, both had a master's degree in interpretation from a renowned European interpretation school, both had lived outside their countries of origin since they had graduated, and both were about the same age. In addition, they both had similar years of experience although one had been a United Nations staff member for less than ten years. This last element was not considered to be relevant as the interpreter in question had a long career as a freelancer in international organizations.

Through semi-structured interviews and open-ended questions according to DiCicco-Bloom and Crabtree (2006) qualitative data was collected using research questions requiring qualitative answers. The topics raised in each narrative were compared in order to gain a better understanding of the variables that outline the positionality of national and non-national interpreters.

However, it is important not to generalize the findings. Such a generalization would require a much larger number of interviewees of the same typology working under similar circumstance. This, to our knowledge, has not occurred during the historical period examined.

Finally, distance with events can cause memory lapses, and the feelings and impressions that interpreters had on the spot may be distorted. This is a very human phenomenon. However, as far as the present essay is concerned, we will presume that the memory of our two narrators did not suffer similar shortcomings, and such a variable is, in any case, beyond the control of respondents and researchers.

6 Interpreters' Positionality

It is important to explain at the outset that neither of the two interpreters was surprised when the purpose of the interview was explained to them. The announced topic was that of "considering the dual position of interpreters as insiders and outsiders". The stage was set by identifying the mission that had been chosen to serve as the background of the interview. Neither of the two interpreters asked what was meant by "dual position" and their answers made it clear that they fully understood the concept. This leads us to think that both respondents had internalized the principles of neutrality and impartiality as a major component of their professional profile in general, but especially as United Nations staff members, but also that being a national may require her/him to double her/his vigilance in order to avoid any misconduct.

> National Interpreter: I had a stake in the mission. I was a national and a United Nations interpreter at the same time (…) but I maintained a great deal of neutrality during the whole mission.
>
> Non-national interpreter: To answer your question, did I feel involved, did I see myself as United Nations staff or as an outsider? I felt that I was a full-fledged member of United Nations staff. The head of mission treated

> us as members of the team, we were included in all the briefings. We were never excluded from any meeting.

The answer of the non-national interpreter shows that for her/him being an insider meant being considered primarily as a United Nations staff member and allowing her/him to understand the "inside story". Such a reflection deserves to be deeply considered in future works, and it supports the thesis of Bos and Soeters (2006) for whom interpreters must acquire a deep understanding of the conflict in which they are interpreting and its dynamics.

The mission had a heavy emotional weight for the national interpreter who said as much at the beginning of the interview.

> National interpreter: I was eager to go and to be part of the international effort of peace and stabilization in my own country, but I had mixed feelings too, how would it feel to be there?

The non-national interpreter did not express a specific emotional state before being explicitly asked to describe her/his own feelings. Then, the overall feeling that did emerge was one of concern and fear for safety. It should be noted that interpreters could hear the sounds of explosion. This significant detail was related only by the non-national interpreter.

> Non-national interpreter: As an interpreter, first you are scared. An attack took place nearby, let alone the fact that the area was bombed from time to time. Mortar shells were falling not far from our hotel. You could look out of the window and see plumes of smoke around the city. You could see fighter bombers in action. You could see and hear them. It was scary.

The emotionally charged expressions used by the national interpreter raised the question about whether he/she was able to discharge her/his duties properly. If the experience was so overwhelmingly trying, did the interpreter feel the need, at any moment, to discuss her/his dual position? It was clear from the answer that the real test was not to recognize the dual position but to maintain confidentiality, another core principal of the interpreter's work. Maintaining confidentiality does not suggest, of course, struggling not to reveal confidential information, but it means avoiding expressing psychological distress during and after the mission.

> National interpreter: I felt the need to express my feelings and I did it with my doctor, with my psychotherapist.

While recognizing the need for psychological support, the national interpreter did not allude to the effect that such an emotional stress had on the quality of interpretation. It is worth mentioning that to express her/his psychological distress, the interpreter chose to entrust a doctor who is another professional who works under oath.

The narratives also showed how, by inverting the situation, the positionality of the interpreter changes. The national interpreter was asked to describe her/his experience during a field mission carried out in the country of the other respondent. Although we inverted the roles, we kept the same nomenclature. Despite recognizing the difficulty of such missions, the interpreter confirmed that it could not be compared to the difficulty of working in her/his own country.

> National interpreter: the missions I had done there [in the country of the other interpreter] had nothing to do with how I felt during the mission in my own country. The latter was a very difficult mission.
>
> (…) When I was on an inquiry mission there [in the country of the other interpreter], it was very, very tough. It was very difficult to hold back your tears when you were interpreting. But then I forgot it. It did not touch me emotionally as much as the mission in my own country.

The non-national made a distinction between working in her/his own country and interpreting for witnesses there. While focusing exclusively on the positive aspects of working in her/his country—where the interpreter was familiar with the dialect, the humor, and so on—interpreting for witnesses was clearly described as being more stressful. This difficulty was recognized also by the national interpreter. Interpreting testimonies seemed to be one of the most stressful exercises for both respondents.

Non-national interpreter: In my country, I am a national, I have a local accent and I understand everything that is being said, I know the sense of humour and the exact way to ask a question to get the information the delegation wants. I convey the message in a culturally sensitive way that is understandable by the other party more than it is in another country. In my country it's different. No one can say that they were misunderstood by the interpreter. Besides, you feel more at ease and you know the situation very well.

On witnesses:

National interpreter: You must be callous not to be emotionally involved. Maybe some people manage to control themselves, I can control myself obviously, but it is very difficult especially when they interview witnesses who tell you about their tribulations and what they have been through.

Non-national interpreter: Interpreting for witnesses is different, of course that has a psychological impact on you, especially if it is reminiscent of something you have experienced.

(…) Since you know the situation in your own country, you know the kind of atrocities that people are going through and the suffering they are facing. You are prepared in advance for what they are going to say. This is a good protection mechanism. Your subconscious is prepared, it becomes easier

The same interpreter then added:

Non-national interpreter: Having been a field interpreter for many years I have had to find a coping mechanism, but it does not work all the time. I had PTSD following a mission that was not to my own country. It was not a particularly difficult mission, but it created a breach that led to an overall explosion. It transformed all the hidden memories into a PTSD.

The same respondent, then, claimed that she/he had a mechanism to cope with painful testimonies, though recognizing that it did not always serve its purpose. And, although working in one's own country in a non-conflictual setting was a factor that facilitated work, for the reasons given above, listening to witnesses to violent events or atrocities in one's own country was an important variable that could shift positionality.

Both interpreters addressed how they were perceived by users especially government officials. The national interpreter told two stories of how government officials has tried to intimidate her/him. On one occasion, an official had publicly told a distorted story about a close relative of the interpreter and had asked her/him to interpret it to the delegation. On another, a relative who had come to meet the interpreter at the hotel had subsequently been interrogated by the authorities. The non-national interpreter considered that he was treated as United Nations staff, on an equal footing with other members of the delegation.

> National interpreter: the story he told was very disparaging and very unprofessional. And it was meant to be disparaging. He said it in Arabic, and he was expecting me, as an interpreter, to translate everything. This is exactly what I did. I translated everything.
>
> Non-national interpreter: The interpreters were the only link between the two sides, but we were seated with the United Nations delegation, so we were part of the United Nations delegation. The government officials looked at us as one opposing negotiating party. They did not draw a distinction between interpreters and non-interpreters we were all United Nations personnel.

Another interesting difference between the two interpreters was the emotional impact that the mission had on them. While the national interpreter placed emphasis on the memories that haunted her/him afterward, the non-national seemed to be more focused on what an interpreter "should" do in such a situation but also acknowledged that stress does have an impact on interpretation quality. It is worth noting that this is the first and last time that interpretation quality was alluded to in either of the two narratives.

A possible explanation of this fact may be that, when exploring their positionality as insiders or outsiders, both interpreters focused spontaneously and exclusively on the psychological effect that the shift in position might have on them. They did not seem to consider the possible pernicious impact it might have on the quality of their work. This might be because they believed that this it was self-evident that their work would be affected. Alternatively, it might be that they considered that the extra emotional stress they felt in the situation of interpreting in their own country was the price they had to pay to maintain the same quality of work in difficult circumstances.

> National interpreter: It was too trying; the memories are still there. I cannot get rid of them.
>
> Non-national interpreter: I didn't feel more involved. Being professional, your main concern is to convey the message. But there are many ways to convey the message. We are human beings, sometimes we are more at ease with some than with others. When you are more at ease, you may be even more accurate.

The respondents were asked, if they had the power to choose who to send on mission, whether they would send interpreters to work in their own home countries. The two interpreters had different opinions. The national interpreter indicated that it would depend on the sensitiveness of the mission, thereby aligning with the non-national interpreter's view that interpreters are most at ease in their own country and may be more helpful for the delegation in a non-violent or conflictual setting. The non-national interpreter stated that no distinction should be drawn between nationals and non-nationals when selecting staff for a field mission, arguing that if she/he can do it, any other interpreter can.

We should add that, in the current case, violence was a new phenomenon in the national interpreter's country whereas the non-national's country has been riven by conflict for many decades. This may have given the non-national interpreter greater exposure to distressing accounts and made her/him more accustomed to such situations.

> National interpreter: An interpreter should always remember that she/he is a United Nations interpreter. I went on other missions to my country and it was great. Being a national who knows perfectly the dialect and the cultural background allowed me to help the United Nations delegation in ways that others would not have been able to. If the interpreters feels that he/she cannot deal with the psychological distress of it it is his/her duty to abstain.

> Non-national interpreter: You are there as a United Nations staff member and you have to have that mindset of serving the United Nations cause which is for me a noble cause. My experience as an interpreter in the field is the demonstration of that it is possible to overcome these difficulties, and being at the United Nations reinforced that kind of feeling.

7 Conclusion

Sooner or later, interpreters working in the field will inevitably come face to face with the positionality dilemma, and United Nations interpreters are not exempted from this rule. Their status as international staff means that they enjoy certain immunities when on duty. This provides them with some degree of protection and makes it less likely that they will fall victim to abusive power relations in the triangle of United Nations users, third-party users and interpreters.

Our findings point to a change in the positionality of United Nations interpreters when they work in their own countries. What emerges from the narratives is that the confidentiality of the information exchanged between the parties was not a challenge the respondents had to face. The position of United Nations interpreters as insiders or outsiders does not appear to be the source of any professional misconduct, and neither of the interpreters in our study reported linguistic shortcomings or behavioral alteration, but their dual position obviously produced emotional stress.

By working during troubled and emotionally charged times such as the "Arab Spring", interpreters working in their own countries found themselves witnessing a dramatic change without having the luxury of knowing beforehand the nature of the context they were embarked on, nor possessing an established coping mechanism to face the challenge. This had an impact on their perception of themselves and of their work. By stressing that she/he acted in full respect of neutrality, notwithstanding the difficulty of her/his position we can likely presume that the national interpreter believed this to be the core challenge. The strong emotional stress may be understood, not only as the natural outcome of interpreting accounts of harsh events, but also as the result of a deliberate effort the national interpreter made to abide by an internalized code of conduct. This indicates that ethical issues are an integral part of the perception interpreter have of themselves and of what they should do.

In addition, the issue of coping mechanisms, which arose during the interviews, points to the need to consider the possibility of offering psychological assistance designed specifically to interpreters. It is true that, when United Nations interpreters are sent into conflict situations in the field, a lot of variables are out of the organization's control, but one constant factor is the changing positionality of the interpreter according to the typology and location of the conflict in question. And it is this constant that the organization should bear in mind when organizing these field missions.

We believe that it is neither necessary nor desirable to establish rules that would prevent United Nations interpreters from working in the field in their own countries. However, we are also of the view that it is not unreasonable to say that interpreters should be offered prior training, in order to guarantee that missions' goal of neutrality and impartiality can be attained at a lower psychological cost.

References

Askew, Louise, and Myriam Salama-Carr. 2011. Interview: Interpreters in Conflict – The View from Within. *Translation Studies* 4 (1): 103–108.

Baigorri Jalón, Jesús. 2004. *Interpreters at the United Nations. A History*. Salamanca: Universidad de Salamanca.

Baker, Catherine. 2010. It's Not Their Job to Soldier: Distinguishing Civilian and Military in Soldiers' and Interpreters' Accounts of Peacekeeping in 1990s Bosnia-Herzegovina. *Journal of War and Culture Studies* 3: 137–150.

———. 2012. Opening the Black Box: Oral Histories of How Soldiers and Civilians Learned to Translate and Interpret During Peace Support Operations in Bosnia-Herzegovina. *Special Issue "Making Educational Oral Histories in the 21st Century". Forum d'histoire orale 32.*

Baker, Mona. 2010. Interpreters and Translators in The War Zone: Narrated and Narrators. *The Translator* 16: 197–222.

Birnbaum, Jean. 2017. Gilbert Achkar face à l'hiver arabe. *Le Monde*, March 2.

Bos, Geesje, and Joseph Soeters. 2006. Interpreters at Work: Experiences from Dutch and Belgian Peace Operations. *International Peacekeeping* 13: 261–268.

Delgado Luchner, Carmen, and Leila Kherbiche. 2018. Without Fear Or Favour? The Positionality of ICRC and UNHCR Interpreters in the Humanitarian Field. *Target* 30 (3): 415–438.

Delisle, Jean, and Judith Woodsworth. 2012. *Translators Through History*. Amsterdam: John Benjamins.

DiCicco-Bloom, Barbara, and Benjamin F. Crabtree. 2006. The Qualitative Research Interview. *Medical Education* 40: 314–321.

Drake, Pat. 2010. Grasping at Methodological Understanding: A Cautionary Tale from Insider Research. *International Journal of Research and Method in Education* 33 (1): 85–99.

Encel, Frédéric. 2014. *Géopolitique du Printemps arabe*. Paris: Presses universitaires de France.

Humphrey, Caroline. 2012. Dilemmas in Doing Insider Research in Professional Education. *Qualitative Social Work* 12 (5): 572–586.

Inghilleri, Moira. 2003. Habitus, Field and Discourse. Interpreting as a Socially Situated Activity. *Target* 15: 243–268.

———. 2010. You don't Make War without Knowing Why. The Decision to Interpret in Iraq. *The Translator* 16 (2): 175–196.

Labaree, Robert V. 2002. The Risk of 'Going Observationalist': Negotiating the Hidden Dilemmas of Being an Insider Participant Observer. *Qualitative Research* 2 (1): 97–122.

Moser-Mercer, Barbara, and Grégoire Bali. 2008. Interpreting in Zones of Crisis and War: AIIC. http://aiic.net/page/2979/interpreting-in-zones-of-crisis-and-war/lang/1.

Palmer, Jerry. 2007. Interpreting and Translation for Western Media in Iraq. In *Translating and Interpreting Conflict*, ed. Myriam Salama-Carr, 13–28. Amsterdam: Rodopi.

Ruiz Rosendo, Lucía, and Manuel Barea Muñoz. 2017. Towards a Typology of Interpreters in War-Related Scenarios in the Middle East. *Translation Spaces* 6 (2): 182–208.

Ruiz Rosendo, Lucía, and Clementina Persaud. 2016. Interpreters and Interpreting in Conflict Zones and Scenarios: A Historical Perspective. *Linguistica Antverpiensia* 15: 1–35.

Shaw, Ian. 2011. *Evaluating in Practice*. Farnham: Ashgate.

Todorova, Marija. 2020. Interpreting in a Refugee Context. In *Legal and Healthcare Interpreting*, ed. Eva Ng and Ineke Crezee, 63–82. London, Amsterdam, and New York: John Benjamins.

12

Interpreter-Mediated Encounters in Complex Humanitarian Settings: Language and Cultural Mediation at Emergency ONG Onlus

Maura Radicioni

1 Introduction

Humanitarian crises are defining elements of the current international geopolitical scene. As a direct consequence of wars, conflicts and migrations, civilian populations are often displaced from their homes and almost always witness a deterioration of their living conditions. This often entails a significant increase in mortality, both in the short term and in the long term. Such crises, defined by the National Research Council (2002) as complex humanitarian emergencies, have grown exponentially in recent years, with Europe facing its greatest migration wave since the end of World War II (OECD Migration Policy Debates 2015). The continent has witnessed a rapid surge in migratory pressure at the southern borders of the European Union (EU) in recent years, according to data as

M. Radicioni (✉)
University of Geneva, Geneva, Switzerland
e-mail: Maura.Radicioni@etu.unige.ch

M. Todorova, L. Ruiz Rosendo (eds.), *Interpreting Conflict*, Palgrave Studies in Languages at War, https://doi.org/10.1007/978-3-030-66909-6_12

recent as that compiled by the OECD's *International Migration Outlook 2018* (OECD 2018), the Study and Research Center of the Italian Caritas (Caritas and Fondazione Migrantes 2017), the UNHCR's and the IOM's *World Migration Report 2018* (IOM 2017), and the 2018 report on migration by the Italian Statistical Office (Istat 2018).

Against this backdrop, refugees and internally displaced people are faced with language and mediation needs which need to be addressed both in the immediacy of the war zone and in faraway areas. A number of entities and organizations play a role in this rapidly evolving scenario. Within the context of humanitarian aid provision, such language and mediation needs are met by several players, in various ways and at different stages of the aid chain. Professional translation and interpreting practices are being implemented alongside other strategies, such as using a lingua franca, resorting to bilingual staff as ad hoc language and cultural brokers or relying on trained cultural mediators and interpreters (Delgado Luchner 2018).

The role played by humanitarian organizations and nongovernmental organizations (NGOs) is paramount in such a context. NGOs are powerful political players that provide assistance to victims of war and conflict, refugees, asylum-seekers and local communities in emergency and crisis situations. As they deal with individuals from a wide variety of language and cultural backgrounds, multilingual communication is vital to them. Translation and interpreting thus play a fundamental role for NGOs, as they are key components of the multilingual activity of these organizations.

In today's geopolitical scene, humanitarian organizations and NGOs also have a crucial role in Italy. The country has several such organizations active in the provision of aid, medical assistance, support to unaccompanied minors, as well as search and rescue operations at sea. In doing so, Italian humanitarian organizations and NGOs have provided valuable help and carried out activities that straddle the lines among a number of fronts: asylum procedures, conflict-related settings, healthcare and support to migrants and refugees, and legal assistance.

As entities active in multilingual and multicultural settings, humanitarian organizations and NGOs often resort to interpreters and cultural mediators (Kherbiche 2009; Moser-Mercer et al. 2013). These language professionals do not only provide language and cultural mediation in triadic settings but also advise and help refugees, migrants and asylum-seekers claim and negotiate their rights in the host country (Taronna 2016) in dyadic scenarios. According to Tesseur (2018, 1–2), "speakers from a wide range of languages come together and providing language mediation often forms part of NGOs' day-to-day work. In other words, translation and interpreting are keys to the functioning of these organisations, as they negotiate and interact between actors from a wide variety of cultural and linguistic backgrounds in the work they conduct."

As Todorova (2020, 64) points out, interpreters working in complex humanitarian settings do not just enable communication "by transferring content from one language into another." The role played by language professionals in complex humanitarian scenarios, specifically those involving migrants and refugees, is that of active participants in a mediation process (Todorova 2020, 74).

In this chapter, I aim to explore language and mediation practices carried out by the Italian medical NGO Emergency ONG Onlus (Emergency) in the complex humanitarian settings in which its interpreters (or cultural mediators, as the organization likes to call them) operate in Italy. Although Emergency is also active in war-torn zones abroad, this chapter focuses on its operations in Italian territory. The reason to concentrate on Emergency's projects in Italy is that the vast majority of its language professionals and cultural brokers work in clinics and mobile units within the framework of the Programma Italia; very few or none of its interpreters are employed in areas of conflict outside Italy, as language needs in war-torn contexts in other countries are often addressed by the use of a lingua franca or the role of bilingual personnel as ad hoc language and cultural brokers. By analyzing the role, profile, training backgrounds and tasks of the cultural mediators employed by Emergency for its Italian operations, I wish to contribute to the understanding of language and cultural brokering by an Italian NGO as a form, first and foremost, of cultural mediation. Based on a case study carried out at Emergency's Castel Volturno clinic, this chapter illustrates the multiplicity of tasks performed by the organization's language professionals in this complex humanitarian setting, as well as their broader role as cultural brokers and, ultimately, as humanitarian aid providers. The analysis reinforces the belief that translation and interpreting are culturally embedded practices and suggests that this is even more so in complex humanitarian settings, where cultural differences between communicating parties may lead to conflicts and exacerbate an already difficult situation and where interpreters operating as cultural mediators are expected to solve conflicts and facilitate communication.

2 Emergency ONG Onlus

Emergency is an independent humanitarian NGO set up in 1994 with the objective of providing free medical and surgical treatment to civilian victims of war, land mines and poverty in war-torn scenarios outside Italy. The organization, currently active in seven countries (Afghanistan, Central African Republic, Iraq, Italy, Sierra Leone, Sudan and Uganda), is in the process of implementing the African Network of Medical Excellence (ANME), an innovative model of humanitarian healthcare designed to promote the construction of medical centers of excellence across Africa. The ANME has received support from the Health Ministries of a number of African countries. The Salam Centre for Cardiac Surgery in Khartoum, Sudan, which opened in 2009, was the first of the facilities in the ANME network. The second, the Centre of Excellence in Pediatric Surgery in Entebbe, Uganda, is scheduled to open in the coming months.

Besides its activities abroad, Emergency has been running projects in Italy within the framework of its Programma Italia since 2006. According to Bellardinelli (2017), the program consists of a number of humanitarian projects whose goal is to give assistance to vulnerable populations and people in need in particular situations of emergency or natural disasters, as well as to provide free healthcare and social and health-related guidance services. The latest official figures published by the organization show that, as of December 2020, Emergency has provided more than 420,000 free-of-charge consultations to individuals who would otherwise have no access to medical care. Consultations are currently provided in a number of outpatient clinics located in Palermo, Marghera, Sassari, Polistena, Castel Volturno, Naples and Brescia, where both general and specialist medical treatment is provided free of charge, as well as nursing, psychological support and health education. Patients are advised on how to gain access to the national healthcare system, as well as on what their rights are and how to assert them.

Programma Italia also makes use of politrucks, that is, mobile clinics that enable access to regions with few services and public healthcare facilities, such as agricultural areas, marginalized urban districts, localities hit by natural disasters and refugee reception centers. The politrucks, therefore, provide essential medical care where it is needed most. So far, mobile clinics have brought medical assistance to people living in deprived neighborhoods of Milan, provided sexual health information for sex workers in Castel Volturno, helped migrants and refugees landing in Sicily, supported the large community of agricultural workers in Latina and aided people affected by earthquakes in the center of the country.

Staff employed by the Italian NGO includes doctors, nurses, logistics experts and cultural mediators, that is, language and cultural brokers who carry out tasks of language and cultural mediation, social orientation and information provision to migrants and asylum-seekers in their dyadic and triadic encounters with the organization's medical staff and/or with authorities. The term *mediatori culturali*, or cultural mediators, is always indicated in the job descriptions for such positions in Programma Italia projects. The reference to the cultural component seeks to highlight the greater importance that the organization and the mediators themselves attach to their role as cultural brokers in comparison to their language mediation tasks.

All clinics, mobile units and centers run by Emergency in and outside Italy serve as highly innovative models of humanitarian intervention. Their aim is to bring high-quality healthcare to the patients treated, while asserting the right of each and every human being to receive such treatment free of charge. This is viewed as a fundamental human right, as enshrined by article 32 of the Italian Constitution[1] and as a "fundamental and inalienable right belonging to each member of the human family," in accordance with the 1948 Universal Declaration of Human Rights

[1] "The Republic protects health as a fundamental right of the individual and in the interest of the community and guarantees free treatment to the destitute" (Costituzione della Repubblica Italiana 1948, 10, my translation).

(United Nations General Assembly 1948). Hence, every day, Emergency offers healthcare based on principles of equality, quality and social responsibility. This is proudly stated in its "Manifesto for a Human Rights-Based Medicine" (Emergency 2020), signed in 2008 with the Health Ministries of the African countries in which it operates and whose reference to the principles of equality, quality and social responsibility also constitute the foundation of the organization's Italian operations.

3 Interpreting as Cultural Mediation

The often-cited and commonly endorsed definition of cultural competence as "a set of congruent behaviors, attitudes, and policies that come together in a system, agency, or among professionals that enable that system, agency, or those professionals to work effectively in cross-cultural situations" (Cross et al. 1989, 13) is particularly relevant when highlighting the competences needed by interpreters and mediators who work in complex humanitarian settings. In these, language professionals are called upon to mediate a variety of complex situations and are faced with numerous cross-cultural differences between the parties involved. This is especially the case when the complexity of a humanitarian scenario is enhanced by the various roles and settings where interpretation occurs, since these can rapidly change and force language and mediation professionals to shift from health to legal, administrative and social domains. Interpreters as cultural mediators take on several roles, such as that of empowering vulnerable individuals, and are active participants in the communicative encounter, with their cultural and ethical contribution being oftentimes necessary. According to Todorova (2020, 76), "the interpreter can assist in creating empowerment for the vulnerable party during the mediation process by providing cultural knowledge, and by being a strong advocate for the refugees when needed." This accurately describes the role of Emergency's cultural mediators in the complex humanitarian settings of the Italian clinics in which they operate. Defining cultural competence in the sense of Cross et al. (1989) can, therefore, help overcome cross-cultural differences in communication and foster effective treatment in interpreter-mediated medical, social and administrative encounters (Leanza 2005), as well as in complex humanitarian contexts.

The role of the interpreter as a cultural agent is now widely acknowledged among scholars (Angelelli 2004; Roy 2002; Wadensjö 1998). When called upon to deal with participants from various cultural backgrounds, interpreters and cultural mediators who work in community settings play different roles based on the context and the surrounding social and cultural values. This is also true for interpreters working for NGOs in complex humanitarian emergencies. They often use a variety of strategies to overcome language barriers in their aid chains as effective communication practices (Delgado Luchner 2018). In an attempt to clarify the definitions and descriptions of the roles of interpreters as discussed in the literature, Roy (2002) proposes a classification of such roles and suggests that interpreters can serve as either helpers, conduits and facilitators of communication or bilingual/bicultural specialists. In a later study, Leanza (2005) adds two additional roles for community interpreters in pediatrics, those of welcomers and of family support, with a clear extension of the function of medical interpreters in view of broader social and cultural spheres.

The role of the bilingual/bicultural specialist is particularly relevant for the purposes of this chapter. In the dyadic and triadic interactions between its health professionals and the migrant patients it treats on a daily basis, Emergency attaches great importance to the cultural skills of its mediators and puts them on an equal footing with language-based ones, as shown by initial research carried out with the cultural mediators working at the Castel Volturno clinic.[2] In the wake of the cultural turn in Translation Studies, which began in the 1980s, the focus has shifted from language mediation to cultural mediation, and translation and interpreting are now viewed as culturally and socially embedded practices. Since then, there is now almost universal consensus among scholars that interpreters need to have knowledge of the cultures of the languages they work with and that they "must be sensitive to the fact that they are

[2] The research study is part of an ongoing PhD project on humanitarian interpreting being carried out by the author under the supervision of Professor Lucía Ruiz Rosendo (Interpreting Department, Faculty of Translation and Interpreting, University of Geneva).

communicating across cultures as well as across languages" (Roy 2002, 351). Mikkelson ([1999] 2009) highlights the need for language intermediaries to be culturally knowledgeable, and Hale (2014, 328) warns against "the many complexities of potential cross-cultural misunderstandings," as community interpreters mediating between participants from various cultural backgrounds may encounter difficulties conveying the source message into the target message accurately due to cross-cultural differences. Hence the need for culturally competent language brokers, who, according to Todorova (2016, 2020), can help explain cultural differences and, in doing so, establish a sense of trust, reach a compromise and strive toward a mutually acceptable solution.

According to Wadensjö (1998, 75), interpreters "cannot avoid functioning as intercultural mediators," since interpreting makes it possible to identify nonlinguistic features and differences between people, such as differences in worldview (1998, 277). This particularly applies to Emergency's cultural mediators employed in Italy, who, within the framework of the research carried out in Castel Volturno, have on several occasions stressed the importance of a shared cultural background between interpreters and migrant patients to ensure effective communication. This attitude confirms that "the mediator actively contributes to the social construction of migrants' problems and to the enhancement of possible solutions thereof by extending institutional support, showing active listening, and reducing the risk of conflicts," especially if the mediator shares the migrant's cultural background and lays emphasis on "the meaning of culture and intercultural mediation in these interactions" (Baraldi 2018, 15).

The focus on interpreting as cultural mediation, with mediation concerning both language and culture, can be further clarified by the three analytical dimensions identified by Pöchhacker (2008) in analyzing interpreting as mediation: linguistic/cultural mediation, cognitive mediation and contractual mediation. According to this classification, linguistic/cultural mediation is basically a synonym for interpreting; cognitive mediation helps interpreters express their subjectivity as interpreters, thereby rejecting the concept of "translation machine metaphor" (Hale 2007) for interpreting; and contractual mediation facilitates communication and conflict management with a view to enhancing cultural understanding and solving (intercultural) conflicts. In Pöchhacker's view, a distinction should be made between interpreters and contractual or cultural/intercultural mediators, with a clear focus on contractual mediation, as this distinction helps avoid the notion that cultural mediators are preferred to professional interpreters in certain systems and institutions because they are considered more competent in managing intercultural relations and conflicts. According to Rudvin and Tomassini (2008, 247, emphasis in the original), the prominence of the cultural mediator over the interpreter and the issue of role are "even more interesting and dynamic in Italy compared to many other countries because of the prominence of the so-called '*mediatore culturale/interculturale*' [cultural/intercultural mediator], the '*mediatore linguistico*' [language mediator], and the '*mediatore linguistico-culturale*' [linguistic-cultural mediator]." The existence of different terms to refer to language and cultural brokers employed in public service interpreting and lately in humanitarian interpreting (HI) for refugees, migrants and asylum-seekers is likely to create general confusion and lack of clarity about the terms used in Italy. The Italian Turco-Napolitano Law no. 40/1998 itself (Parlamento italiano 1998) uses the Italian terms *interprete*, *mediatore culturale*, *mediatore interculturale* and *mediatore linguistico* (interpreter, cultural mediator, intercultural mediator and language mediator, respectively) as apparent synonyms, thereby highlighting "the existence of a multifarious, hybrid nomenclature [...] this spectrum simply reflects the complexity of role-definitions and definitions of the profession/discipline across sectors" (Rudvin and Tomassini 2008, 246).

In the humanitarian sector, in particular, the existence of hybrid nomenclature stresses the importance of interpreters' cultural skills, since the adjective "cultural" or "intercultural" is always referred to when indicating the language and cultural brokers active in complex humanitarian settings. This shows the need for them to possess cultural competence to cope with potential cross-cultural differences and solve intercultural conflicts.

4 Interpreting as Cultural Mediation for Emergency's Programma Italia: Roles, Responsibilities and Expected Tasks

Within the context of its Italian activities and specifically of Programma Italia, Emergency hires language and cultural professionals to carry out language and cultural mediation, as well as health and social service orientation. The language and cultural brokers employed by the organization are referred to as *mediatori culturali*, that is, cultural mediators, not as interpreters, which highlights the greater importance that both the NGO and the mediators themselves attach to their role as cultural brokers when compared to language mediation.

The tasks performed by Emergency's cultural mediators in the outpatient and mobile clinics in Italian territory are well described by the job announcement published in the organization's website.[3] The announcement states the same requirements in terms of skills and duties to be met in all outpatient and mobile clinics, where these professionals are to operate. Differences between individual job advertisements depend on the location where the cultural mediator is to be employed and mainly refer to language requirements, which vary depending on the different ethnic groups targeted by the clinic concerned (Italian, English and French are generally required, whereas Arabic, Romanian and some African languages and dialects are needed in a number of cases). Although relevant experience appears to be a necessary requirement in the social and health sectors, it is less demanded with regard to language mediation. According to the job announcement, the position requires both specific skills relevant to the professional role in question (i.e., to match the needs of migrant people with health and social services available in the area where they live) and a good knowledge of Italy's healthcare and social service facilities.

Other requirements include flexibility and a cooperative problem-solving approach, with the ultimate aim of finding the best way to help people access the care or assistance they need. To achieve this goal,

[3] Emergency (2020). "Cultural Mediator." Accessed 21 February 2020. https://en.emergency.it/job-descriptions/cultural-mediator.

cultural mediators are expected to mediate between patients and healthcare providers, as well as to liaise with local authorities, regional associations and the facilities of the National Health Service.

Interpreting is never mentioned among the duties and responsibilities that applicants are expected to carry out in Emergency's outpatient and mobile clinics in Italy. However, specific mention is made of cultural mediation in a number of instances, with the main duties and responsibilities of applicants including, inter alia, linguistic and cultural mediation in compiling medical files and linguistic and cultural mediation prior to and during medical examination. Even if not explicitly mentioned in the job requirements, cultural mediation is viewed as more relevant than language mediation, as has been expressed by the health professionals and cultural mediators working for Programma Italia and, specifically, in Castel Volturno, over the course of this case study. Candidates are expected to provide cultural mediation in carrying out duties, such as welcoming patients and/or health and social service users; proposing treatment options and provision of healthcare education, where necessary and always in agreement with the doctor (where present); accompanying patients in need of hospital treatment and offering assistance with reception and admissions procedures; and performing health and social service orientation activities (e.g., creating individual itineraries aimed at helping people integrate into the region, advising on regulations and rights regarding health or residency issues, cooperating with regional public and civil services, such as registry offices and health service registration, migrant services, police stations, prefectures, etc.). In this respect, Emergency's cultural mediators carry out several tasks and take on different roles. They amount to the model of the mediator as a "bridging figure," following which the cultural mediator "is given a great deal of responsibility—his/her mandate is not only to help the interlocutors avoid misunderstandings and anticipate areas of conflict, but also to construct, no less, a shared basis or cultural-cognitive platform between the interlocutors by facilitating comprehension and reciprocal understanding/agreement" (Rudvin and Tomassini 2008, 246).

Specific requirements include, among others, (1) qualifications (preferably in social sciences or economics, or a relevant professional diploma—no specific mention is made of translation, interpreting or cultural mediation courses), (2) professional experience in the field of health and social services or in organizations (public or private) that deal with immigrants or poverty alleviation, (3) willingness to work as part of a multidisciplinary team and (4) fluency in a number of languages (varying depending on the job's location). The minimum duration of cultural mediators' employment in the project is 3–6 months, after which Emergency may decide to offer a contract extension of up to 12 months.

4.1 Interpreting for NGOs in Complex Humanitarian Emergencies as a Form of Humanitarian Aid Provision

For the purposes of this chapter, the author maintains that the dialogue interpreting and mediation activity performed by cultural mediators working for Emergency in its Italian clinics, specifically in Castel Volturno, should be considered a form of humanitarian interpreting (HI), as defined by Delgado Luchner and Kherbiche (2018, 17):

> The term "humanitarian interpreting" describes interpreting practices that fall within the legal framework of International Humanitarian Law (IHL) and International Refugee Law and aim to enable humanitarian organisations to communicate with public authorities and protected individuals/beneficiaries, in order to allow the latter to access their rights. Humanitarian interpreters are members of the humanitarian field (aid providers, beneficiaries or both), who work in contexts characterized by human suffering, vulnerability and stark power asymmetries.

Emergency's cultural mediators do not perform only medical interpreting or interpreting in community settings; they take on various roles and carry out tasks that are at the intersection between health mediation, humanitarian aid provision and social service provision. The interactions they mediate are more varied than encounters in institutionalized medical contexts or administrative settings with authorities, which indicate that these cultural mediators operate in a much broader spectrum.

Emergency's own bylaws confirm the status of the cultural mediators it employs as aid workers. In them, the organization explicitly indicates that its activities should be contextualized within the legal framework of International Humanitarian Law (IHL), including the 1949 Geneva Conventions and the 1954 Hague Convention. Furthermore, the NGO refers to the International Human Rights Law (IHRL) as one of its major reference areas of legislation, including the 1948 International Declaration of Human Rights and the 1951 Refugee Convention. Article 32 (paragraph 1) of the Italian Constitution is yet another reference piece of legislation that Emergency aid workers refer to. It states that the Italian Republic "safeguards health as a fundamental right of the individual and as a collective interest and guarantees free medical care to the destitute" (Costituzione della Repubblica Italiana 1948, 10, my translation). Emergency, therefore, considers the right to health as a human right, with this principle representing the very foundation of all its actions, including the ones performed by its cultural mediators.

According to Delgado Luchner and Kherbiche (2018), HI is a suitable umbrella definition and reference framework for the encounters mediated by cultural mediators who work for Emergency. As further explained below in the case study of Castel Volturno, their activities include only language and cultural mediation in medical settings, as well as social and health orientation for migrants, to be carried out in both dyadic and triadic encounters. This allows language intermediaries working for Emergency to be viewed as actual aid workers along the entire aid chain followed by the organization.

4.2 Case Study: Castel Volturno as an Example of Cultural Mediation in Interpreter-Mediated Medical Encounters

Based on a case study of Emergency's Castel Volturno outpatient clinic, this chapter illustrates the language and cultural mediation practices of the Italian medical NGO. The Castel Volturno clinic is taken as an example of the work performed by the organization's cultural mediators within the more general complex humanitarian scenario of a highly degraded area, home to a large number of migrants and refugees.

Castel Volturno, in the southern province of Caserta, has some of the highest numbers of migrants in Italy and is characterized by urban degradation, illegal housing and businesses, environmental pollution and the strong presence of organized crime. A recent report by the Study and Research Center of the Italian Caritas (Caritas and Fondazione Migrantes 2017) estimates that foreigners represent a third of the resident population. Most of them are migrants who disembarked in the country's southern ports and have gone to Castel Volturno to work as farmworkers and prostitutes, mainly illegally, attracted by job and accommodation prospects offered by a widespread network of informal and illegal activities. Castel Volturno can be considered a frontier town, which is difficult to interpret and manage due to a number of reasons, such as the large numbers of migrants from several nationalities, the speed with which the population has settled down and the precarious living conditions in an area where rules are dictated by organized crime. The social context is characterized by low trust toward institutions, informal activities, very low employment rates (especially with regard to young people and women) and educational levels. Against this backdrop, extremely active and strong associations have started working in Castel Volturno over the years, providing a first emergency response to urban degradation and social exclusion. Emergency ONG Onlus is one of them.

Within the framework of its Programma Italia, Emergency has been active in Castel Volturno with a mobile unit since 2013 and a clinic since 2015. The staff includes four cultural mediators, one of whom is the clinic coordinator, a doctor, a nurse, an apprentice nurse and a pediatrician working on a part-time basis. At the clinic, migrants and other vulnerable groups receive free basic healthcare with the help of the NGO's cultural mediators. Social and healthcare services include general medicine, child healthcare, nursing, social and health orientation, health education and training. Besides the sex workers, who are mainly women from Africa (of Nigerian and Ghanaian origin), there is a large community of Romanians who have settled in the nearby Mondragone.

In addition to the outpatient clinic, a mobile unit also operates in Castel Volturno and the wider Caserta area, carrying out information-gathering and disease prevention activities targeted at this group of migrants: the aim is "to facilitate the access of sex workers to health services and to increase awareness of sexually transmitted diseases and behaviours to prevent risk."[4]

The patients treated at the Castel Volturno clinic are mostly migrant women (sex workers or women with gynecological problems), children and men employed in construction and agriculture, often in conditions of severe exploitation (a direct consequence of the unhealthy living conditions that these people experience). The social orientation service provided by cultural mediators is also extremely important, since most of the patients have illegal status and need to be referred to administrative offices for their documents to be issued.

As of August 2019, four cultural mediators work at the Castel Volturno clinic: two male (Italian) and two females (one Nigerian and one Romanian), whose ages range between 40 and 49 years. They have different backgrounds and qualifications in areas other than language mediation or translation/interpreting (political science, economics and cultural heritage). The Nigerian and Romanian mediators have a formal qualification in cultural mediation (900-hour course in intercultural mediation). Before working for Emergency, all four mediators had worked as cultural mediators for other NGOs (MSF and Save the Children, local NGOs), the public sector (local health companies and prisons) or international organizations. The languages mastered by the four mediators are Italian, English, French, Romanian and a number of Nigerian languages (Esan, Bini and Pidgin English).

As is the case with the other outpatient and mobile clinics of Programma Italia, the cultural mediators in Castel Volturno carry out language and cultural mediation activities in triadic settings, for example, supporting Emergency doctors and nurses during examinations, assisting migrants during external medical consultations or examinations, accompanying migrants to information and counseling centers or to hospital emergency wards, and dealing with the issuing of documents on behalf of patients, which will allow them access to the National Health Service. They also

[4] Emergency (2020). "Castel Volturno Outpatient Clinic." Accessed 21 February 2020. https://en.emergency.it/projects/italy-castel-volturno-clinic.

provide social and health orientation to migrant patients in dyadic settings: for instance, they take care of their registration at the clinic, inform them of their rights, help them get access to the National Health Service and give them basic health and social information. In short, by providing a wide range of services along the aid chain, including language and cultural mediation and social and health orientation, the cultural mediators at Castel Volturno fall within the definition of HI proposed by Delgado Luchner and Kherbiche (2018).

The case study being carried out at Castel Volturno has so far yielded interesting results. Participants in the doctoral research project are the interpreters and mediators hired by Emergency, the health personnel and the refugees/migrants requesting assistance. So far, a number of e-mails and telephone conversations were exchanged with the clinic's coordinator, a mediator himself and the other cultural mediators at the beginning of the project (Spring 2018). In October–November 2018, questionnaires with semi-structured interviews were administered to the cultural mediators. Finally, a preliminary visit was paid to the facility in the summer of 2019 to prepare and pave the way for the upcoming ethnographic work.

The research carried out so far has highlighted, among other factors, the importance of a strong focus on culture for interpreting practice, the role that cultural differences between migrant patients and Emergency health professionals might play on language mediation, the related difficulties for interpreters to ensure an effective transfer of meaning, and ultimately, the close correlation between the ability to successfully mediate between different cultures, on the one hand, and the effectiveness of care and compliance with treatment, on the other hand. According to one cultural mediator, "we are more effective if we share the culture of the migrant patient" (personal communication, 12 July 2018, my translation), which suggests that cultural differences are better overcome when mediation is carried out by a language professional with a shared cultural background.

There is a clear need for an intercultural approach that accounts for the differences in migrant patients' perception of certain parts or functions of their bodies, since all cultural mediators working in Castel Volturno have highlighted that migrant patients have an intimate, sometimes pantheistic and definitely spiritual view of medicine and healthcare. Only through the adoption of a truly intercultural approach in interpreter-mediated encounters can interpreters' cultural patterns be adequately translated into the patterns of individuals from different cultural backgrounds, and vice versa. This paves the way for what Quaranta and Ricca (2012) define as "intercultural medicine," that is, the set of linguistic and practical processes aimed at promoting the adoption of clinical protocols and a positive approach to treatment for migrants. Intercultural medicine is needed to integrate foreign patients' cultural patterns into Western health practices and narratives and avoid descriptions and information that might lead to the rejection of treatment.

A shared cultural background between mediators and migrant patients can coordinate and create a common ground with patients' system of values and beliefs and, ultimately, create a relation based on trust. In the words of one of the mediators working in Castel Volturno: "Language comprehension is definitely necessary; however, it is the ability to mediate between cultures [...] that can contribute to establish a relation based on trust and help the patient understand that treatment is needed" (personal communication, 21 November 2018, my translation).

Culturally competent mediators in the sense of Cross et al. (1989) are strongly needed, as cultural traditions and practices permeate the way in which interactions are conducted and have a strong influence on interpreter-mediated encounters. Cultural differences are also seen in the knowledge and practices that belong to migrant patients' culture of origin. Such practices show a parallel universe of care (acquaintances, relatives and friends) based on superstition, the evil-eye and specific cultural patterns. Therefore, forms of translation capable of mediating cultural differences and, ultimately, fostering trust and ensuring effective treatment are needed:

> when faced with complex languages full of [culturally embedded] metaphors and symptoms based on another symbolic logic, in their daily practice [cultural mediators] opt for solutions that tend to repeat consolidated strategies and select what information should be kept (because it is deemed meaningful) and what information should be rejected, as it is deemed to express superstition, beliefs, and prejudice. (Taliani and Vacchiano 2006, 105, my translation)

This clearly emerged during the visit to the Castel Volturno clinic, making it possible to detect strategies and tactics used by Emergency's cultural mediators that go in the direction illustrated by Taliani and Vacchiano (2006): use of more informal register and direct forms of treatment to establish a closer link with migrant patients and create a relation based on trust; use of simplified language in the description of procedures/treatments by health professionals; involvement of family members to convince migrant patients of the "goodness" of certain treatments and ensure their compliance; and use of figures of speech (metonymies and metaphors) to refer to names of places in a non-Western style, but following the logic of the migrant being cared for.

5 Conclusions

This chapter is a first attempt to describe the language and cultural mediation strategies of the Italian NGO Emergency ONG Onlus, through the investigation of mediation practices implemented at its Castel Volturno clinic. The aim was to stress the importance of an intercultural approach to healthcare and interpreter-mediated encounters in the specific humanitarian context of a clinic run by an NGO that provides healthcare services. The initial findings of the qualitative study and ethnographic observation confirm the importance of cultural issues, as interpreters and language mediators working in humanitarian settings are the first to be/become aware of potential cultural differences that might hinder communication. Cultural issues have to be accounted for to overcome cultural differences that might pose problems for effective communication and to reach a "cultural compromise" for health prevention, promotion, education and treatment.

While the present study has concentrated on the language strategies within a single NGO clinic, additional research in other clinics of the same organization or in other NGOs employing cultural mediators or resorting to similar language and mediation strategies is necessary for a more precise mapping of the language and cultural mediation strategies adopted in the complex humanitarian settings in which NGOs operate. Furthermore, the specificities of the context in which the cultural mediators at Castel Volturno operate warrant a more critical and detailed engagement with their roles, tasks and challenges, and require further analysis of issues such as ethics, neutrality, confidentiality and impartiality.

Acknowledgments The author would like to thank Emergency ONG Onlus, specifically its Programma Italia, for granting authorization to access the Castel Volturno clinic. The author would also like to thank the clinic's coordinator, Sergio Serraino, and all the cultural mediators working in Castel Volturno for the information shared and support given.

References

Angelelli, Claudia V. 2004. *Medical Interpreting and Cross-Cultural Communication*. Cambridge: Cambridge University Press.

Baraldi, Claudio. 2018. Interpreting as Mediation of Migrants' Agency and Institutional Support. A Case Analysis. *Journal of Pragmatics* 125: 13–27.

Bellardinelli, Andrea. 2017. Le attività di Emergency 'Programma Italia' rivolte ai migranti e persone in stato di bisogno. In *Conflitti, guerre civili, vittime e diritto internazionale*, ed. Maria Immacolata Macioti, 76–83. Roma: Mediascape/Edizioni ANRP.

Caritas, and Fondazione Migrantes. 2017. *XXVII Rapporto Immigrazione 2017–2018*. Roma: Centro Studi e Ricerche IDOS.

Costituzione della Repubblica Italiana. 1948. https://www.cortecostituzionale.it/documenti/download/pdf/Costituzione_della_Repubblica_italiana.pdf. Accessed 21 February 2020.

Cross, Terry L., et al. 1989. *Towards a Culturally Competent System of Care: A Monograph on Effective Services for Minority Children Who Are Severely Emotionally Disturbed*. Washington, DC: Georgetown University Child Development Center.

Delgado Luchner, Carmen. 2018. Contact Zones of the Aid Chain: The Multilingual Practices of Two Swiss Development NGOs. *Translation Spaces* 7 (1): 44–64.

Delgado Luchner, Carmen, and Leila Kherbiche. 2018. Without Fear or Favour? The Positionality of ICRC and UNHCR Interpreters in the Humanitarian Field. *Target* 30 (3): 415–438.

Emergency. 2020. The 'Manifesto for a Human Rights-Based Medicine'. Document 23. https://en.emergency.it/what-we-do/medicine-and-human-rights. Accessed 21 February 2020.

Hale, Sandra B. 2007. *Community Interpreting*. Basingstoke: Palgrave Macmillan.

———. 2014. Interpreting Culture. Dealing with Cross-Cultural Issues in Court Interpreting. *Perspectives* 22 (3): 321–331.

International Organization for Migration (IOM). 2017. *World Migration Report 2018*. https://www.iom.int/wmr/world-migration-report-2018. Accessed 21 February 2020.

Istat Archivio Migrazioni. 2018. *Mobilità interna e migrazioni internazionali della popolazione residente*. 13 dicembre. https://www.istat.it/it/files//2018/12/Report-Migrazioni-Anno-2017.pdf. Accessed 21 February 2020.

Kherbiche, Leila. 2009. Interprètes de l'ombre et du silence: entre cris et chuchotements (Réflexion sur l'interprétation dans un contexte humanitaire auprès du CICR). MA dissertation, Université de Genève.

Leanza, Yvan. 2005. Roles of Community Interpreters in Pediatrics as Seen by Interpreters, Physicians and Researchers. *Interpreting* 7 (2): 167–192.

Mikkelson, Holly. (1999) 2009. Interpreting Is Interpreting – Or Is It? *aiic.net*, December 14. http://aiic.net/page/3356/interpreting-is-interpreting-or-is-it/lang/1. Accessed 21 February 2020.

Moser-Mercer, Barbara, Carmen Delgado Luchner, and Leila Kherbiche. 2013. Uncharted Territory: Reaching Interpreters in the Field. In *CIUTI-Forum 2012: Translators and Interpreters as Key Actors in Global Networking*, ed. Martin Forstner and Hannelore Lee-Jahnke, 403–422. Bern: Peter Lang.

National Research Council. 2002. *Demographic Assessment Techniques in Complex Humanitarian Emergencies: Summary of a Workshop*. http://www.nap.edu/catalog/10482.html. Accessed 21 February 2020.

OECD. 2015. *Migration Policy Debates*, no. 7. Document 23. https://www.oecd.org/migration/Is-this-refugee-crisis-different.pdf. Accessed 21 February 2020.

———. 2018. *International Migration Outlook 2018*. http://www.oecd.org/migration/international-migration-outlook-1999124x.htm. Accessed 21 February 2020.

Parlamento italiano. 1998. Legge 6 marzo 1998, n. 40: 'Disciplina dell'immigrazione e norme sulla condizione dello straniero'. *Gazzetta Ufficiale* no. 59, 12 marzo. https://www.camera.it/parlam/leggi/98040l.htm. Accessed 21 February 2020.

Pöchhacker, Franz. 2008. Interpreting as Mediation. In *Crossing Borders in Community Interpreting. Definitions and Dilemmas*, ed. Carmen Valero-Garcés and Anne Martin, 9–26. Amsterdam: John Benjamins.

Quaranta, Ivo, and Mario Ricca. 2012. *Malati fuori luogo: medicina interculturale*. Milano: Raffaello Cortina Editore.

Roy, Cynthia B. 2002. The Problem with Definitions, Descriptions, and the Role of Metaphors of Interpreters. In *The Interpreting Studies Reader*, ed. Franz Pöchhacker and Miriam Shlesinger, 344–354. Abingdon: Routledge.

Rudvin, Mette, and Elena Tomassini. 2008. Migration, Ideology and the Interpreter-Mediator: The Role of the Language Mediator in Educational and Medical Settings in Italy. In *Crossing Borders in Community Interpreting. Definitions and Dilemmas*, ed. Carmen Valero-Garcés and Anne Martin, 245–266. Amsterdam: John Benjamins.

Taliani, Simona, and Francesco Vacchiano. 2006. *Altri corpi: antropologia ed etnopsicologia della migrazione*. Milano: Edizioni Unicopli.

Taronna, Annarita. 2016. Translation, Hospitality and Conflict: Language Mediators as an Activist Community of Practice across the Mediterranean. *Linguistica Antverpiensia* 15: 282–302.

Tesseur, Wine. 2018. Researching Translation and Interpreting in Non-Governmental Organisations. *Translation Spaces* 7 (1): 1–19.

Todorova, Marija. 2016. Interpreting Conflict Mediation in Kosovo and Macedonia. *Linguistica Antverpiensia* 15: 227–240.

———. 2020. Interpreting for Refugees: Lessons Learnt from the Field. In *Interpreting in Legal and Healthcare Settings. Perspectives on Research and Training*, ed. Eva N.S. Ng and Ineke H.M. Creeze, 63–82. Amsterdam: John Benjamins.

United Nations General Assembly. 1948. The Universal Declaration of Human Rights – Preamble. December 10. https://www.un.org/en/universal-declaration-human-rights. Accessed 21 February 2020.

Wadensjö, Cecilia. 1998. *Interpreting as Interaction*. London: Longman.

[illegible] 2008. [illegible] *Community Interpreting* [illegible] Amsterdam: John Benjamins.

[illegible]

[illegible]

13

Andalusia, the Principal Gateway to Europe for Migrants and Refugees Arriving by Sea: Access to the Right to Interpreting Services in Reception Entities for International Asylum Seekers

Estela Martín-Ruel

1 Introduction

In the following sections, we will look at some useful basic facts about international protection, highlighting those aspects that differ in Spain in comparison with other EU countries which receive people from third countries, and focusing in particular on the situation in Andalusia, one of the most important points of entry for migrants arriving in Europe. This will help us understand existing interpreting needs. We will then briefly describe Spain's refugee reception system and see how it addresses the provision of interpreting services, from a regulatory perspective, looking at the conclusions of some studies into the actual situation on the ground.

E. Martín-Ruel (✉)
Interglosia, Universidad Pablo de Olavide, Sevilla, Spain
e-mail: estelaruel@upo.es

M. Todorova, L. Ruiz Rosendo (eds.), *Interpreting Conflict*, Palgrave Studies in Languages at War, https://doi.org/10.1007/978-3-030-66909-6_13

Finally, we present our own results, obtained by extending the scope of an earlier study and then applying that study to almost all the international asylum seeker reception organizations in Andalusia.

2 Aim and Methodology

The study described in this chapter was preceded by a preliminary work (Martín-Ruel and González Rojas forthcoming) aimed at finding out and detailing how interpreting services are made available to migrants at the CAR (Refugee Reception Centre) in Seville.

CARs are public establishments regulated by the Ministerial Order of 13 January 1989 (BOE 1989). The Seville CAR, the only one in Andalusia, is one of four such establishments in Spain. T&I services in the CARs are governed by public invitations to tender organized by the *Junta de Contratación* (Contracting Board) of the Ministry of Employment and Social Security. That is one of the basic differences between CARs and the other entities mentioned further on in this paper. The technical specifications which accompany each invitation to tender describe the interpreting services required (Junta de Contratación 2017). However, they do not specify the training or qualifications the prospective interpreters are expected to have.

In this preliminary study, we focused on the nature of interpreting for international asylum seekers reception, as a specialized area of public service interpreting. The study highlighted the need for familiarity with bilateral interpreting techniques, awareness of the degree of formality appropriate to each situation, and awareness that the role played in this field of interpreting by factors like fidelity, impartiality and neutrality is not always comparable to that found in conference interpreting. It also underlined the need for a strict code of professional ethics which, considering the possible consequences of misinterpretation in situations of vulnerability where people's future is at stake, must be respected. We are, after all, talking about situations which "take the interpreter into the most private spheres of human life" (Hale 2010), where communication is going to be affected by feelings of shame, terror, guilt, suspicion, fear… and even by things like honor, respect, group identity and religion (Lázaro

2008). It is therefore necessary to maintain a difficult balance between empathy and the minimal degree of reservation needed to be able to maintain a professional attitude (Las Heras 2010). The interpreter needs to know when to adopt the role of *conduit*, *clarifier*, *culture broker* or *advocate* (Niska 2002), a scale of intervention in which *conduit* implies the lowest level of involvement and the highest level of invisibility and *advocate* implies the highest level of involvement and the lowest level of invisibility. This sensitivity is vital for both parties to understand each other at both linguistic and cultural levels (Kalina 2015) and can only be achieved through appropriate training and experience.

We found that manuals do exist which attempt to make good the lack of regulations governing the interpreter's role in international protection scenarios. For example, the Australian Refugee Appeals Court and Immigration Appeals Court manuals, *Methods and Techniques for Interviewing Applicants for Refugee Status* (UNHCR 1995), and the *Handbook for Interpreters in Asylum Procedures* (UNHCR 2017).

To observe how these guidelines are followed in the CAR in Seville we carried out a qualitative study based on a semi-structured interview with one of its officers. The main findings were that:

- Most interpreting services are accompaniment interpreting, with 198 being carried out at medical appointments, training venues, employment interviews, and so on as opposed to 73 on the CARs' own premises in 2017.
- Telephone interpreting is hardly ever used, and only in urgent cases.
- When CAR personnel ask for interpreters, they usually specify the sex and ethnic origin they require to avoid situations of conflict.
- English and French are often used as *lingua francas*.
- The languages in most demand in 2017 were: Arabic, Ukrainian, French, Kurdish, Sorani, Russian and English.
- Interpreters of French and English are usually Spanish nationals. Other interpreters usually have the foreign language as their mother tongue.
- CAR personnel often get the impression that the interpreters have received no professional training in T&I.
- Interpreting problems mentioned included: speaking or answering as the interpreter rather than for the asylum seeker, maintaining parallel

conversations without informing the other party of what is being said, summarizing information, not respecting the foreigner's cultural conventions.
- On occasions, ad hoc interpreters are used in emergencies or for little spoken minority languages, and this leads to problems of partiality.

Taking this first study as a point of departure, we extended its scope to look at the other entities involved in receiving international asylum seekers in Andalusia. The objective was to obtain a more general overview of how the right to interpreting services is being exercised in the region which constitutes the biggest point of entry for migrants arriving in Europe by sea.

The study was extended to cover another five entities apart from the CAR. This meant that it now covered almost all the organizations involved in the international protection program at regional level. The entities studied were the Red Cross, the Federación Andalucía Acoge, Accem, the Fundación Cepaim and the Fundación SAMU (specialized in unaccompanied children). All these foundations and NGOs include specific budget allocations for T&I in international protection. To protect their anonymity, the agencies will be referred to henceforth as: Entity A, Entity B, Entity C, Entity D and Entity E (not necessarily maintaining the same order in which they are listed above).

In February 2019, members of the Interglosia research group at the Universidad Pablo de Olavide set about making the operationalization of the construct, having first collected data drawn from existing literature and from our first results in the CAR. The aim was to outline the information we hoped to obtain in the interviews, taking into account theory and our own research interests.

We then designed a semi-structured interview. Since we were using a qualitative research technique, our goal was to describe a phenomenon on the basis of its characteristics and through detailed observation of the object of study. This was done by processing the collected data in a non-standardized way (Corbetta 2003, 66–67). Although this way it is more difficult to obtain generalizable data than in the case of quantitative research (Corbetta 2003, 391–392), the technique served as a support for constructing hypotheses and theories.

The interview included 17 questions on interpreting, 17 on translation, 4 on training for interaction with translators and interpreters and 1 last question about improvable aspects. This chapter focuses exclusively on interpreting.

A total of nine people were interviewed: a head of training, a psychologist, a center manager, a lawyer and head of a T&I service, a center coordinator, two people in charge of the international protection program, a social worker and the head of a legal department. The interviews were conducted and recorded in April 2019, having first obtained the corresponding permission. For each entity the recorded material had a duration of approximately 1 hour. In June 2019, all the interviews were transcribed and anonymized.

The results obtained were the product of a triangulation process (Denzin 1970), because the data used came from different sources and different times: existing research documents on the subject, the preliminary, preparatory interview done at the CAR in 2018 and the interviews done at the other entities in 2019.

3 International Asylum Requests in Spain

Before delving into the results of the study, it is first important to establish what exactly *right to asylum* means and to differentiate between international asylum seekers and refugees.

The *right to asylum* is a fundamental human right enshrined in Article 14 of the Universal Declaration of Human Rights, in the Geneva Convention of 1951 and in the New York Protocol of 1967. At European level, it is addressed in the 2017 European Union Charter of Fundamental Rights, while in Spain it was first recognized in the 1978 Constitution and legislated in more detail in the Asylum Law of 1984, this latter law being replaced by the current Asylum Law of 2009 (Ley 12/2009, of 30 October). It is defined as:

> Every person's right to seek protection outside their own country when fleeing from conflict or persecution which places their life at risk because

> of their race, religion, gender, sexual orientation, social class, nationality or public opinion. (CEAR 2018b)

According to UNHCR, the UN Refugee Agency, an *asylum seeker* is a person:

> [...] whose request for sanctuary is yet to be processed. Any current expulsion, deportation or extradition process will be halted pending a decision regarding the asylum request. (ACNUR 2014, 4)

A *refugee* is a person whose request for asylum has already been granted and who enjoys full refugee status in the host country. This implies a whole series of rights and obligations. Analysis of figures for asylum applications in Spain reveals certain trends which differ from those found in the other EU countries. These need to be explained before describing our study.

3.1 Countries of Origin

In Spain, for the past three years, the nationality of the majority of international asylum seekers is Venezuelan. In 2018, their numbers rose by 86% in comparison with the previous year (Accem 2019). Actually, five South American countries account for 63% of the total number of asylum applications: Venezuela, Honduras, El Salvador, Nicaragua and Colombia (Eurostat 2019). We believe these asylum seekers' main reason for choosing Spain is the common language, a crucial factor for integration in a host country. As Spanish speakers, they will be able to communicate with no need for interpreting services.

But people seeking asylum in Spain are not all from Spanish-speaking countries. The third country of origin in terms of asylum requests is Syria and the sixth is the Ukraine, followed by Palestine, while just behind Nicaragua (in eighth place) come Morocco and Algeria (Eurostat 2019).

In the EU as a whole, for four years running, the main countries of origin have been Syria, Afghanistan and Iraq. Of the top ten sender countries, five are in the Near and Middle East and Nigeria is the only African country. In 2018, Venezuela appeared on the list for the first time, due precisely to the number of Venezuelans seeking asylum in Spain (Accem 2019). If figures for the rest of the world are considered, 57% of all refugees received by UNHCR (2019a) come from Syria, Afghanistan and South Sudan.

3.2 Number of Applications

Another important peculiarity in Spain is that whereas in the EU the tendency in recent years has been for asylum applications to decrease (numbers fell by 9% between 2017 and 2018, and by even more in comparison with 2015 and 2016), here just the opposite has occurred: there has been a continuous increase, with numbers rising by 48% between 2017 and 2018. By 2018, Spain had very quickly become the fifth country in the EU in terms of the number of asylum applications received (Eurostat 2019).

The main host country in the EU over the last few years has been Germany, with 29% of the total number of asylum applications in 2018, although this figure represents a fall of 17% compared to the previous year. At global level, the country with the biggest increase in asylum applications in 2018 was the United States (254,300), followed by Peru (192,500), Germany (161,900), France (114,500) and Turkey (83,800). Surprisingly, Turkey was by far the country which actually hosted the highest number of refugees (3.7 million), followed by Pakistan (1.4 million), Uganda (1.2 million), Sudan and Germany (1.1 million each) (UNHCR 2019a).

As is well known, applications are one thing: decisions on applications are another. In Spain, while asylum applications increased, the number of decisions fell by 11%. Favorable decisions decreased too, with only 24% of all requests being granted as opposed to 35% the previous year. In other words, most applications—76%—were rejected. This figure is similar to that for the rest of the EU, where the number of decisions also decreased in 2018 (40% fewer than the previous years), 37% of the requests being admitted and 63% being rejected (Accem 2019).

3.3 The Situation in Andalusia

Particular attention should be paid to the figures for migrants arriving in Andalusia because it is here that the entities included in our study operate.

In Spain, the principal points of entry are Ceuta, Melilla, Andalusia and part of the Mediterranean coast. Most migrants arrive by sea, as can be seen in the UNHCR Spain Weekly Snapshot (UNHCR 2019b). Indeed, the Andalusian coast has become the principal route for migrants and refugees arriving in Europe by sea (CEAR 2018a).

4 Access to Interpreting Services in Spain's Reception and Integration System

International asylum applications in Spain are processed at national level, through the *Oficina de Asilo y Refugio* (Asylum and Refugee Office), of the Ministry of the Interior. The process of receiving and integrating asylum seekers pending decisions on their applications is run by the Ministry of Labor, Migrations and Social Security. Reception comprises of the following three phases, controlled by different entities, government agencies or NGOs (Dirección General de Migraciones 2017):

- Reception Phase, the first six months. Applicants are provided with accommodation and helped with health care, schooling, work training, Spanish-language classes and subsidies for food and clothing. Applications are also submitted for documentation, they are informed about the corresponding legal processes, and so on.
- Integration Phase, up to 12 months. The applicants' stay at the reception units comes to an end, but they continue to receive support to make them as independent as possible: for example, assistance with job-hunting or grants to help pay the rent for a home.
- Autonomy Phase, up to 18 months. The person may continue to receive one-off or sporadic assistance.

In all these phases, people arriving in Spain need to be able to communicate. That is, it is extremely important for them to be able to understand all the processes they need to negotiate and to express themselves sufficiently accurately in their given situation, because that may well be decisive for the granting or non-granting of refugee status and, therefore, the possibilities of staying or being deported to their countries of origin. It may even be a matter of life or death. Especially in the early stages when they still have not had enough time to learn the language. Everyday situations like going to the doctor, registering on the census or schooling their children, and more complicated things like receiving psychological treatment, interview coaching with a lawyer and the asylum interview itself with the police—which will require a meticulously detailed account of their lives—can therefore only be done with the linguistic and cultural mediation of an interpreter.

This may seem a very basic consideration, but reality shows that it is not afforded the importance it warrants. According to León Pinilla et al. (2016), in Spain "interpreting for refugees is carried out 'as best as can be'", and few people are aware of the problems that may be caused by misinterpretation. This is corroborated in the conclusions of the most recent university case studies to have been carried out in Spain in this field, which constitutes a relatively new line of research (Arroyo Philpott 2019; Chafchaouni 2019; Cruz-Contarini López 2019; Sabuquillo Jiménez 2019; González Rojas 2018).

Access to translation and interpreting (T&I) services in international asylum scenarios is guaranteed under several regulatory frameworks. At European level, Article 22 of *Directive 2011/95/EU of the European Parliament and of the Council of 13 December 2011* states that information will be provided to beneficiaries of international protection "in a language that they understand or are reasonably supposed to understand" (OJ 2011), while several sections of *Directive 2013/32/EU of the European Parliament and of the Council of 26 June 2013* speak of ensuring an asylum seekers' "right to the services of an interpreter" and "interpreting services" (OJ 2013). *Regulation (EU) No 516/2014 of the European Parliament and of the Council of 16 April* establishing the Asylum, Migration and Integration Fund also mentions "the provision of support services such as translation and interpretation" (OJ 2014). In Spain, the right to an interpreter is addressed, for example, in *Ley Orgánica 4/2000 (11 January)* regarding rights and freedoms of foreigners in Spain and their social integration, several articles of which establish the right to "assistance from an interpreter if they do not understand or speak the official language being used" (BOE 2000). *Ley 12/2009 (30 October)* governing the right to asylum and subsidiary protection also covers the "right to an interpreter" and to the "translation and interpreting of documents" (BOE 2009).

The problem, however, lies in the fact that none of these regulations specify what training and experience these interpreters should have. The criteria used when selecting them is therefore arbitrary and usually results in the recruitment of people who are not specifically qualified to do the job, with no assurance of an appropriate level of professionalism or ethical conduct. Very often, ad hoc interpreters are used: volunteers, "family members, people without the necessary training or skills who try to make up for their lack of knowledge with motivation and commitment" (Pérez Estevan 2017, 180). They are usually called on in emergencies, or to cover minority languages for which it is difficult to find professional interpreters, but their involvement generally creates problems since there are "[…] a high number of situations in which family members, often children, friends, neighbors or even staff from the institutions themselves who speak the user's language are asked to act as interpreters" (Hicheri 2008, 213).

5 Access to Interpreting Services in Reception Entities for International Asylum Seekers and UASCs (Unaccompanied or Separated Children) in Andalusia

In the next section, we will analyze the information we obtained about interpreting needs during interviews with managers from the refugee reception organizations which took part in the study.

5.1 Interpreting Situations

Of all the situations in which reception entities require interpreting services, one of the most important is the interview with an asylum seeker who has just arrived at the center. This interview is held within the first 15 days following the person's arrival: admission into the system, explanation of rights and duties, and legal, psychological and social services. Other important situations are the preparation of the asylum interview and all interviews with lawyers. Interpreters may also be needed for progress interviews or interviews to decide the extension of a person's stay at the center. Although beneficiaries attend Spanish language classes as a means of achieving the priority objective of becoming as autonomous as possible, their level is usually still elementary.

Outside the center, accompaniment interpreting may be required during visits to census offices, health facilities, schools, and so on. Entity D even employs interpreters in contextualization (Spanish cuisine, culture, etc.) and health (health services cards, childcare) workshops.

5.2 Types of Interpreting

Entity E is the only one that habitually uses telephone interpreting. All the others work with interpreters in face-to-face situations. In fact, they totally reject remote interpreting and only request it when there is no alternative due to the difficulty of finding an interpreter for a less common language (Entity D has eliminated it altogether). Their justification is that it is too cold and impersonal for extremely delicate, intimate conversations where the lack of non-verbal language removes a crucial element of communication and results in a loss of interpreting quality.

With regard to interpreters' resources, none of the entities reported that their interpreters work with notebooks, notes or glossaries except Entity D, where they had occasionally been seen writing notes in a diary or notebook. Entity B even preferred its interpreters not to take notes for fear that what they had written may later be disclosed.

5.3 Languages

In all the entities, Arabic (in all its different dialects) stands out as one of the languages most in demand, together with Ukrainian and Russian (often used for Ukrainians). English and French are also required, but these languages are usually covered by the entity's own personnel. To a lesser extent, there is also demand for Bambara, Urdu, Tigrinya, Georgian and Armenian.

All the entities except Entity C, which only has interpreters for French and Arabic, usually request the mother tongue of the beneficiary (even though it may be difficult to find an interpreter) rather than use *lingua francas*, which are sometimes used in cases of emergency or when dealing with very minority languages. The mother tongue of the interpreters employed is usually the foreign language.

5.4 Requesting an Interpreter

All the entities (except Entity C, which has its own staff interpreters) specify not only the language required but also the dialect and even the nationality when requesting an interpreter. For more sensitive situations (visits to a doctor or a psychologist), even the interpreter's gender. The aim is to make communication as comfortable as possible for the beneficiary, because he/she will be disclosing very personal information.

Interpreters are not usually informed about the situations in which they will be working. At most, they may be provided with the basic facts of a case just before the interview starts. Entity B conducts an initial interview in which the interpreter is given general information furnished by the Ministry of the Interior about international protection, basic vocabulary and habitual subjects, but no information is provided after that about specific cases. Entity D offers interpreters no specific information for reasons of confidentiality, and because they are not considered privy to such information. In Entity E, which offers telephone interpreting services, interpreters are only informed about the situation at the beginning of the call. Volunteers are provided with a little more information.

None of the entities reported cases of interpreters themselves asking for information beforehand.

5.5 Interpreter Profile

Entity C is the only one with its own staff interpreters. As employees, their role is very peculiar insofar that they act as mediators, intervening directly when they become aware of any conflict. They report conversations they may have heard in the center to their superiors, and sometimes the beneficiaries themselves turn to them for help with certain issues. They are also expected to translate internal documents.

The other entities outsource interpreting services for their more formal interviews to external companies, while for accompaniment interpreting in everyday situations, they usually rely on members of their own staff who speak the languages in question. Entity B has a T&I service controlled centrally from Madrid and Entity D also has an interpreter pool.

Nearly all the entities say they avoid ad hoc interpreters (family members, friends or other refugees) at all costs, except in emergency situations or for very minority dialects, and that they turn to volunteers only very occasionally. One exception is Entity D, which does use volunteers, usually university students who speak languages, but not necessarily T&I undergraduates.

Generally speaking, the different entities know nothing about the training and experience of the interpreters they hire, trusting in the company that provides them and neither insisting on or checking their credentials. Entity B does claim to seek "trained" individuals, but simply states by way of specification that "the French translator [...]is a person with two degrees, one in Journalism and one in Philology". The training required to work as a staff interpreter in Entity C is in mediation, social integration, primary education or social education.

5.6 The Ideal Profile

When asked about the skills the ideal interpreter would display, the following things were mentioned: Entity A: languages, care with non-verbal conduct, fidelity to the source language and preferably, although not as the main priority, prior experience in asylum situations and T&I; Entity B: trained people, prioritizing neutrality even above language competence, people with no vocation as a mediator, just "as accurate as possible" when interpreting; Entity C: above all, languages, and preferably an ex-user, of the same nationality and with training in social education or T&I; Entity D: familiarity with the social context, a certain amount of sensitivity, cultural and language competence, respect for the beneficiaries, ability to control their emotions (knowing their own limits so they can turn down participating in certain particularly harrowing interviews), people non-judgmental about the reasons for the asylum application; Entity E: ability to differentiate an interpreting job from a normal conversation, impartiality, people who will not express value judgments.

5.7 Interpreting Problems

The reception agency personnel interviewed highlighted the following major problems experienced when providing interpreting services:

- Parallel conversations, that is to say, exchanges which take place between the interpreter and one of the parties without the other party being informed or being able to understand what is being said. Sometimes so blatant that it is obvious that the beneficiary and the interpreter have been in contact outside the entity, exchanged telephone numbers, and so on. These are not allowed in Entity B, where they are automatically cut short.
- Impartiality; attempts to benefit the asylum seeker.
- Excessive empathy, interpreter's lack of control over his/her own emotions when transmitting sensitive information, especially when they share nationality.

- Tendency to intervene, to add information of their own, to answer on behalf of one of the parties, to be judgmental or to make personal comments.
- Excessive concision, giving the impression that information has been lost.
- Availability problems regarding dates, emergency cases or languages required.
- Mistrust in the interpreter's role: both by the entity (for fear that the interpreter is going to disclose information) and by beneficiaries (who fear that the interpreter may disclose information to the police, especially if it is the same interpreter in the asylum interview at the police station).

It should be noted that no entity made any mention of budget problems, because the international protection program has ministerial budget allocations which specifically cover T&I in reception entities.

5.8 Training for Interaction with Interpreters

No entities have ever received any kind of training for interaction with interpreters. Over the years, all of them have worked intuitively with interpreters or relied on self-learning through trial and error or from reading manuals. Neither do they have specific internal procedures for how to act, speak, position oneself or address the parties.

However, all the entities except Entity B (which believes it operates smoothly thanks to its long years of experience) would consider it very useful to receive this type of training. They all agree that the most ideal form of training would be short and intensive—so as not to paralyze their staff's activity—but also eminently practical.

6 Discussion and Conclusion

The main conclusions drawn after analyzing the information obtained in the interviews were:

Situations in which entities require interpreting services seem to be divided into two main groups: more formal interventions (reception interviews, interviews with psychologists and social or legal services), which usually need a paid, external interpreter; and more day-to-day interventions (accompaniment in appointments with doctors, schools, administrative agencies), where interpreting tasks are usually performed by employees of the entity who speak the required languages.

Nearly all the entities reject telephone interpreting, citing loss of non-verbal information. Non-verbal communication is always important, and even more so in delicate asylum-related situations. It also contributes to the climate of trust and empathy the entities seek to create to make it easier for beneficiaries to express themselves.

Interpreters do not usually use notes or glossaries. This may suggest that they are not accustomed to working with consecutive interpretation, preparation or documentation techniques—resources habitually employed in professional interpreting and which help transmit information as fully, faithfully and accurately as possible: one of the major problems observed in our study. One entity even prefers its interpreters not to write anything down for fear the information may be disclosed, indicating ignorance of the interpreter's professional deontology and duty to always safeguard confidentiality. This ignorance ties in with the fact that prior information about a situation (to allow proper preparation by the interpreter) is neither provided by the entities nor requested by the interpreters. Admittedly, sufficient preparation time is more difficult to get in this field of interpreting than in conference interpreting, but even so it constitutes a phase in the interpreting task that is fundamental for assuring the quality of the process.

The languages most in demand are Arabic (in all its different dialects) and Ukrainian. Russian is also often requested, but we found that it is usually requested for Ukrainians because it is easier to find Russian-speaking interpreters. If the five Spanish-speaking countries are removed from our list of the ten sender countries with the largest number of people seeking asylum in Spain in 2019 (Sect. 3.1), the remaining countries are Syria, the Ukraine, Palestine, Morocco and Algeria. Our data, therefore, concurs with that of Eurostat. Interpreters of French and English are also often requested, but to a lesser extent: not because fewer beneficiaries speak these languages but because they are usually covered by the entities' own personnel, reflecting a belief that a person who speaks a language will automatically be a good interpreter.

One positive thing about the way interpreting services are requested is that entities usually specify not only the language but also the dialect required, and even the nationality of the interpreter, thus anticipating possible conflicts or suspicions which may arise between beneficiaries and interpreters who speak the same language but are of nationalities such as Moroccan and Sahrawi, Turkish and Armenian, or Ukrainian and Russian. The same thing happens with gender. In the case of an appointment with a gynecologist or an interview about trafficking of women or gender violence, for example, the decision to request a woman interpreter will help beneficiaries from some cultures express themselves more easily and comfortably.

With regard to interpreter profiles, we found that interpreters are sourced from external companies or in-house pools or language services where no thought has been given to checking up on prior experience or training in T&I. We realize that it may be difficult for some minority languages, but for Arabic, French or English it would be perfectly feasible to use trained professionals. Furthermore, when training is required, the stipulation refers to general university-level training or, at best, training in mediation, social services or primary education. It is not considered necessary for the interpreter to have received training in T&I, even though such training would solve many of the problems that were reported. Admittedly, entities value training in social issues and this is not usually included in T&I training syllabuses in Spain. Nevertheless, considering the increase in demand, perhaps it should be introduced as a specialization or complementary skill.

The role required of interpreters by the different entities varies greatly in terms of the higher or lower levels of visibility and intervention mentioned earlier (Niska 2002). At one end of the scale is the *conduit role* required by Entity B, in which literality and neutrality are paramount, and at the other, the *advocate role* favored by Entity C, which seems to go beyond the strict remit of an interpreter in that it also involves acting as mediator, source of knowledge, educator and translator. As a happy medium, most entities require a certain amount of empathy, flexibility and awareness of the context of each job, together with an ability to adapt to cultural conventions without becoming emotionally involved, taking sides with the beneficiary or judging their situation.

The entities say they hardly ever use volunteers, and when they do it is only for informal or very urgent situations. Ad hoc interpreters like family members or friends are usually avoided, indicating an awareness of potential problems of biased interpreting.

Nearly all the problems the entities mentioned—related to impartiality, neutrality, adding or omitting information, emotion management—have to do with lack of training and professionalism, and even with the absence, among both agencies and beneficiaries, of a clear idea of the interpreter's role and professional ethics. Clarification of some of these issues could avoid misunderstandings regarding things like trust and confidentiality.

One noticeable fact was the absence of any economic problems. It would be easy to assume that interpreting problems in a social sector concerned with immigration, have their roots in the amount of money available, because non-profitmaking humanitarian associations like these may find it difficult to pay for well-trained professionals. Surprisingly, however, no entity reported not being able to afford to hire professional interpreters since, as part of a nationwide international protection program, they receive specific funding to cover their T&I needs. The problems, therefore, stem more from ignorance about the profession and its minimum requirements and, above all, from the outsourcing of interpreting services to companies which neglect both the training and the remuneration of the interpreters they hire. Entities usually trust in these companies' criteria and seem to know nothing about what is being offered or about what they should insist on.

Despite this lack of awareness and knowledge about the profession, however, the entities display a keen interest in receiving specific training and learning how to work with professional interpreters. They are open to improving the quality of the services they offer as much as possible. In other words, there may be ignorance but there is no lack of will. To paraphrase Las Heras (2012, 213), it can be said that hardly any quality services exist in this sector, and that those that do achieve any success do so thanks to the support of different organizations fighting for migrants' rights and to the effort and commitment of individuals who frequently interpret either "voluntarily or for a very low fee".

In the light of these conclusions, we are now working on an even broader study which will cover the largest possible number of reception agencies all over the region. Analysis of the results obtained in the face-to-face interviews will be extended to those obtained from a survey conducted electronically among reception professionals working in all the provinces of Andalusia (social and community workers, psychologists, lawyers, mediators, reception center coordinators, trainers, etc.). This more quantitative analysis is expected to provide information that will offer a more extensive and at the same time more detailed insight into the reality of how interpreting needs are met in refugee reception agencies.

References

Accem. 2019. *Informe 2018 sobre Protección Internacional en España y en la Unión Europea*. https://www.accem.es/dia-mundial-del-refugiado/refugiados-datos-2018/#tab-id-1. Accessed 3 July 2019.

ACNUR. 2014. *Los Medios de Comunicación y las Personas Refugiadas*. http://www.acnur.es/PDF/folletomedios2014_final_241014_20141112113618.pdf. Accessed 10 March 2018.

Arroyo Philpott, Almudena. 2019. *Estudio de caso: La visión y el papel del intérprete en la Asociación Comisión Católica Española de Migración (Accem) en la provincia de Córdoba*. Unpublished MA thesis. University Pablo de Olavide.

BOE. 1989. *Orden de 13 de enero de 1989*. https://www.boe.es/boe/dias/1989/02/02/pdfs/A03187-03187.pdf. Accessed 20 December 2018.

———. 2000. *Ley Orgánica 4/2000, de 11 de enero*. https://www.boe.es/buscar/pdf/2000/BOE-A-2000-544-consolidado.pdf. Accessed 20 December 2018.

———. 2009. *Ley 12/2009, de 30 de octubre*. https://www.boe.es/buscar/pdf/2009/BOE-A-2009-17242-consolidado.pdf. Accessed 20 December 2018.

CEAR. 2018a. *Informe 2018: Las Personas Refugiadas en España y Europa*. https://www.cear.es/wp-content/uploads/2018/06/Resumen-Ejecutivo-Informe-CEAR-2018.pdf. Accessed 23 April 2019.

———. 2018b. *El Derecho de Asilo*. https://www.cear.es/derecho-de-asilo/. Accessed 23 April 2019.

Chafchaouni, Safa. 2019. *Interpretación en contexto de asilo y refugio: el caso de Melilla*. Trabajo de fin de Grado. UPO.

Corbetta, Piergiorgio. 2003. *Social Research: Theory Methods and Techniques*. London: SAGE Publications.

Cruz-Contarini López, Carmen. 2019. *La labor del intérprete social en los contextos de asilo y refugio en los procesos de interpretación en las ONG de Sevilla*. Unpublished MA thesis, University Pablo de Olavide.

Denzin, Norman K. 1970. *Sociological Methods. A Sourcebook*. Chicago, IL: Aldine Publishing Company.

Dirección general de migraciones. 2017. *Sistema de Acogida e Integración para Solicitantes y Beneficiarios de Protección Internacional*. http://extranjeros.mitramiss.gob.es/es/Subvenciones/anos_anteriores/area_integracion/2016/sociosanitaria_cetis/manuales_comunes_gestion/documentos/Manual_de_Gestion_Sistema_acogida_2016.pdf. Accessed 16 January 2019.

Eurostat. 2019. *Asylum and Managed Migration*. https://ec.europa.eu/eurostat/web/asylum-and-managed-migration/data/database. Accessed 3 July 2019.

González Rojas, Carolina. 2018. *Estudio de Caso: el Servicio de Interpretación de Idiomas en el Centro de Acogida a Refugiados (CAR) de Sevilla*. Unpublished MA thesis, University Pablo de Olavide.

Hale, Sandra. 2010. *La interpretación comunitaria. La interpretación en los sectores jurídico, sanitario y social*. Granada: Editorial Comares.

Hicheri, Leila. 2008. Traducción e interpretación en instituciones públicas. *Actas del IV Congreso de Esletra*: 213–218.

Junta de Contratación. 2017. *Pliego de Prescripciones Técnicas que Regirá la Contratación del Servicio de Interpretación, Interpretación de Acompañamiento e Interpretación Telefónica, Traducción y Traducción Jurada por Lotes, para los Residentes de los CAR*. https://mnhlicitaciones.com/wp-content/uploads/2017/10/DOC20171003111718PPT-FIRMADO.pdf. Accessed 23 April 2018.

Kalina, Sylvia. 2015. Ethical Challenges in Different Interpreting Settings. *MonTI Special Issue* 2: 63–86.

Las Heras, Carmen. 2010. Solicitantes de asilo, refugiados, apátridas: un Babel invisible. In *La traducción y la interpretación contra la exclusión social*. Madrid: Centro Virtual Cervantes.

———. 2012. Derecho a servicios de traducción e interpretación, in *la situación de las personas refugiadas en España*. https://cear.es/wp-content/uploads/2013/05/Informe-2012-de-CEAR.pdf. Accessed 23 February 2018.

Lázaro, Raquel. 2008. Dilemas éticos del traductor / intérprete en los servicios públicos. In *I Foro Internacional de Traducción / Interpretación y Compromiso Social.* http://www.translationactivism.com/articles/Raquel_Lazaro.pdf. Accessed 6 May 2019.

León Pinilla, Ruth, Eivor Jordà Mathiasen, and Vicente Prado Gascó. 2016. La interpretación en el contexto de los refugiados: valoración por los agentes implicados. *Sendebar* 27: 25–49.

Martín-Ruel, Estela, and Carolina González Rojas. forthcoming. El servicio de interpretación en la acogida de solicitantes de protección internacional: el caso del CAR en Andalucía. In *Comunicación Interlingüística e Intercultural en Contextos de Asilo y Refugio*, ed. Francisco J. Vigier Moreno. Granada: Editorial Comares.

Niska, Helge. 2002. Community Interpreter Training. In *Interpreting in the 21st Century*, ed. Giuliana Garzone and Maurizio Viezzi, 133–158. Amsterdam and Philadelphia: John Benjamins.

Official Journal of the European Union. 2011. *Directive 2011/95/EU of the European Parliament and of the Council of 13 December 2011.* http://data.europa.eu/eli/dir/2011/95/oj. Accessed 20 December 2018.

———. 2013. *Directive 2013/32/EU of the European Parliament and of the Council of 26 June 2013.* http://data.europa.eu/eli/dir/2013/32/oj. Accessed 20 December 2018.

———. 2014. *Regulation (EU) No 516/2014 of the European Parliament and of the Council of 16 April.* http://data.europa.eu/eli/reg/2014/516/oj. Accessed 20 December 2018.

Pérez Estevan, Elena. 2017. Interpretación en contextos de asilo y refugio: una lucha hacia el bienestar. *FITISPos International Journal* 4: 174–182.

Sabuquillo Jiménez, Ángela. 2019. *Estudio de caso: ¿Cómo se valora en una ONG la figura del intérprete en la fase de acogida con mujeres procedentes de Costa de Marfil?* Unpublished MA thesis, University Pablo de Olavide.

UNHCR 1995. *Metodología y técnicas para entrevistar a solicitantes de la condición de refugiado.* https://www.refworld.org/cgi-bin/texis/vtx/rwmain/opendocpdf.pdf?reldoc=y&docid=50ac91d82. Accessed 23 April 2018.

———. 2017. *Handbook for Interpreters in Asylum Procedures.* Viena: UNHCR Austria.

———. 2019a. *Figures at a Glance.* https://www.unhcr.org/figures-at-a-glance.htm.l. Accessed 3 July 2019.

———. 2019b. *Spain Weekly Snapshot.* https://reliefweb.int/sites/reliefweb.int/files/resources/70146.pdf. Accessed 3 July 2019.

14

Interpreting for Refugees in Hong Kong

Marija Todorova

1 Introduction

Interpreting for refugees is a topic that has been gaining more prominence in the past decade due to the increased patterns of migratory movements toward Western Europe caused by conflicts in the Middle East and Africa. However, instances of large number of people being forced to flee their homes in order to protect their lives have not been unknown throughout human history. Over the last century, global population displacements have been caused by the two world wars, regional conflicts, and many civil wars throughout the world. Although these movements have been well documented and studied by historians, the importance of interpreting for refugees has long been invisible in the academic context. Still, interpreting is essential in order to obtain the status of refugee and receive the necessary legal and humanitarian protection and assistance.

M. Todorova (✉)
The Hong Kong Polytechnic University, Hung Hom, Hong Kong
e-mail: todorova@uacs.edu.mk

M. Todorova, L. Ruiz Rosendo (eds.), *Interpreting Conflict*, Palgrave Studies in Languages at War, https://doi.org/10.1007/978-3-030-66909-6_14

In my previous work on interpreters in conflict-related scenarios, I have discussed aspects of the work of interpreters in refugee camps taking on the role of mediators between the refugees and assistance providers (Todorova 2014, 2016, 2017, 2019). Most of this work has been focused on the working conditions and training of interpreters engaged by UNHCR and other international organizations to support the management of large numbers of refugees crossing the borders into North Macedonia and being accommodated in refugee camps on two occasions, that is the conflict in Kosovo in 1999–2000 and the European refugee crisis in 2014–2015. My research identified some specific roles undertaken by interpreters working in refugee crises, and in particular, how these differ from the roles taken by community interpreters, with the intention to raise the question that there is a need to improve training tailored to their unique needs.

This chapter extends the previous discussion by examining the role of interpreters during another major refugee crisis affecting the world in the period 1970–2000, namely the Vietnamese boat people crisis in the aftermath of the Second Indochina War. I will particularly look at the situation in Hong Kong as one of the first destinations for the refugees from Vietnam, together with Indonesia, Malaysia, the Philippines, Singapore, and Thailand (UNHCR 2000, 81).

In my analysis of the employment and working conditions of interpreters during the Vietnamese refugee crisis in Hong Kong, I rely on interviews conducted and documented in the context of an oral history creative project (Hoang 2018). In the course of her creative doctoral thesis, Hoang conducted a total of 27 interviews with diverse actors, including social workers, immigration officers, relief volunteers, police officers, and refugees, involved in the Vietnamese boat people crisis in Hong Kong. They have been presented in full, as part of an oral history website, together with other artifacts, to represent the history of the refugees from Vietnam who arrived in Hong Kong and to "provide a more comprehensive account of what had happened to [Hong Kong] and the [Vietnamese boat people] during the twenty-five years of this crisis" (Hoang 2018, 4). Hoang provides her own exegesis for the archival material, whereas I will use the interview transcripts in order to trace the stories about interpreters and interpreting. Although no interpreters were interviewed, from the total of 27 interviews, I have identified eight interviewees who mention the work of interpreters. By analyzing their accounts and supplementing it with other available documents from that period, I will try to point to the main issues relevant to the work of the interpreters.

Additionally, the study also compares the employment and working conditions of interpreters during the Vietnamese boat people crisis with the current situation of interpreting for refugees in Hong Kong. The existing working conditions of interpreters assisting refugees and asylum seekers in Hong Kong are analyzed by looking at existing documents, supplemented by semi-structured interviews with two experienced interpreters who have worked for UNHCR and are now part-time interpreters for the Hong Kong government. The comparison uncovers any similarities or changes in the present-day conditions of work. The interviewed interpreters work with variety of languages, including Tamil, Urdu, and Punjabi, and assist asylum seekers from different conflict regions, including Sri Lanka, Nepal, and Pakistan in their application for refugee status with the Hong Kong Immigration Department. The interviews were conducted in person and in English and are anonymized for the purposes of this paper. The participants in this study were asked to share their experiences in terms of their education, their views of the role they played in the refugee assistance process, the availability of institutional support for their work, the most challenging and most rewarding examples of their work, and the areas in which they believed interpreters should receive training. I strongly believe that my past experience working as an interpreter for refugees has benefited the interviews significantly, as "personal involvement is more than a dangerous bias—it is the condition under which people come to know each other and admit others into their lives" (Oakley 1981, 58).

2 Background

In the post-World War II era, another war that significantly influenced world affairs and Southeast Asia in particular, is known by several different names: in Western history, it is known as the Vietnam War, while in Vietnam it is more often referred to as the American War. This war lasted for about two decades, from 1955 to 1975 and brought more than 3 million in military and civilian casualties. The Vietnam War took a devastating toll on the Vietnamese population due to many massacres of civilians, as well as on the economy and the infrastructure. In 1976, Vietnam was unified as the Socialist Republic of Vietnam, though sporadic violence continued over the next 15 years, including conflicts with neighboring China and Cambodia. Even as the war ended, about 12 million Vietnamese became refugees.[1]

Between 1975 and 2000, more than 213,000 Vietnamese Boat People sought asylum in Hong Kong, of these 143,000 were resettled in other countries, more than 67,000 were repatriated to their country of origin and 1368 were resettled locally.[2] The first group of Vietnamese refugees arriving in Hong Kong were 3743 people rescued in the South China Sea by the Danish container ship, Clara Maersk.

At the very beginning, when the Vietnamese refugees started arriving at the shores of Hong Kong, they were automatically regarded as refugees. Many of them were being resettled by Western countries almost immediately without any special procedures. However, gradually, as time went on and the number of refugees increased, the Western countries were slowing down the resettlement rate (Law 2014, xiv). On the other hand, many of the Vietnamese immigrants in Hong Kong were believed to be people who were not eligible for refugee status. Detailed interviews with applicants for refugee status had proven that many of them actually came from Northern Vietnam or China[3] who were trying to reach Western countries in a pursuit for better life.

In 1998, the Hong Kong SAR government announced the cancellation of the First Port of Asylum policy, and in 2000, the last Vietnamese refugee camp in Hong Kong, Pillar Point, was closed. The government announced a Widened Local Resettlement Scheme to allow about 1400 Vietnamese refugees and eligible Vietnamese migrants to apply for settlement in Hong Kong.

[1] The data presented has been retrieved from http://www.history.com/topics/vietnam-war/vietnam-war-history (Accessed 7 October 2019).

[2] http://vietnameseboatpeople.hk/about-us/ (Accessed 7 October 2019).

[3] http://vietnameseboatpeople.hk/about-us/ (Accessed 7 October 2019).

Currently, despite the city's longstanding history of refugee flows, it is one of the regions of the world with the slowest pace of claims processing and one of the lowest degrees of acceptance of claims. According to the Hong Kong Immigration Department, there are presently 10,477 outstanding protection claims in the Hong Kong Special Administrative Region, and only 65 out of close to 30,000 cases have been deemed substantiated since 2004, which amounts to less than 0.4 percent of applications (Lau and Gheorghiu 2018, 21). These refugees are from different ethnic backgrounds fleeing violent conflicts and political prosecution in Asia, Africa, and the Middle East.

The discussion that follows acknowledges the work of interpreters for refugees in an attempt to amend the situation where "even on those occasions when their presence is mentioned, interpreters working in conflict zones are rarely referred to by name or singled out for detailed description or comment" (Ruiz Rosendo and Persaud 2016, 2). If we listen to their stories, we may be able to learn a lot about how they perform their day-to-day duties (Allen 2012) and use this in providing them with the most appropriate support and training. Many of the people working as interpreters within refugee emergencies are non-professionals and often former refugees themselves. They are dedicated staff members, but often without adequate training for dealing with emergency humanitarian situations.

3 Non-professional Interpreters

Interpreters employed to work in conflict- and emergency-related scenarios are often non-professional linguists yet play a key role in the communication. They are hired ad hoc and informally and thus enjoy lesser status than professional interpreters. The work of non-professional interpreters in conflict-related scenarios has been documented by Baker (2010), who explored the training provided to individuals providing linguistic support to the NATO peacekeeping forces in the aftermath of the war in Bosnian and Herzegovina. Similar situation has been noted across other conflicts in different periods in time (Salama-Carr 2007; Inghilleri 2008; Kujamäki 2012). As identified in my study (Todorova 2019) on bilingual local staff employed by UNHCR and other local and international stakeholders to assist with two refugee crises in North Macedonia, most staff providing interpretation have never been trained as professional interpreters. However, relatively little academic attention has been given to non-professional interpreting in war and in conflict. Delgado Luchner and Kherbiche (2018) identify the term humanitarian interpreters which is closely linked to interpreting for refugees in crises as a result of war and conflict. A lot still needs to be done to examine the activities of bilingual or multilingual individuals providing language support for military forces and international humanitarian organizations (Antonini 2015). In what follows, I examine the background and working conditions of interpreters engaged to work with refugees during two different time periods in Hong Kong, an immediate large-scale crisis situation and lower-scale asylum applications due to conflicts and war.

3.1 Vietnamese Boat People (1975–2000)

The analysis of the oral history about the Vietnamese boat people crisis in Hong Kong shows that interpreters who spoke Vietnamese and English or Chinese were indispensable for both the work of the Immigration Department processing a large numbers of people arriving collectively into the Hong Kong port, as well as for the humanitarian assistance efforts provided in the refugee camps.

In terms of the work of the Immigration Department, language was not perceived as a major issue at the very beginning. Paul Lok, training officer at the Immigration Department, remembers the first refugees arriving on the Clara Maersk ship saying that the interpretation was not much of a problem then since "the stories they told [contained] very fundamental information that we required [and] their backgrounds were not being investigated into" (January 2013). With the arrival of the other boats, the need for interpreters increased. First, interpreters were informally recruited among the refugees themselves. These were not professionally trained interpreters, but rather "people with an educated background, i.e. some were teachers from a middle-class background" (Paul Lok, January 2013).

The need for formally recruiting interpreters first arose when the Hong Kong government introduced the screening process and interviews in order to grant refugee status to eligible applicants. Some of these interviews were conducted in English or Chinese, as some refugees could speak English or Chinese. However, when they did not have sufficient understanding of English or Chinese there was a need to involve interpreters, who were often "other Vietnamese refugees [engaged] to assist in order to get [applicants'] particulars *as accurately as possible*" (Henry Siu, September 2013, my emphasis). At this stage, the procedure for the Vietnamese immigrants in Hong Kong to be granted refugee status involved "interpreters provided by the Hong Kong Government" (Davis 1991, 34). The Hong Kong Immigration Department "employed more than 200" Vietnamese interpreters (Henry Siu, September 2013) who facilitated the interview process of applicants. The Vietnamese migrants who were not eligible to get refugee status were repatriated under the comprehensive plan of action as agreed by the United Nations. The Hong Kong Immigration Office took charge of processing the arrivals and granting them refugee status based on detailed interviews that depended on interpreters:

> And one time, a lot of people were stuck in Hong Kong. The resettlement rate was getting very slow. So, we had to introduce what was called a screening system [in order to be] able to screen out those who were not eligible for refugee status. And so, we needed to introduce a screening system for these people. And there were obviously a lot of legal issues around the screening process, whether or not we had done it right. So, how could we actually talk to the people? If you communicate through a different media, you may not get the story right. You may not be able to pick up the *true facts*, because you don't speak the language. So, at one point in time, we had to use a lot of translators and interpreters. (Eddy Chan, January 2013, my emphasis)

The procedure later also involved a so-called readback policy used for verification of the received information in translation. The procedure involved a step in the interview process during which "after the interview, through the interpreters we had to 'read-back' what our officer had written in the report to the refugees, before obtaining a signature [from them] to agree on their story and assessment" (Henry Siu, September 2013).

The issue of trust was one of the most frequently raised problems during this process. On one hand, the Immigration Officers felt that "there were not many Vietnamese-speaking Hong Kong people that we have confidence to allow them to be interpreters. And we didn't have many interpreters. We had to rely on our judgment within the group. I mean, firstly, the faction leaders will not be interpreters" (Paul Lok, January 2013). In order to have confidence in the interpreter the Immigration officers expected the interpreter to able to assist not only with passing the message from one language to another, the interpreters were also used in the process of determining the status of the refugee applicants by determining the origin based on the knowledge of the accents:

> We have entry condition given to us by the UNHCR. Up-to-date information about Vietnam. Even news from a week ago, and we try to ask questions to determine their place of domicile to see whether they speak [the language]. We have Vietnamese interpreters who can even tell which part of Vietnam their language is from. … And the most important thing of our work is status determination. It's to determine whether they are refugee or not. (Peter Choy, January 2013)

On the other hand, there were increasing number of "reports that Vietnamese boat people helping in the running of detention centers and acting as interpreters were being 'terrorised' by other boat people" (Davis 1991, 212) since they were seen as collaborators of the Hong Kong officials against the refugees. Thus, interpreters who were witnessing screening interviews had to balance their loyalties and were often among the ones who reported immigration officers as unhelpful (Davis 1991, 38).

Apart from the immigration process at the Hong Kong government, interpreters were needed for providing humanitarian assistance and community service in the refugee camps. Similarly, better-educated refugees with language knowledge were used as interpreters in these situations.

Kathleen Malone, who worked as a volunteer teacher at the Sham Shui camp, remembers one of the refugees she encountered "who was very well-educated. He spoke five languages including French, Vietnamese, Mandarin, Cantonese and English. And he was an interpreter in the camp" (January 2013). James Ginns, a manager for a refugee camp adjacent to Pillar Point, says that he "employed quite a number of Vietnamese people who had been involved with different NGO's [for] refugees over the years. And they had been refugees themselves. And they came onto the team and did community work and interpreting work and that kind of thing" (January 2013). One of the organizations involved in providing assistance, Caritas, used their Vietnamese-speaking staff to provide interpreting services:

> UNHCR took Caritas seconded staff to the UNHCR office to work with the Vietnamese. But at that time, our staff couldn't speak Vietnamese. So I requested the religious Vietnamese speaking Sisters and Priests to go and help in each of the camps. So every Sunday, for those who are Catholic, they have mass. [They held mass] every Sunday in the refugee camps. And the Sisters go on weekdays to teach them English and act as interpreters also. (Joyce Chang, January 2013)

One of the oral history accounts acknowledges the difficult condition in which the interpreters worked, especially the emotional burden of relieving the traumatic experiences. When describing her work, Penelope Mathew from the Jesuit Refugee Service said:

> We would go in each day and we would interview maybe five or six people and spend around an hour with each person. And of course, you've got your interpreters for who this is a really exhausting day. They're sitting there trying to listen to the story, and they're trying to translate for both the lawyer and explaining to the client as well. It is a very long and exhausting process. Sometimes really emotionally draining because of the kinds of things you are being told, some are quite horrible. (Penelope Mathew, August 2013)

3.2 Refugees and Asylum Seekers in Hong Kong (2000–2019)

Over the past two decades, interpreting for refugees and asylum seekers in Hong Kong has been mainly provided by locally engaged interpreters registered with the Hong Kong Judiciary. The Vietnamese boat people crisis was the last major refugee crisis in Hong Kong. After that crisis, most of the refugee claimants have been arriving to Hong Kong either individually or in smaller groups fleeing conflicts in different regions of the world, but mainly from Sri Lanka, Pakistan, and Nepal. The new refugees' situation has been much different compared to that during the Vietnamese crisis as "the refugees arrived on planes and were well off, often able to pay for their stay while their application was being processed" (interpreter 2). However, this has not always been the case, and some refugees depend on government assistance for basic living needs, as they are not allowed to work during the process of application (interpreter 1).

The interpreters I interviewed for this study both stated they had never been formally trained as interpreters. They were invited to join the Hong Kong Judiciary because of their language skills. It should be noted here that while these interpreters are non-professionals in terms of their lack of formal training in the field, the very concept of what constitutes a professional interpreter remains nebulous, as many interpreters work part-time, have other commitments, such as self-owned companies, or engage in other part-time work, such as teaching. As an interpreter with seven years' experience explained, "most existing interpreters [in Hong Kong] do not have academic training in interpreting, as they did not originally plan to enter the field" (Gurung 2017, 93).

Both interviewed interpreters have completed higher education and have worked in the field of secondary and tertiary education. Currently, they are working as interpreters for the Hong Kong Judiciary and other government offices on a part-time basis. After being recruited, both interpreters were provided with a few hours of induction into court procedures and the code of ethics, issued with a handbook containing a glossary of legal English terminology, court procedures and court addresses and were expected to take on courts interpreting assignments. Although not formally trained as interpreters they both have long-term experience as interpreters for the Hong Kong Judiciary and UNHCR. Both UNHCR and the Hong Kong government have provided them with short-term informal training in interpreting at different points in time.

When working with the judiciary, the interviewed interpreters state that officials prefer "interpreters with knowledge of dialects, extensive educational background and long years of experience in the field" (interpreter 2). Because they do not share the same refugee background as the claimants the interpreters are "seen as more neutral" (interpreter 2). However, they are still expected to share their "knowledge of the country situation which helps in making an informed judgment of the refugee claim" (interpreter 2). This knowledge and experience "allow [the interpreter] to explain the processes and give advice to junior lawyers and other officials" (interpreter 1). The interpreters agree that their knowledge has often times proven to be beneficial for the screening process. Although both interpreters were aware of the requirement for neutrality, they expressed that their role was not to "just blindly interpret but are an indispensable part of the team and can contribute to the effectiveness of the screening process" (interpreter 1).

When asked if they have any other role in the process of providing interpreting services for refugees, both interpreters expressed readiness to assist the refugees beyond their job responsibilities as they see it as "service to humanity" (interpreter 1). Sometimes this service is provided after the asylum seeker is granted refugee status, whereas "before the applicant is given the refugee status, during the process of their screening, there is more caution" (interpreter 2). During the initial screening process, the interpreters have to stay "as neutral as possible and have no attachments to the claimant" (interpreter 2). The reason for this is that "very often asylum seekers who come to Hong Kong are generally well off and do not have very grounded fear, they are more economic migrants" (interpreter 2).

The support interpreters provide to refugees can vary, from "explaining how to get around and where to find different offices" (interpreter 2) to "providing monetary assistance" (interview 1). One of the interviewed interpreters recalls a situation when she had bought food for a young refugee applicant who had not eaten for days, as the food provided for him by the immigration was not culturally suitable. She has also helped refugee applicants on several other occasions by contacting family members, lending them money, donating clothes, buying groceries, and even teaching them to cook and take care of themselves.

However, both interpreters agree that in some cases "working with refugees involves a lot of emotions as refugees flee tragic circumstances, trauma, and torture" (interpreter 1). Through experience they learn "what to expect and although no support is provided, can cope with the emotionally heavy situations. However, some of the younger colleagues find it much more difficult and sometimes break down and require a break" (interpreter 2).

4 Discussion

Comparing the two periods looked at in this study brings us to several observations. First, using non-professional interpreters has proven to be one of the recurrent traits when working in humanitarian refugee crises arising from violent conflicts and war. The interpreters provided by the government were often non-professional and had received little to no training. Non-professional translators are contributing to "the consolidation of new paradigms of linguistic, cultural and religious mediation in new sites of cross-cultural contact and interaction—resulting from voluntary migration flows as well as the involuntary displacement and resettlement of populations affected by armed conflict or humanitarian tragedies" (Pérez-González and Susam-Saraeva 2012, 152). Their decision to interpret in a specific situation frequently involves factors that differ significantly from their professional counterparts. Most of the interpreters working with refugees are self-taught practitioners not provided with comprehensive training. Often interpreters are refugees themselves, as were most of the cases during the Vietnamese crisis, who were hired for their linguistic skills, but also for the ability to empathize with the refugees because they shared similar experience with them. Others were hired for their linguistic skills but also knowledge of the culture and current political situation in the countries of origin of the refugees and asylum seekers. Although, commonly considered as lacking professional training in interpreting and thus not familiar with ethical codes and practices of the profession, these individuals proved to be very highly educated and knowledgeable. By having the bilingual skills and the willingness to interpret they help fill in a gap that exists in the large demand for interpreting services in refugee camps and working with less common language combinations among professional interpreters. The need to employ non-professional ad-hoc interpreters brings about the need to provide these bilingual and multilingual individuals with ongoing training specific to interpretation for refugees.

In addition to providing interpretation during meetings, some of the other activities performed by interpreters involve "establishing a sense of trust and providing encouragement to the parties involved reaching an acceptable solution" (Todorova 2016, 238). Interpreters should develop trust among all parties in the process, which assumes developing trust with people belonging to different cultural backgrounds. The interviews I conducted helped shed light on the fact that the interpreters who worked with the refugees in an emergency situation are committed to helping the refugees receive assistance and were capable of engaging with their emotions. This established trust between the interpreter and the refugee, in a situation when the capacity to trust was diminished. It also helped to better understand their needs, but also motivated the interpreters to provide direct assistance. Interviewed interpreters showed a strong self-perception as not only enablers of communication but also assistants in the effort to bring vulnerable groups to safety.

The issue of trust is intrinsically linked to the issue of ethics. Interpreters recruited from within the refugees they served and contracted to serve a foreign government or an international organization, often find themselves in a position to choose between their employer and the community they belong to. In these situations, they operate without the guidance of a code of ethics or any ethics training, where they rely on their personal judgement. Challenges in refugee interpreting situations occur when interpreters themselves share the same experiences as the clients they work with. Although, most Codes of Ethics demands that interpreters are accurate and impartial at all times the fact that interpreters might share the similar experiences as the refugees they work with, may make it problematic for interpreters to be impartial at all times, which may present ethical concerns (Crezee et al. 2011).

Building on the current research in community interpreting, Martin and Valero-Garcés rightfully note that regardless of the level of professionalization, community interpreters will continue to work in "circumstances in which it would be difficult for any human being to remain unperturbed" (2008, 2). Defining an ethical and efficient community interpreters, Zhang (n.d.) maintains that they are "impartial yet empathetic, which presents an obvious contradiction at face value: being impartial implies distance, whereas empathy denotes a connection". The work of a community interpreter is unique in its context: they often have the privilege of seeing people at their most vulnerable. Their ethics training guide them as they seek a right course of action, and they navigate between their roles as conduits, clarifiers, cultural brokers, and advocates. Decisions are made swiftly, and adjustments are made based on moment-to-moment dynamics. The distinction between an "impartial" interpreter and an "advocate" one is a simplification which may carry some theoretical value but has little applicability to the practice of community interpreting having in mind the very different contexts in which it takes place.

Interpreting in emergencies does have its own distinctive characteristics arising from the iterative and prolonged contact with individual refugees, as well as the highly emotional content of the mediated communication resulting from the trauma of conflict and forced migration. Non-professional interpreters, especially those who have experienced a life of a refugee themselves, are exposed to a significant amount of emotional trauma that accompanies witnessing or hearing atrocities (Pillen 2016, 17). This can be ameliorated by providing appropriate training and counseling. Proposed training may include mock interpreting sessions on testimony of violence, torture, and so on (Cappelli 2014). Additionally, psychological counsellors can help interpreters "understand the suffering of the victims and embrace it in their minds before the actual assignments with a view to reducing the degree of emotional involvement" (Cappelli 2014, 23).

5 Conclusion

No matter when or where a humanitarian disaster involving large numbers of refugees occurs the demand for interpreters will be immediate and large. In this research, I have tried to identify common issues arising in interpreting for refugees across temporal and special boundaries. Interpreting for refugees, especially in big crises, seems to be done by non-professional ad-hoc interpreters who, although have strong educational background, have receive little or no training in interpreting. However, these interpreters show another important skill that has helped them in effectively conducting their job and in addition helping others in need. Empathizing with the others they have been able to assist the legal and humanitarian officers and work with them in a team in order to maximize the assistance provided for the refugees. In this process, the issues of neutrality, objectivity and trust all gain a different meaning which needs to be renegotiated. Regardless of whether they were trained or untrained interpreters, these language brokers were expected to perform duties in situations that were neither clearly defined nor explained in formal or informal interpreting training, often quite contrary to any instruction and preparation the interpreters got, primarily in regard to their neutrality, impartiality, and invisibility (Todorova 2016, 2017). Furthermore, working for the vulnerable and traumatized exposes interpreters to vicarious trauma that needs to be addressed in training and counseling support.

Although the study is by no means a comprehensive presentation of the situation, in a situation when very little studies of this kind are available, it serves to provide a glimpse into the background and working conditions of interpreters for refugees in Hong Kong. It can be used as a starting point for further investigations of the interpreters for refugees at various locations and time periods. Additionally, when compared to other studies of interpreting for refugees it can lead to more general discussion of the specific needs for training and support.

The findings of the study can be used to highlight common issues facing interpreters for refugees across geographical and temporal divides. They can also assess the need for policy and training for interpreters working with refugees in a situation when the numbers of refugees fleeing violent conflicts around the world are on the constant rise.

References

Allen, Katharine. 2012. *Interpreting in Conflict Zones*. NAJIT. http://najit.org/blog/?p=229. Accessed 5 February 2021.

Antonini, Rachele. 2015. Non-Professional Interpreting. In *Routledge Enciclopedia of Interpreting Studies*, ed. Franz Pöchhacker, 2–26. New York: Routledge.

Baker, Catherine. 2010. The Care and Feeding of Linguists: The Working Environment of Interpreters, Translators, and Linguists During Peacekeeping in Bosnia-Herzegovina. *War & Society* 29 (2): 154–175.

Cappelli, Paolo. 2014. Wartime interpreting: exploring the experiences of interpreters and translators. In *(Re)concicerando etica e ideologia en situaciones de conflict/(Re)visiting Ethics and iIeology in Situations of Conflict*, ed. C. Valero Garcès, 15–24. Alcalà de Henares: Servicios de Publicaciones Universidad de Alcalà.

Crezee, Ineke, Shirley Jülich, and Maria Hayward. 2011. Issues for Interpreters and Professionals Working in Refugee Settings. *Journal of Applied Linguistics and Professional Practice* 8 (3): 253–273.

Davis, Leonard. 1991. *Hong Kong and the Asylum-Seekers from Vietnam*. New York: St. Martins Press.

Delgado Luchner, Carmen, and Leïla Kherbiche. 2018. Without Fear or Favour? The Positionality of ICRC and UNHCR Interpreters in the Humanitarian Field. *Target* 30 (3): 415–438.

Gurung, Sangi. 2017. Legal Interpreters for Ethnic Minorities in Hong Kong: Identities and Cultural Mediation. In *Open Access Theses and Dissertations*. Hong Kong: Hong Kong Baptist University.

Hoang, Carina Oanh. 2018. From Both Sides of the Fence: Vietnamese Boat People in Hong Kong 1975–2000. In *Open Access Theses and Dissertations*. Bentley: Curtin University.

Inghilleri, Moira. 2008. The Ethical Task of the Translator in the Geo-Political Arena. *Translation Studies* 1 (2): 212–223.

Kujamäki, Pekka. 2012. Mediating for the Third Reich: On Military Translation Cultures in World War II in Northern Finland. In *Languages and the Military. Alliances, Occupation and Peace Building*, ed. Hilary Footitt and Michael Kelly, 86–99. Basingstoke: Palgrave Macmillan.

Lau, Pui Yan, and Iulia Gheorghiu. 2018. Vanishing Selves Under Hong Kong's Unified Screening Mechanism. *Cultural Diversity in China* 3 (1): 21–35.

Law, Sophia Suk-mun. 2014. *The Invisible Citizens of Hong Kong: Art and Stories of Vietnamese Boatpeople*. Hong Kong: Chinese University Press.

Martin, Anne, and Carmen Valero-Garcés. 2008. Introduction. In *Crossing Borders in Community Interpreting: Definitions and Dilemmas*, ed. Anne Martin and Carmen Valero-Garcés, 1-8. Amsterdam: John Benjamins.

Oakley, Anne. 1981. Interviewing Women: A Contradiction in Terms. In *Doing Feminist Research*, ed. Helen Roberts, 30–58. Boston: Routledge & Kegan Paul.

Pérez-González, Luis, and Şebnem Susam-Saraeva. 2012. Nonprofessionals Translating and Interpreting. *The Translator* 18 (2): 149–165.

Pillen, Alex. 2016. Language, Translation, Trauma. *Annual Review of Anthropology* 45 (1): 95–111.

Ruiz Rosendo, Lucía, and Clementina Persaud. 2016. Interpreting in Conflict Zones Throughout History. *Linguistica Antverpiensia* 15: 1–35.

Salama-Carr, Myriam. 2007. *Translating and Interpreting Conflict*. Amsterdam: Rodopi.

Todorova, Marija. 2014. Interpreting Conflict: Memories of an Interpreter. In *Transfiction: Research into the Realities of Translation Fiction*, ed. Klaus Kaindl and Karl Spitzl, 221–232. Amsterdam: John Benjamins.

———. 2016. Interpreting Conflict Mediation in Kosovo and Macedonia. *Linguistica Antverpiensia* 15: 227–240.

———. 2017. Interpreting at the Border: 'Shuttle Interpreting' for UNHCR. *CLINA* 3 (2): 115–129.

———. 2019. Interpreting for Refugees: Empathy and Activism. In *Intercultural Crisis Communication: Translation, Interpreting, and Languages in Local Crises*, ed. Federico Federici and Christophe Declercq, 153–173. London: Bloomsbury Academics.

UNHCR. 2000. *The State of the World's Refugees 2000: Fifty Years of Humanitarian Action*. https://www.unhcr.org/publications/sowr/4a4c754a9/state-worlds-refugees-2000-fifty-years-humanitarian-action.html. Accessed 5 October 2020.

Zhang, Tianyi. n.d. *Empathy and Interpreting: The Curious Case of Healthcare Interpreting*. Available at https://www.interpreterslab.org/empathy-and-interpreting-the-curious-case-of-healthcare-interpreting/

15

Latin American Interpreters Working in a Safe Country: Specific Training and Emotional Implications

Lorena Guadalupe Baudo
and Gabriela Fernanda Lorenzo

1 Introduction

This work reports an experience in which we participated as simultaneous in-booth interpreters, in an event organized by the Ministry of Culture, Presidency of the Argentine Nation, in conjunction with the United Nations Development Program, called Global Dialogues. This event presents annual editions in different sites of the world; this time we were lucky that our home city—Córdoba, at the very heart of our country—was chosen as the venue and that the actors—speakers, refugees and migrants—were invited to our province, otherwise the core of the event is in Buenos Aires and in different Latin American capitals, although it also circulates as a world tour. This edition was intended to address two triggering questions: What does it mean, culture-wise, for a society to open its doors to others? That is, to analyze the fears and anxieties

L. G. Baudo (✉) • G. F. Lorenzo
National University of Córdoba, Córdoba, Argentina
e-mail: lorena.baudo@unc.edu.ar; gabriela.lorenzo@unc.edu.ar

M. Todorova, L. Ruiz Rosendo (eds.), *Interpreting Conflict*, Palgrave Studies in Languages at War, https://doi.org/10.1007/978-3-030-66909-6_15

generated by *Strangers at our door* (Bauman 2016),[1] along with the origins and impact of migratory waves. The other question was: How can we see the migrant as someone who arrives to a place to contribute and enrich in a society that is constantly evolving and not, on the contrary, as a mere spectator of the pre-established culture? In other words, the migrant swings between being a problem and contributing or enriching according to the convenience of State policies, to what is perceived as regression or progress, according to the order of globalization. Not only the linguistic, cultural and technical skills sets needed, but also the emotions, values and subtleties that occur in this type of context from the interpreter's perspective is what we will present in this work since interpreters are key actors in the refugee and migrant integration in host societies.

2 Topics of the Event

Before the event, we had almost none of the information that we have and present today; we will talk about the realities of the interpreter later, but this particular event was based mainly on four thematic points:

a) stereotypes; how refugees are represented in the media and how, depending on media representation, we have generated in ourselves the image of a refugee;
b) "the poor refugee"; how we perceive refugees as victims or as survivors; how we characterize them, what attributions or characteristics we assign to them;
c) Eurocentrism, since the situation is such that although many countries in the world receive refugees, it is the countries of Europe that receive the greatest number; and
d) security, analyzed from a dual perspective: both the security of the people who arrive to a country and the security of the people in the host country.

[1] *Extraños llamando a la puerta* (Zygmunt Bauman 2016), the Spanish version we used for reference.

No explicit distinction between forced displacement and voluntary migration was made at the event; notwithstanding mostly refugees' stories and account were present.

3 Historical Basis

For the interpreter it is key to situate themselves in a space and time, to complete their mental map of all the possible terms and discussions that will emerge in an instance of cultural mediation. For this reason, it is important to remember the socio-historical context that surrounded us.

Since the last two decades of the twentieth century, on the world and Latin American scene, migration has escalated to a highly relevant place in the international agenda.[2] Migration encompasses issues ranging from the situation of internally displaced people and groups, the dynamics between development and migration patterns, the consequences of human displacement on the environment, or the unfounded fear that terrorist cells may leak into migration.

The migration crisis in Europe is the biggest humanitarian crisis since the Second World War,[3] which was exacerbated in 2015 by the increasing flow of refugees, asylum seekers, economic migrants and other vulnerable migrants, who arrive (or try to arrive) in the Member States of the European Union, through dangerous crossings in the Mediterranean Sea and South-East Europe, from countries in the Middle East, Africa, the Western Balkans and South Asia. At the beginning of 2017, a travel ban to the United States of Syrian refugees and immigrants from seven nations with a majority Muslim population, imposed by the administration of President Donald Trump, would add on top of the European panorama.

The peak of the problem in the media was the death of Aylan Kurdi, a three-year-old Syrian boy, on September 2, 2015, who was found

[2] Taking into account, for example, the discussions proposed mainly by the UN and its related agencies, such as the United Nations High Commissioner for Refugees (UNHCR) and the International Organization for Migration (IOM), global reference bodies in the discussion on Migration and Refugees: http://www.acnur.org/; https://www.iom.int/.

[3] As we prepare this chapter, the COVID-19 pandemic is in the process of developing, which might become the greatest crisis since the Second World War.

drowned on the beach of Turkey. However, in 2016, Bauman warned: "There are growing signs that public opinion, in conspiracy with eager media, is slowly but surely approaching the point of exhaustion from the tragedy of the refugees" (10).

There we were, at a turning point in history.

4 Interpreting Assignment

In an ideal world, the interpreter should receive in advance the lectures, information about the speakers, the objectives of the event among other vital aspects for a good preparation. In reality, this almost never happens. How do you interpret in an event of this nature, with a multiplicity of speakers, and therefore a multiplicity of voices? How do you get all the information? The organizers only provided us with the names of the speakers two days before the event. Very diverse geographical areas were represented, as well as many visions or world views on this situation: Paola Gómez Restrepo is a Colombian refugee living in Canada who runs an NGO called Sick Muse Art Projects that works to encourage and build a connection between artists and other community partners to promote artwork and arts education that engages communities in social justice and community development issues. Marco Romero, Colombian, director of CODHES, a Colombian NGO that promotes the enforcement of the human rights of displaced persons, refugees and migrants. Michelle Brané is one of the United States' leading experts on immigration reform. As director of the Migrant Rights and Justice Program at the Women's Refugee Commission, she advocates for the critical protection needs of immigrant women, children and other vulnerable migrant populations in the United States and opened our eyes to the reality of Latin America. Felicia Waldman is the deputy director of the Romanian delegation to the International Alliance for Holocaust Memory. Her experience covers Jewish mysticism, Holocaust education and public policies in Romania, and Romanian Jewish heritage. Dismas Nkunda is the Founder and CEO of Atrocities Watch Africa, an NGO focused on research, dissemination and prevention of atrocities in Africa. He is also the Founder and former Director of the International Refugee Rights Initiative, an NGO advocating for refugee rights abroad. Joel Bubbers is Director of the British Council in Syria. He currently coordinates the organization's response to the refugee crisis. Previously, he worked for the British Council in Egypt and Lebanon, in the European Union delegation in New York and in the NATO Civil Coordination area based in Mons, Belgium. Hatice Akyuen is one of the leading journalists and speakers on the integration debate in Germany. She was awarded the Berlin Award for Integration for her contribution as an author and journalist to the migration and integration debate, as well as for her commitment to democratic cooperation. Mohammad Al-Khafaji is an Iraqi refugee living in Australia and CEO of Welcome to Australia, an NGO dedicated to the integration of migrants through projects of inclusion, diversity and openness.

An additional challenge was having to interpret the account of refugees forced to flee their countries of origin—Haiti, Syria and Nigeria—and whose host city is now Córdoba. Their names remained unrevealed until we heard them for the first time at the very moment of rendering their testimonies. As language mediators, we found ourselves in an intercultural dialogue, with one foot on each side of the border (Mignolo and Tlostanova 2009, 14), among a vulnerable groups of refugees, the keynote speakers who have already gone through that path and memories, and local policy makers and the civil society responsible of transforming the uncertain conditions of refugees into a welcoming place of settlement.

5 Challenges and Strategies

We will now detail five challenges we sometimes faced during the exercise of the profession, but this was particularly the case in the event on migrants and refugees. We will also break down the strategies that we used in the booth to deal with these difficulties thanks to previously acquired skills:

Challenge 1: Lack of access to information in due time

The day proved to be a great confluence of speakers and realities, nourished by different visions or *lifeworlds*. According to Martina Rienzner:

"lifeworlds" can be described as "horizons of interpretation" including all aspects which are experiences taken as accepted fact without question. These "horizons of interpretation" are the result of actions and experiences. Both a person's own experiences as well as those of others create that basis upon which another person's actions can be interpreted and ensure that people can interact with others. (2017, 152)

For this type of highly sensitive and cultural events, to be well-trained and professional is a given, as clearly specified in the introduction to the *Handbook for Interpreters in Asylum Procedures* (2017); and nonetheless, previous knowledge and previous linguistic and communicative experiences might not be enough. This type of interpretation without almost any information provided beforehand is called by Tolosa and Gallego *groping interpretation* and the challenge is very well described by the authors when they state: "No matter how much specialization, culture, linguistic competence, intuition, flight hours, chameleon-like capacity and reaction that the interpreter has, he or she may be surprised by the thematic and terminological specificity of the conference" (2012, 34).

Strategy 1: In our preparation, when we only had the names of the potential speakers and the overall theme of the event, we first used a technique called *Context Reinsertion*, which implies a component of *Analysis* as well (Gillies 2015). What did we do? We looked for newspaper headlines in electronic journals on Migration. All the headlines have a lot of information behind them, a lot of background that is not explicit in the headline itself. With this logic, we practiced exercises to reinsert contexts in headlines on the topic by asking ourselves questions about the specific situation of each country involved, of each region, of each continent; about the biography of each speaker and their relation to the topic; about the fields and subfields that are intersected by the topic; about the position of migration in the international agenda. We reinserted the context to the extent of our knowledge and when we were not able to answer our questions, we completed the gaps with specific research, both terminological and thematic. We carried out this task leaving aside any kind of prejudice or judgment on the data found. This type of exercise helps to anticipate potential problems, as well as the perspectives from which the speakers will approach the topics. At the moment of truth; that is, our booth time, we just had to leave aside theoretical considerations on *contextualization* effectively summarized by Rienzner (2017, 153): *contextualization cues* (Gumperz 1982), *inter* and *transcultural misunderstandings* (Sarangi 1994) and *communicative expectations* (Jacquemet 2011), and we took a very practical approach in relation to diverging pronunciations and culture-specific terms—we lean on each other's strengths: Gabriela excels at grasping more diverse pronunciation schemes and Lorena is a terminologist.

Challenge 2: Thematic complexity and information mining

Taking into consideration the vast array of speakers, their lifeworlds and countries of origin, displacement and destination: What is too little information? What is too much information? How far do we go, for example, in the case of the Holocaust?

Strategy 2: The interpreter cannot start from scratch with every subject or field they are asked to interpret, so they have to read constantly and be aware of everything that is happening to them at the moment and of their potential knowledge gaps. On the other hand, what we should aim at is trying to understand the concepts. We focus on the concepts and not on the ideas. Migration is a cross-cutting theme that touches upon politics, sociology, demography, human rights and ecology. Therefore, a good preparation practice can be concept maps around thematic areas, such as the ones suggested by Maria Eder, et al.: circumstances in the country of origin (institutions, culture-specific terms, special forces, etc.), phraseology (including taboos and euphemisms) and timetables and geographical areas (2017, 180–181), which can be used in two instances and for two different purposes. From the point of view of terminology, the glossaries that we would find on the areas converging to migration would exceed the interpreter's possibilities of study, what we can do is to look for a basic limited material (in any textual typology: article, video) that informs and describes the foundations of the subject. From that material, we extract key terms from which we expand the terminological network in logical and ontological relationships between the terms that will ultimately constitute our mental dictionary at the time of interpretation (Baudo 2016, 7). To practice—and for the sole purpose of practice—we can select and listen to a video that we consider useful for our preparation, we write down the main topic (e.g. Migration in South America) in a circle in the center of a page of our notebook. From that circle outward, we project a number of branches or subareas for each major part of that speech, and from each branch more subsections emerge. This gives us an overview of the discourse because we sometimes lose the comprehensive perspective of the ideas we hear. It is an exercise that forces us to analyze the structure of the discourse, how the ideas are connected, what cause-consequence relations arise between the adjacent and partially overlapping areas (Gillies 2015).

Challenge 3: Non-localized conflict

Speakers who were part of the round tables came from multiple geographical area. Therefore, we could not focus our research on a particular situation because it is not the same what happens in Europe, what happens in Australia, in the USA, in Argentina. It encompasses almost all realities in some way, which are to a certain extent, opposing situations regarding the information that can be found in the media, since, although migration is a very relevant topic in the international agenda, the media coverage is scarce these days. The stories of migrants that we interpreted made the numbers and experiences visible, especially in the case of Latin America, where the conflict is under-reported and hardly recognized by local governments and the press.

Strategy 3: The funnel-like preparation of the topic; that is, from the general to the specific, focusing on the general concepts and conceptual network around migration, politics, economics and international human rights policies. Later on, when we were close to the date of the event and we had access to the names of the speakers, we started from each speaker to extend the preparation to the more general, delimited by the place of action of each speaker. A clear example of this would be the preparation for Hatice Akyuen's dissertation/participation, the research began with her origins, reasons for her migration, background and position regarding the refugee conflict mainly from her position of having grown up in Germany despite having been born in Turkey. This structuring allows us not only to incorporate terms but rather to understand the concepts that this renowned journalist is likely to include in her participation.

Challenge 4: The interpreter's visibility

"It is a fiction that I am neutral and invisible" as the cover of the UNHCR's *Handbook for Interpreters in Asylum Procedures* (2017, 4) cites from the words of an interpreter. The day of the event, we kept in mind our mission: we played a key part in rendering the messages of refugees in front of an audience that was made up mainly of people of interest for them, people with the power to make their settlement smoother in the host country: Argentina. Our main challenge was to produce verbatim interpretation of the accounts to touch people's hearts; that meant to render the testimonies of vulnerability and resilience of both keynote speakers and refugees. By doing so, we ran the risk of being overwhelmed by extremely intense emotions, which could in turn be exposed in our voice and the clarity of our message.

Strategy 4: Eduardo Kahane has stated that

> plain repetition, if it exists, is useless, because its effect on the listener of the original language will be by definition different from the effect it would have on the listener of the interpretation. It is necessary, therefore, to transform. The value of such a transformation requires more detailed study, but it largely depends on the resources of style and character of the interpreter. (1986, 184)

It is then the responsibility of the professional interpreter to develop the capacity to strike a balance that allows them to connect emotionally with the story in order to be able to transmit the emotions, descriptions, sensations of the speaker without these emotions invading us and making it difficult for us to continue with the interpretation. Some of these emotional accounts included vivid passages describing a refugee having to literally walk on dead bodies as he fled a war zone, a family surviving an impossible sea odyssey, teenage girls in peril as crossing borders unaccompanied...

> The interpreter—rather than the asylum seeker—is often (...) the principal person the decision maker listens to during an asylum interview, and the emphasis placed on credibility gives their role greater prominence: credibility relies on their words, and they can make things better or worse. They actively participate. Hearing a disjointed account, the interpreter can decide to depart from the applicant's words, in order to optimize communication. (Craig and Gramling 2017, 93)

We were not at an asylum-seeking interview; however, many decision makers from the political sphere were present at the conference, where their impressions on refugees could have been tilted on the positive or the negative side. We decided not to depart from the refugees' oral account; much on the contrary, we involved deeply in their stories. We decided on a twofold strategy: the interpreter in charge would use loanwords for culture-specific terms, while her booth partner would look for descriptive equivalent or explanation, which we would insert later in the account when time permitted. Particularly in this event, which was loaded with emotions, we anticipated the moments in which these emotional stories will be produced, and we choose to reduce the duration of the interpretation times in order to recover our breath, metaphorically and literally, and continue. In booth times like these is when we really value working with our colleagues and it is essential that there is synergy between them.

Challenge 5: The Unexpected

The last challenge we are going to address is the unexpected. There is an unwritten rule that says the interpreter must be prepared for the worst; that way when unforeseen situations arise, the preparation of the professional interpreter gives them tools to face the difficulty in the best possible way. The last speaker was the unexpected factor. Totally out of the program, five minutes before the closing time of the event, we were informed by the organization that this renowned journalist was going to give a brief lecture to close the event, which then turned out to be 45 minutes: a historical-political overview of the conflict of refugees and migrants from the beginning to the present. A succession of names, countries, conflicts, political and war events that culminated in the situation of the conflict. Without a doubt, it was totally unexpected and yet we had to face up to what was presented to us.

> **Strategy 5**: We decided to take turns every 5 minutes, instead of the standard 20 minutes to maintain the quality of interpretation, shifting turns with each new idea. How to prepare to implement this strategy? A very useful exercise is what Andrew Gillies proposes and calls *chunking* (2015). When you listen to a speaker who is speaking at a faster than average speed, sometimes it seems like an uninterrupted flow of words coming in your direction at full speed. It is like watching a text all in one go. The idea is to work in pairs: take written texts on the topic you need to prepare, put them in a plain document, for example, and remove all punctuation marks, even paragraph divisions. The interpreter who prepares the exercise hands it to the other interpreter, and the latter has to reconstruct the spaces following the logic of the ideas. It is a simple exercise, but it debunks some myths about non-stop speech and helps in the preparation for the case we had to deal with.

6 Conclusion

In this intercultural and multicultural dialogue, as interpreters we find ourselves "living on both sides of the border" (Mignolo and Tlostanova 2009, 14). It is this kind of situation that leads us to go beyond our learning about short-term and long-term memory to seek a place in the emotional memory. The stories of migrants and refugees are part of what is called *Community Interpretation* or *Humanitarian Interpretation*, a topic for which various strategies of anticipation and preparation can be developed. Nevertheless, at the very moment of interpretation, the topic ceases to be a mere theme and becomes a question that challenges us in our entire human dimension: we must strip ourselves of every place of enunciation in order to assume another skin, a nomadic and wandering walk, a story that overflows with emotions, but that cannot overwhelm us. The human dimension of the interpreter—"men (and women[4]) as the only being of language"—must urge us to think and to make others think "of cultures, their diversity, their differences, their possible and impossible dialogues; to think of the fractures and explosions", focusing "on their capacity to respond and to be responsible against the fabric of violence, and an imperious need of claiming for transformation towards a more just future society" (Barei 2014, 19).[5] At the border, we find ourselves trying to cross it, enriching it with a perspective of ethical commitment.

References

Barei, Silvia. 2014. Desde esta frontera. In *Iuri Lotman in memoriam*, ed. Silvia Barei, 9–22. Córdoba, Argentina: Facultad de Lenguas, Universidad Nacional de Córdoba.

Baudo, Lorena. 2016. *La preparación del intérprete en el discurso especializado. El caso de la crisis económica europea*. http://hdl.handle.net/11086/6188. Accessed 5 October 2020.

Bauman, Zygmunt. 2016. *Extraños llamando a la puerta*. Buenos Aires: Paidós.

Craig, Sarah, and David Gramling. 2017. Is There a Right to Untranslatability? Asylum, Evidence and the Listening State. *Tilburg Law Review* 22: 77–98.

Eder, Maria, Alexandra Jantscher-Karlhuber, Irmgard Soukup-Unterweger, Gernot Hebenstreit, Frank Austermuehl, and Students of the MA Translation in a European Context at Aston University. 2017. Information Mining for Interpreters. In *Handbook for Interpreters in Asylum Procedures*, ed. UNHCR, 169–186. Vienna: UNHCR Austria.

[4] Our insertion.

[5] Our translation.

Gallego, Daniel, and Miguel Tolosa. 2012. Terminología bilingüe y documentación ad hoc para intérpretes de conferencias. Una aproximación metodológica basada en corpus. *Estudios de Traducción* 2: 33–46.
Gillies, Andy. 2015. *Analysis Exercises for Consecutive Interpreting.* https://www.youtube.com/watch?v=mSqw3e1ddM0.
Gumperz, John J. 1982. *Discourse Strategies.* Cambridge: Cambridge University Press.
Jacquemet, Marco. 2011. Crosstalk 2.0: Asylum and Communicative Breakdowns. *Text & Talk – An Interdisciplinary Journal of Language, Discourse & Communication Studies* 31 (4): 475–497.
Kahane, Eduardo. 1986. La interpretación de conferencias o el teatro como metáfora. *Cuadernos Hispanoamericanos* 431: 175–190. http://www.cervantesvirtual.com/obra/la-interpretacion-de-conferencias-o-el-teatro-como-metafora. Accessed 5 October 2020.
Mignolo, Walter, and Madina Tlostanova. 2009. Habitar los dos lados de la frontera/teorizar en el cuerpo de esa experiencia. *Revista Ixchel.* http://www.redkatatay.org/sitio/talleres/mignolo_frontera.pdf. Accessed 5 October 2020.
Rienzner, Martina. 2017. Interpreters as Experts in Multi-lingual and Transcultural Communication. In *Handbook for Interpreters in Asylum Procedures*, ed. UNHCR, 152–168. Vienna: UNHCR Austria.
Sarangi, Srikant. 1994. Accounting for Mismatches in Intercultural Selection Interviews. *Multilingua – Journal of Cross-Cultural and Interlanguage Communication* 13 (1–2): 163–194.
UNHCR Austria. 2017. *Handbook for Interpreters in Asylum Procedures.* Vienna: UNHCR Austria.

Part IV

Conclusion

16

Pressing Issues and Future Directions for Interpreting in Conflict Zones

Marija Todorova

Despite an increasing interest and research into the specifics of interpreting in conflict zones (e.g. Inghilleri 2005; Baker 2010; Moser-Mercer et al. 2014; Kelly et al. 2019; Ruiz Rosendo 2020), more research is still needed to elucidate key concepts, such as ethics, neutrality, positionality and identity, that are of paramount importance to interpreters in conflict scenarios regardless whether they work with the army or humanitarian organizations. The roles that interpreters in conflict zones adopt vary based on context, the participants in the interpreted event and the power relations that develop between them, and the specific tasks they carry out in each stage and communicative situation. These tasks frequently exceed the basic responsibility of linguistic transfer of the message to incorporate a role of cultural mediators and sometimes active participants in their own right or participants in the mediation process. Consequently, more discussion is needed regarding the categories of interpreters working in each stage of different conflict situations.

M. Todorova (✉)
The Hong Kong Polytechnic University, Hung Hom, Hong Kong
e-mail: todorova@uacs.edu.mk

M. Todorova, L. Ruiz Rosendo (eds.), *Interpreting Conflict*, Palgrave Studies in Languages at War, https://doi.org/10.1007/978-3-030-66909-6_16

In order to examine these specific roles of interpreters in conflict zones, researchers are often confronted with the difficulty of identifying relevant sources of information. Historical references to interpreters in conflict are often found in sources that do not explicitly focus on interpreting activities (Ruiz Rosendo and Persaud 2016). Moreover, interpreters in conflict are either not mentioned in historical documents as they were not seen as significant, or when their performance has been mentioned they have not been referred by name. The research presented in this volume tends to change this situation by identifying individual interpreters and presenting their stories.

Furthermore, the present volume has put emphasis on the role of interpreters in conflict scenarios, expanding the scope beyond Europe, to include primary conflicts located in the Middle East, Africa and Asia. Given the circumstances and conditions under which interpreters in conflict zones and related scenarios perform their work, more interdisciplinary discussion is needed in order to analyze the different factors that have an impact on the concept of neutrality. Thus, this volume includes scholars specializing in the field of Translation Studies, but also researchers with background in Conflict Resolution and Peacebuilding Studies. The volume also features articles that present the perspectives of practicing interpreters, interpreter advocates, and military personnel.

1 Interpreting for the Military

The eight chapters included in the first part of this volume share one powerful common finding: that interpreters are and have been crucial actors in wars throughout history. Another noteworthy core idea is that the positionality of interpreters who work for the military is always complex.

1.1 Trust and Loyalty

As Ruiz Rosendo argues, interpreters are paradoxically considered to be an ambivalent resource: on the one hand, they are indispensable for communication but, on the other, they usually belong to the community in conflict and therefore arouse the mistrust of the military. Along these lines, Takeda's chapter highlights the risky issues faced by interpreters as dual citizens of warring states. Related to this, she emphasizes the ethical implications of language mediation in criminal acts, as well as the complex language issues in environments of international armed conflict.

Trust and loyalty are issues closely related to ethics, the latter an aspect being thoroughly analyzed by Luo and Jiaotong, who conclude that the interpreters' choices of loyalty in war are shaped by an entangled web of factors whose relevance and prominence varies. The view that ethnicity or nationality determines the interpreter's loyalty appears as a simplistic one. In such challenging contexts as conflicts, interpreters find themselves under severe pressure, an argument that Kim agrees on in his study of the role of the interpreter and the interpreting habitus. He explains how the lack of qualified interpreters in the Korean War led to the pressure put on the interpreters by the American military. The complexity of these interpreters' positionality was due to the fact that they were themselves US military personnel and, as such, were obliged to abide by the norms dictated by their superiors. Additional consequence was that the interpreters had to perform myriad tasks that went beyond interpreting, another common aspect to be found in the chapters of this volume. Indeed, Gómez Amich also comes to this very same conclusion, adding the lack of consensus among the military personnel as to what responsibilities should be given to the interpreters and how to set boundaries to their work. The complex positionality of the military interpreter is also described my Méndez Sánchez in her study of the Spanish armed forces, although she adds on the advantages that this positionality entails. She argues how the presence of military interpreters is relevant because they know and understand the profession and are more familiar with the different topics and with the military jargon and discipline.

Loyalty is an issue also approached by Gómez Amich who argues that one key aspect that all military interviewees in her study agreed on was the fact that the interpreters had to defend the interests of the armed forces, acting as their tool and prioritizing their needs, inasmuch as they were the recruiters of the interpreters. Moreno Bello echoes this statement and declares that interpreters channel their loyalty to the contracting armed forces. This result is related to the ethical principle of neutrality, also analyzed by Moreno Bello, who comes to the conclusion that interpreters are never a neutral conduit, and who highlights how they tend to intervene to explain cultural elements. This aspect is also underscored by Ruiz Rosendo who posits that the interpreter's role goes beyond translating the linguistic message to include cultural mediation, which is essential in military operations taking place in a country with a diametrically distinct culture.

Finally, the distrust in the interpreter is clearly presented by Hass who points to the "translator-traitor" mentality that marked the prosecution of interpreters as traitors in US military and federal courts in the aftermath of the 9/11 attacks. Examining the court proceedings, Hass concludes that they were marked by the fact that the interpreters were seen as sympathetic to the opposite side in the conflict due to their cultural and religious background, and not just based on evidence.

2 Humanitarian Interpreting

One of the main contexts in which post-conflict humanitarian interpreting takes place includes providing interpreting services to refugees and asylum-seekers primarily working with UNHCR or other humanitarian NGOs that provide support to these groups. The six chapters included in this section identify several common issues raised by interpreters working with refugees and asylum seekers.

2.1 Interpreters as Insiders

Belonging to the conflict is seen as a one of the most common characteristics of interpreters for refugees. As noted by Todorova, very often the interpreters engaged in humanitarian interpreting are refugees themselves, who were hired for their linguistic skills but also for their ability to understand the cultural codes, and that could empathize with the refugees because of their shared experiences. However, we can notice a difference in the perception of how their cultural background affects interpreters. While Radicioni concludes that "a shared cultural background between mediators and migrant patients can coordinate and create a common ground with patients' system of values and beliefs and, ultimately, create a relation based on trust", Haidar points out "to a change in the positionality of United Nations interpreters when they work in their own countries". Interviewing Arabic speaking United Nations interpreters that worked during "emotionally charged" circumstances of the Arab Spring, Haidar has identified that national interpreters report greater emotional impact and stronger emotional stress while performing their duties that may have affected their performance.

Being inside the conflict affects the interpreters' positionality, thus putting into question the notion of neutrality typically associated with the interpreting practice. The roles required of interpreters by the different parties vary greatly in terms of the higher or lower levels of visibility and intervention mentioned earlier (Niska 2002). However, Martin Ruel stresses that often interpreters working with organizations providing assistance to asylum seekers are in a position or even expected to assume an advocate role, which seems to go beyond the strict remit of an interpreter in that it also involves acting as mediator, source of knowledge, educator and translator. Similarly, Todorova points out that the distinction between an "impartial" interpreter and an "advocate" has little applicability to the practice of community interpreting when providing service for the most vulnerable.

This positionality of humanitarian interpreters in conflict-related situations often reflects in the development of empathy during the interpreted event. Interpreters are also expected to show a certain amount of empathy, flexibility and awareness of the context of each job, together with an ability to adapt to cultural conventions without becoming emotionally involved, taking sides with the beneficiary or judging their situation. This not only affects the interpreters' performance but could cause a substantial emotional impact with personal and professional consequences. Examining the Israeli-Palestinian conflict, Barea notes the emotional effect that the interpreting assignment has on the professional interpreter who is situated inside the conflict. Furthermore, non-professional interpreters, especially those who have experienced a life of a refugee themselves, are exposed to a significant amount of emotional trauma that accompanies witnessing or hearing atrocities (Pillen 2016). The emotional stress that arises from interpreting raises the need for offering psychological assistance designed specifically for conflict interpreters. Baudo and Lorenzo find that interpreters in contexts of conflict often report that during a mediated event they assume "another skin" and experience a high degree of emotional stress when conveying "a story that overflows with emotions". We can conclude that working for the vulnerable and traumatized exposes interpreters to vicarious trauma that needs to be addressed in training and counseling support.

3 Lack of Access to Information

Finally, a common issue arising from research in both military and humanitarian interpreting is the fact that there is a lack of timely information available to locally recruited interpreters. Kelly and Baker (2013) claim that this lack of resources is due to concerns related to confidentiality. Baudo and Lorenzo agree that the lack of timely information in order to adequately prepare for interpreting events creates an obstacle for interpreters engaged in refugee interpreting. Also challenging is the important need for background knowledge when confronted with protracted conflicts in different parts of the world. In addition to information related to a specific event, interpreters must be aware of associated religious, political and socioeconomic intricacies, historical evolution of the conflict, and past developments. Martin Ruel also identifies that prior information about a situation (to allow proper preparation by the interpreter) and sufficient preparation time are not provided by the organizations providing services to asylum seekers.

4 Future Directions

This volume contributes to the growing body of systematic and multiperspectival research of interpreting in conflict and post-conflict zones and adds further insight into the roles played by interpreters in conflict. However, there are still issues that need to be addressed with further research. We would like to especially draw attention to two topics that are emerging as pressing in the near future.

4.1 Training Needs

One of the issues identified in most of the articles in this volume as relevant to all interpreters in conflict and post-conflict situations is the need for specialized training that corresponds to the specific roles that they perform and addresses the specific contexts in which they perform their duties. Most researchers agree that "despite the position the interpreter has played in conflict scenarios, no provision has been made for training interpreters specifically to work in those settings, with few exceptions" (Ruiz Rosendo and Persaud 2016, 28). Research across geographical and temporal divides has identified that interpreters recruited to work with the military or as local staff of international humanitarian organizations are self-taught practitioners, recruited for their language skills, who often have strong educational background, but have not been provided with comprehensive training in interpreting skills. Furthermore, interpreters in conflict-related contexts who have the expertise in translation and interpreting often find themselves expected to perform duties in situations that were neither clearly defined nor explained in training, and often quite contrary to any instruction and preparation the interpreters got. Most of the identified issues related to neutrality, emotional stress, and positionality can be ascribed to the lack of appropriate training.

Mendez identifies that participation in international military missions tends to be qualified as a generally positive and professional experience. However, she concludes that the work of the "military interpreter" warrants better training and more appropriate regulation. The training needs for military interpreters include specific interpreting training, but also mediation skills to enable them to successfully intermediate between the national and the military culture. On the other hand, one of the training needs identified by Martin Ruel is training in social issues. Previous research has identified a number of specific roles undertaken by interpreters working in refugee emergencies (Todorova 2020), and in particular, how these differ from the roles taken by community interpreters, with the intention to bring to attention the need to provide training tailored to their unique needs. Although training in interpretation is understandably important for non-professional interpreters during conflict situations, other types of training are also (or even to a greater extent) necessary when working in emergency situations. Given the unique tasks performed by interpreters working in emergency situations, interpreters and those who want to specialize in work with refugees in humanitarian emergencies should be provided with appropriate training which will draw not only on the most recent developments in interpreting studies, but also in conflict resolution and peace-building studies. Training in managing risk, dealing with high levels of stress, and effective decision-making in crisis, as well as specialized training in working with children and other vulnerable groups can prove highly effective to interpreters working in humanitarian contexts. Additionally, special attention should be given to training on how to handle sensitive situations and how to respond to personal trauma.

Training is not only needed for current and future interpreters in conflict, moreover, there is an absence, among organizations and beneficiaries, of a clear idea of the interpreter's role and professional ethics. Clarification of some of these issues could avoid misunderstandings regarding things like trust and confidentiality. Training should be made available to users of interpreting services who are keen to learn how to work with interpreters more effectively.

In order to provide more appropriate training, Ruiz Rosendo and Persaud identify the need for more exploration of the "categorization of interpreters in conflict" (2016, 29). We believe that the conclusions presented in this volume can further contribute in the development of tailored training programs that will lead to future professionalization of interpreters in conflict.

4.2 Environmental Conflict

Wars and violent clashes are at the center of the current research on interpreting in conflict. Wars are habitually understood to be caused by differences in ethnicity or religion. Due to this cultural dimension of conflict, the parties involved in war and violent clashes perceive themselves as belonging to a common group that shares ethnic or religious background, and they understand that the main reason they are fighting for is to maintain their national sovereignty. For this reason, there is a tendency "to attribute wars to 'primordial' ethnic passions, which makes them seem intractable" (Stewart 2002, 324). However, these cultural reasons for the conflict can serve to divert attention from the more essential causes that include political, economic, and social inequalities. Recently, environmental issues are considered to be increasingly important causes of violent conflicts, as part of a complex web of social, political, and economic factors that can result in the presence (or absence) of direct violence. Though overwhelmingly present in times of war and armed conflict, physical or direct violence is not the only kind of violence. New definitions of violence also include structural violence, indirect violence, referring to a condition where "violence is built into the structure and shows up as unequal power and consequently as unequal life chances" (Galtung 1969, 171). In this context, it becomes relevant to bring into the debate the concept of ecological violence, that is, injury against the environment caused by pollution, deforestation and overexploitation (Kyrou 2007). Violence against the environment tends to be perpetrated over time and in multifarious ways, threatening nature, humans and livelihoods in the long term. Irreversible damage to the earth's environment threatens the very survival of humankind, making environmental violence a topic of great urgency (Lee 2015, 106).

Researchers have defined "environmental conflict" as a conflict resulting from degradation caused by human activity or mismanagement, rather than just the exploitation of resources (Dokken and Graeger 1995; Benjaminsen et al. 2012); a category of social conflict that is characterized by the qualitative or quantitative reduction of available environmental resources. Management of natural resources, disposing of hazardous waste, controlling pollution and future development plans have created settings for environmental conflicts due to unequal power between affected parties, as well as differences in definition of the problems and solutions. The concept of environmental conflict encompasses a broad spectrum of empirical phenomena ranging from disputes between individuals to wars between states, between radical environmentalists and industry, or wars over renewable resources such as agricultural land, forests, water, raw materials and fishing stocks. Examples of the role that the environment has played in the creation of armed conflicts are not only present today, and anticipated in the future, but have been identified throughout history. For example, Westing (1986) identified 12 international conflicts over natural resources, both renewable and finite, in the period between 1914 and 1980. Moreover, the aim to control resources has also been seen as motivation for the aggressive behavior of colonial powers when faced with indigenous struggles. This leads to a vicious circle in which the control over natural resources leads to armed conflicts which in turn have a devastating impact on those resources.

Although they have many similarities with social and political conflicts, environmental conflicts have specific features, related with triggering events, progress, consequences, involvement of the stakeholders, management or resolution processes. All these are intrinsically linked to linguistic and translation practices, which so far have not been included in the debate on interpreting in conflict. Researchers working on the intersection of language, translation practices and environment bring to attention the conflicts between indigenous knowledge and national policies, such as the "colonial encounter in north Norway between Sámi practices for fishing and knowing the natural world, and the conservation policies of state policy makers" (Østmo and Law 2018). Other examples examine the differences in presenting environmental issues on the Greenpeace websites in China, Japan and Germany (Heinz et al. 2007, 16–36). The examination of the websites in different languages, leads to a conclusion that environment is considered in fluctuating ways across cultures. For example, "the Japanese site appear to invoke guilt as a major motivation for mobilizing action. In contrast, the concept of nature created on the Chinese sites invokes the notion of unspoiled, pure state of nature. An emotional appeal to protect unspoiled nature is also a strong aspect of the German discourse" (Heinz et al. 2007, 31).

Cronin (2017) identifies "food security, climate justice, biodiversity loss, water depletion, energy security, linguicide, eco-migration, resource conflicts, global monocultures [as] some of the issues that will be at the heart of environmental debates in the twenty-first century and that will need to be addressed by scholars and practitioners of translation alike" (3). Future research on the specifics of interpreting practices in environmental conflicts could include topics such as: the linguistic implications of environmental conflicts, interpreting for climate refugees, importance of interpreting in peacebuilding efforts to resolve an environmental conflict, including indigenous populations in scientific debates, and interpreting environmental activism.

Having in mind these current developments and emerging trends in the field of interpreting in conflict, we can conclude with confidence that research in this area is likely to continue to grow and expand. Research involving collaborations among scholars, interpreting practitioners, as well as users of interpreting services can prove beneficial for closely identifying training needs. In the future, we can also expect to see more interdisciplinary research collaborations involving scholars from the field of translation studies and those in sociology, psychology, peace and conflict studies, as well as development and environmental studies, addressing the complexities of conflict contexts that require interpreting in conflict zones.

References

Baker, Mona. 2010. Interpreters and Translators in the War Zone. *The Translator* 16 (2): 197–222.

Benjaminsen, Tor Arve, Koffi Alinon, Halvard Buhaug, and Jill Tove Buseth. 2012. Does Climate Change Drive Land-Use Conflicts in the Sahel? *Journal of Peace Research* 49 (1): 97–111.

Cronin, Michael. 2017. *Eco-Translation: Translation and Ecology in the Age of the Anthropocene*. London: Routledge.

Dokken, Karin, and Nina Græger. 1995. *The Concept of Environmental Security – Political Slogan Or Analytical Tool?* PRIO Report 2. Oslo: PRIO.

Galtung, Johan. 1969. Violence, Peace, and Peace Research. *Journal of Peace Research* 6 (3): 167–191.

Heinz, Bettina, Hsin-I (Cynthia) Cheng, and Ako Inuzuka. 2007. GreenpeaceGreenspeak: A Transcultural Discourse Analysis. *Language and Intercultural Communication* 7(1): 16–36.

Inghilleri, Moira. 2005. Mediating Zones of Uncertainty: Interpreter Agency, the Interpreting Habitus and Political Asylum Adjudication. *The Translator* 11 (1): 69–85.

Kelly, Michael, and Catherine Baker. 2013. *Interpreting the Peace: Peace Operations, Conflict and Language in Bosnia-Herzegovina*. New York: Palgrave Macmillan.

Kelly, Michael, Hilary Footitt, and Myriam Salama-Carr. 2019. *The Palgrave Handbook of Languages and Conflict*. Palgrave Macmillan.

Kyrou, Christos. 2007. Peace Ecology: An Emerging Paradigm in Peace Studies. *International Journal of Peace Studies* 12 (1): 73–92.

Lee, X. Bandy. 2015. Causes and Cures I: Towards a New Definition. *Aggression and Violent Behavior* 25: 199–203.

Moser-Mercer, Barbara, Leila Kherbiche, and Barbara Class. 2014. Interpreting Conflict: Training Challenges in Humanitarian Field Interpreting. *Journal of Human Rights Practice* 6 (1): 140–158.

Niska, Helge. 2002. Community Interpreter Training: Past, Present and Future. In *Interpreting in the 21st Century: Challenges and Opportunities*, ed. Giuliana Garzone and Maurizio Viezzi, 133–144. Philadelphia: John Benjamins.

Østmo, Liv, and John Law. 2018. Mis/translation, Colonialism, and Environmental Conflict. *Environmental Humanities* 10 (2): 349–369.

Pillen, Alex. 2016. Language, Translation, Trauma. *Annual Review of Anthropology* 45: 95–111.

Ruiz Rosendo, Lucía. 2020. Translation and Interpreting in Conflict. In *The Oxford Handbook of Translation and Social Practice*, ed. Meng Ji and Sara Laviosa. Oxford University Press.

Ruiz Rosendo, Lucia, and Clementina Persaud. 2016. Interpreting in Conflict Zones Throughout History. *Linguistica Antverpiensia* 15: 1–35.

Stewart, Frances. 2002. Root Causes of Violent Conflict in Developing Countries. *BMJ* 324 (7333): 342–345.

Todorova, Marija. 2020. Interpreting in a Refugee Context. In *Legal and Healthcare Interpreting*, ed. Eva Ng and Ineke Crezee, 63–81. Amsterdam: John Benjamins.

Westing, Arthur J., ed. 1986. *Global Resources and International Conflict: Environmental Factors in Strategic Policy and Action*. Oxford: Oxford University Press.

Index[1]

[1] Note: Page numbers followed by 'n' refer to notes.

M. Todorova, L. Ruiz Rosendo (eds.), *Interpreting Conflict*, Palgrave Studies in Languages at War, https://doi.org/10.1007/978-3-030-66909-6

The manufacturer's authorised representative in the EU is Springer Nature Customer Service Centre GmbH, Europaplatz 3, 69115 Heidelberg, Germany. If you have any concerns regarding our products, please contact ProductSafety@springernature.com

Printed and bound by CPI Group (UK) Ltd, Croydon, CR0 4YY

30/09/2026

02225457-0016